BAMA
UNDER
BEAR

Alabama's Family Tides

BAMA
UNDER
BEAR

Alabama's Family Tides

By Tommy Ford

THE STRODE PUBLISHERS
HUNTSVILLE, ALABAMA 35801

Photographs Courtesy Of: The University Of Alabama Sports Publicity Office; The **Corolla,** 1960-1974; The **Gadsden Times;** The **Chattanooga News-Free Press;** Barry Fikes, Calvin Hannah, And Dave Stueber Of The **Tuscaloosa News;** Jim Harris, Bill Killian, R. D. Moore, And Brad Sparks Of The **SEC Sports Journal;** The California Angels; The Miami Dolphins; Tom Croke Of The New England Patriots; The New York Yankees; The San Diego Chargers; The Tampa Bay Buccaneers; Dan Bowers; Chip Cooper; Jimmy Smothers; Crosby Thomley; And Rickey Yanaura.

First Edition 1982
Revised Edition 1983

CONTENTS

FOREWORD

There's an old saying of "how time flies when you're having fun."

I always smiled when I heard it years ago but really didn't understand the meaning of it until I left the University of Alabama in the spring of 1982 after 18 years of basking in the glory of Crimson Tide athletics, specifically the Bama football program.

Now that Tommy Ford has asked me to write the foreword to his book, *BAMA UNDER BEAR: Alabama's Family Tides*, and I've had a chance to read the proofs, many fond memories pour over me. Some are sad, some are funny, and some bring back moments that I had forgotten about or didn't realize the importance of until I read what so many members of the Alabama football family had to say about things that happened during their days at Bama.

This book doesn't cover all of the family stories because that would require several volumes. But it does have some sparkling stories about Sid and Billy Neighbors; Gerald, Charlie, and Bruce Stephens; Mike and Steve Ford; Tommy and Steve Wade; Richard and Jimmy Grammer; Butch and Clell Hobson; Gary and Jeff Rutledge; the great Hannah family; and Woodrow and Eddie Lowe.

Hitting some of the highlights. . . Billy Neighbors was one of the first Tide All-Americans under Coach Paul Bryant. He was a great player and a great person. We all have an image of an All-American lineman being someone bigger than life. But Tommy brings out a funny story about when Billy had finished his eligibility and Northport was going to honor him on "Billy

Neighbors Day.'' Billy learned they were going to give him a car
...but he didn't know how to drive!

The Stephens brothers all wore national championship
rings and that is something special.

The Ford brothers were walk-ons and Mike became an All-
American. Coach Bryant and his staff had to change their thinking about walk-ons after that and now encourage them.

Richard and Jimmy Grammer were fine young men and typical of the small, courageous players who played above their
ability in the Bama system. Richard tragically drowned right after
his senior season in a hunting accident, only one week before he
was to be married. I remember Coach Bryant crying when he got
the news.

The Hannah family is truly one of the great sports stories in
American football history. I doubt if any family ever contributed
more to one program before. Not only were they All-American
players, but they are All-American citizens now.

Gary and Jeff Rutledge gave all of us so many thrills as they
quarterbacked Bama to victory after victory and helped carry on
the heavy burden of tradition as the Alabama quarterback. Both
are still among my favorite people in the world. Solid citizens.

There are other families that jump to mind, like the great
Davis kicking contingent, the Singtons, and the Higginbothams,
but perhaps Tommy will write another book after this one and include those he unfortunately had to leave out this time.

Let me tell you a little about the author.

My first recollection of Tommy Ford is his covering of press
conferences for the *Crimson White* during his student days. He
came by my office a lot and even asked for interviews with Coach
Bryant, which was something new for student writers. He was
just a shy and young cub reporter then, but he was well-
organized, very polite, and obviously did a lot of homework on
the questions he wanted to ask. They were direct and to the point.
Coach Bryant appreciated that because some writers don't come
in prepared. And Tommy had a little twinkle in his eye that
Coach Bryant noticed, too.

Coach invited Tommy to travel on the team plane several
times on long trips when he knew the *Crimson White* didn't have
the money to pay his expenses. His conduct was very professional
and he had a maturity about him you don't always see in young-

sters his age.

There is no doubt that this book is a labor-of-love for him. He isn't in it to make money. I hope he does because he spent several years researching his product, spent a lot of time and money, and he deserves it. But it makes me proud to see a youngster that I like to think I helped back when he was a student have the devotion and pride in his alma mater to want to help record some of its great athletic heritage. I hope you enjoy it as much as I did.

Charley Thornton

EDITOR'S NOTE: Charley Thornton served the University of Alabama from 1964 until the spring of 1982 as the sports information director and then assistant athletic director. He won numerous national and regional awards and was chosen the best in his profession by his peers. He is best remembered, however, as serving as the co-host of the "Bear Bryant TV Show" for the last 14 years. Charley is now the associate athletic director at Texas A&M, working with another former Tide standout, Jackie Sherrill.

PREFACE

I've always thought the phrase "mommas and poppas" had a special ring to it, especially when spoken by Alabama head football coach Paul "Bear" Bryant. As long as I can remember, I've heard him talk about the family concept, and how winning on the football field starts in the home of each and every Crimson Tide player.

Many former players under Bryant have told me of their first team meetings as wide-eyed freshmen. Whether it was 1958 or 1978, the results were the same—without fail Bryant would first tell them to write home to their parents. In his book, *Bear*, Bryant recalled his "talking to each player individually...and asking how they were doing, and talking about their brothers and sisters." That was 1958, and he's been doing it ever since.

This family concept Bryant treasures and teaches so much is the theme of *BAMA UNDER BEAR, Alabama's Family Tides.* In this volume nine "families" of Alabama football are highlighted, either in father-son or brother relationships. Of the 22 men I have written about, all but two played under Bryant. Those two, Herb Hannah and Clell Hobson, played under Red Drew in the late forties and early fifties, then passed the Alabama family tradition on down to their sons.

This is a book of "brotherly love" at its best. Through comments and stories by the players themselves, the reader can formulate his or her own reasons as to why the family concept has helped make University of Alabama football so successful. No one may ever put a finger on it, but the results are evident—the Alabama football program has been greatly enhanced by the "family" concept.

Alabama's football family tradition stretches far beyond these nine, however. The calendar can be turned back to the early 1900s to see some of the inaugural families of Alabama football—the Burkses, the Vandergraafs, the Sewells, and the Browns. The late twenties gave us Fred Sington and Albert Elmore, both of whom later contributed offspring to the Alabama football program. The late forties and early fifties, a period of ups and downs for Crimson Tide football, brought us the pass-catching Lary brothers, Ed and Al.

Many of these families will be featured in Volume II of *Alabama's Family Tides*, to be published in the fall of 1984. Add to these several more that played under Bryant, such as the "kicking" Davises, the Kelleys, and the Higginbothams, and the result is a history of Alabama football from an entirely different perspective.

I'm excited about the upcoming Volume II and know that it will be a worthy follow-up to Volume I. In this one you'll read about Sidney Neighbors and Billy Neighbors going through the worst and best of Alabama football. The Stephens brothers—Gerald, Charlie, and Bruce—all won national championships; Mike Ford and Steve Ford walked on and were big hits; and Tommy Wade and Steve Wade displayed their versatility in the turbulent late sixties and promising early seventies.

The Grammers experienced tragedy; Butch Hobson experienced a change of heart; and the Hannahs, the greatest family name in Alabama football history, experienced winning and losing, crying and dying. Gary Rutledge and Jeff Rutledge helped make Alabama's wishbone famous, while Woodrow Lowe and Eddie Lowe both "experienced" Coach Bryant's record-breaking 315th win. Eddie in 1982 is adding to the historic record.

This book was started in 1980 in my hometown of Gadsden and was concluded this spring in Tuscaloosa. In the words of former *Birmingham News* sports editor Zipp Newman, "I can't begin to thank all—but I am making an attempt."

First I wish to thank God for giving me the patience to keep it all going. I have Him to thank for everything.

I want to thank Mark Mayfield for getting me started in sportswriting back in 1976 with the *Crimson White*. My first assignment was to cover a swim meet, a relatively routine task for the experienced writer, but not for a finance major who hadn't written more than four paragraphs since English 101. I hardly knew the difference between the butterfly and the breaststroke, and when I had to ask the coach how to keep score, I knew I was in trouble. But Mark stuck with me and taught me enough to become *CW* sports editor in 1977-1978. For that I am grateful.

The idea to write about the families of Alabama football popped into my head in the spring of 1980. I would not have proceeded had I not received the green light from Charley Thornton of the University's sports publicity office. Charley thought the idea had potential and he was tremendous in helping my project get off the ground. Charley, best wishes at Texas A&M. Jackie Sherrill is fortunate to have you on board.

Ben Cook of the *SEC Sports Journal,* Al Browning formerly of the *Tuscaloosa News,* Jimmy Smothers of the *Gadsden Times,* and Jim Hunter of NASCAR were also instrumental in the early stages of *BAMA UNDER BEAR, Alabama's Family Tides.* Ben and Al are noted authors themselves, but more important to me, they are true friends.

Through Jimmy Smothers I met Jim Hunter of the Alabama International Motor Speedway and now assistant to the president of NASCAR. Jim, one of the nation's top sportswriters, is a pro at whatever he does. He's written five books, and I felt like the luckiest guy in the world when he offered to edit this book. I compare it to Jack Nicklaus offering me free golf lessons or Julius Erving asking me to shoot some hoops. Somewhere in between the Talladegas and the Charlottes and the Daytonas and the Indianapolises, Jim bent over backwards to help me.

Several people in Gadsden contributed immensely, the most important being my mother. She supported me from day one and helped me along so much that I will never be able to repay her. Thanks, Mom.

Bill Cardwell, Diane Coleman, John Croyle, Forney Daugette, Peggy Jones, Bobby Junkins, Rex Keeling, David Kelly, Wayne Owen, and Fred Sington, Jr., helped me with the "little things" that turned out to be "big things." And no one provided more inspiration and moral support than Robin, a very special person in my life.

Eighteen months before I began working for the University of Alabama Alumni Association, Betty Morrison of the alumni staff was providing me with countless names and addresses of all the Tide "families." I sincerely thank Betty and her staff, as well as my current bosses, Larry Keenum and Robert H. Kirksey. Larry and Mr. Kirksey were my "cheerleaders" from the start, and I greatly appreciate their support. Also, I want to thank Jeff Coleman, former director of alumni affairs and historical expert of Alabama football, for assisting me in the early stages.

A big "thank you" also goes out to Jack Perry, University of Alabama assistant athletic director; Clyde Bolton of the *Birmingham News;* Jim Murray and Rich Roberts of the *Los Angeles Times;* Jim Selman of the *Tampa Tribune;* Jim Bell, sports information director at UT Chattanooga; David Housel, sports information director at Auburn University; R.D. Moore of the *SEC Sports Journal;* Dr. Charley Scott of the University of Alabama; Daniel J.J. Ross of the University of Alabama; Mrs. David (Mary) Mathews, a fine author in her own right; Dr. J. Gregory Payne, the biggest Alabama fan in all of Los Angeles; and Dr. John Morgan of West Point, Georgia, perhaps the biggest Alabama fan anywhere.

The sports publicity offices of the following were most helpful: Boston Red Sox, California Angels, Los Angeles Rams, Miami Dolphins, New England Patriots, New York Yankees, San Diego Chargers, Tampa Bay Buccaneers, and the Senior Bowl in Mobile.

Then, there are the people I call the "supporting actors" of this book. I am grateful to each and every one for their comments—Bill Battle, Tommy Brooker, J.P. Cain, Steve Clay, Richard Cole, Paul Crane, Reverend Sylvester Croom, Sylvester Croom, Jr., Jerry Duncan, Pat Dye, Marlin "Scooter" Dyess, Danny and Deborah Ford, Mrs. Ruth Grammer, Clem Gryska, Mrs. Geneva "Coupe" Hannah, Buddy Helton, Darwin Holt, Scott Hunter, Cecil "Hootie" Ingram, Billy Jackson, Pat James, Jim Krapf, James Lowe, Henry "Sang" Lyda, Mal Moore, Billy Richardson, Jeff Rouzie, Jack and Mary Rutledge, Alvin Samples, Jimmy Sharpe, Steadman Shealy, Jackie Sherrill, Dr. Bob Sittason, Steve Sloan, Tom Somerville,

Dr. Gary White, and Kenny Wilder.

Of this group I must single out Pat Dye and Jimmy Sharpe. Very few people know more about Alabama football than those two. Of course, Pat's allegiance is now with the Orange and Blue of Auburn, but he went overboard to help me, and I greatly appreciate that. He's a super individual and has a bright future ahead.

Jimmy Sharpe was around Alabama football for 16 years, and there's not a season, game, quarter, or play he can't remember. He's a walking encyclopedia of Crimson Tide football, and through my experience and interviews with him, we became close friends. I hope he doesn't send me a bill for his services, because I would be in debt forever. Thanks, Jimmy.

And of course, a book on families of Alabama football wouldn't be possible without the help of the families themselves. All were absolutely super and cooperated to the fullest. Many were flattered that I would include them in the book, but in reality I'm the one who's flattered to be doing it. I'm not doing them a favor—they're doing me one. They've earned their places in Alabama football history and deserve some recognition. I hope *BAMA UNDER BEAR, Alabama's Family Tides* accomplishes this.

And last, but not least, I want to thank the "father" of all these families—Coach Paul "Bear" Bryant. My dream in early 1980 would have remained just a dream if Coach Bryant had not given me his nod of approval. I can't say enough about what this man means to me.

For all his help and support, I dedicate *BAMA UNDER BEAR: Alabama's Family Tides* to Paul W. Bryant, a great coach—but a greater man. It is people like him that make people like me work a little harder.

Here it is, a history of Alabama football under Coach Bryant—through the eyes of 20 "family members" that have worn the Crimson and White.

I hope you like it.

Tommy Ford
Fall 1982

NEIGHBORS

Sid • Billy

From the worst to the best in seven seasons—that's the era of Alabama football covered by Sidney and Billy Neighbors, a pair of brothers from Taylorville, Alabama, a small community just outside Tuscaloosa. The once mighty Tide lost every game in 1955, Sid's freshman year. In 1961, Billy's senior season, Alabama won every game.

Sid had the unfortunate distinction of playing at Alabama just prior to the arrival of Coach Paul "Bear" Bryant. This pre-Bryant era was a period of history many Bama fans choose to ignore, or have forgotten about quicker than anyone can yell, "Roll Tide."

Billy, on the other hand, came to Alabama in 1958, the same year Bryant showed up on campus. Bryant was not a teammate of Billy Neighbors. Bryant was the leader, the mentor, the bossman. His nickname of "Bear" described him mildly.

This "Bear" would become the greatest coach in college football history. Billy would have a part of that history, including a national championship in 1961. Billy's successes would continue into eight years of professional football with the Boston Patriots and Miami Dolphins.

Sid's and Billy's father, Sidney, Sr., played football at Tuscaloosa High School in the late twenties under the legendary Paul Burnum. From 1925 through 1929 Burnum coached Tuscaloosa High to an unbelievable 44-0-1 record, and Sidney, Sr., was a part of that milestone. To say the least, the eldest Neighbors was a sports enthusiast, especially when it concerned Alabama football.

"He (Sidney, Sr.,) was nuts about football," Billy

remembers. "He used to always listen to Washington Redskins games when (former Tide star) Harry Gilmer was playing up there. He would go berserk listening to Alabama games. He even went out to the (1935) Rose Bowl to see Alabama beat Stanford."

It was no surprise, then, that Sid and Billy took a keen interest in football. It was natural for them—they didn't know otherwise.

Both graduated from Tuscaloosa County High School in Northport. Sid began his football career at age eight in the typical sandlot games of Tuscaloosa County. He started at the tackle position as a ninth grader, then made All-County as a sophomore. Playing as "the biggest high school player in the state (at 250-260 pounds)" he earned All-State honors his junior and senior years.

"I signed with Alabama right after high school," Sid said, "but I waited a year before going there. My daddy had passed on when I was a sophomore (in high school), and my momma was having trouble making ends meet.

"I was the oldest of six children and Momma had all the kids at home. I just couldn't afford to go to school that year, so I went to work at the Goodrich Tire Plant (in Tuscaloosa) to help things out at home."

After a year with Goodrich, Sid asked Alabama athletic director Hank Crisp if his scholarship was still good. Crisp understood the circumstances behind Sid's request and granted the scholarship without hesitation in the fall of 1955.

The 1955 team, under new head coach J.B. "Ears" Whitworth, began the season with a 20-0 loss to Rice. It was a sign of things to come as it proceeded to lose nine more, including a 26-0 finale to Auburn. The 0-10 record was the worst in Alabama football history, quite a contrast to Whitworth's 10-0 record as a Tide player in 1930.

"The Alabama team (in 1955) had its problems," Sid said. "We couldn't play on the varsity because we were freshmen, but we practiced against them every day. When we scrimmaged them, we whipped them every time. It was really a pitiful thing. The morale was awful."

The freshman class completed its schedule with a 4-1 record, so things were looking better for the next season. Things did improve, but going from 0-10 in 1955 to 2-7-1 in 1956 was not anything to write home about.

"We were optimistic going into the 1956 season," Sid said. "We thought we would have a good football team, but the problems remained.

"The organization was poor. Ears Whitworth was the head football coach. Hank Crisp was athletic director and also line coach. So off the field, Coach Crisp was Whitworth's boss. On the field, Whitworth was Coach Crisp's boss. Things just couldn't (and didn't) work that way.

"Also," Sid continued, "we had a mixture of an old (former head coach) Red Drew staff and the ones that Ears brought in. That was a problem, too. Anytime you have that kind of internal conflict, it's going to affect the players. That's exactly what happened to us."

Sid Neighbors was on hand at the dawn of the Bryant era at Alabama.

The Tiders did manage to break a 20-game losing streak against Mississippi State in late October, but that didn't last long. "It was a great feeling to finally win one," Sid said. "We thought we were going to turn it around then, but it didn't happen that way."

Sid started at tackle in every game of the 1956 and 1957 seasons. The 2-7-1 record in 1956 was duplicated in 1957, Sid's junior year.

"More problems came up in 1957," Sid recalled. "They started tightening down on the money (for the football program) because of poor attendance at the games. We had a strike that year, and all the football players, led by the seniors, walked out of the dorm in the middle of the season. We were protesting living conditions, the food, and the way we were being treated. There were conflicts with the assistant coaches.

"I liked Ears Whitworth," Sid continued, "but he had some poor assistant coaches. He was good to me, giving me the chance to start as a sophomore. Whitworth tried to play the best people instead of the ones that others wanted him to play."

Auburn crushed the Tide, 40-0, in 1957, finishing a perfect season that earned the Tigers a national championship. Auburn would beat Alabama in 1958 also, but after that the tables would turn.

Ears Whitworth had seen his last days at Alabama. His overall three-year record of 4-24-2 was the worst by any coach in Alabama's illustrious football history. The Alabama program needed a break, a helping hand—anything.

On December 3, 1957, help came. Paul William Bryant, the "other end" to legendary Tider Don Hutson in the early thirties, announced he was heading back to the University of Alabama because, as he said, "my school called me."

Before coming to Alabama, Bryant coached one year at Maryland, eight years at Kentucky, and four years at Texas A&M, compiling an overall 91-39-8 record. But most important, he had turned every program around, and that's what the Alabama following was starving for.

Bryant had a reputation Alabama players didn't particularly like. They had heard horrendous stories of Bryant's "boot camp" in 1954 at Junction, Texas (in which only 27 players of two busloads returned), and they were scared, to say

18

the least.

"We were as scared as rattlesnakes," Sid said, "because of what we heard he had done at Texas A&M. Coach Bryant put the fear of God in us that (1958) spring practice. We went through a torture test that almost killed two or three people."

Bryant gave most of the linemen a weight in which to report back the next fall. During the spring Sid weighed around 240 pounds and was told to come back weighing 218. He lost ten pounds over the summer and reported back at 230 pounds. To say Bryant was upset is an understatement.

"I came back weighing 230 pounds, which was the lowest I had ever weighed at Alabama," Sid said. "Coach Bryant told me I was too fat to play. He told me I had to lose another ten pounds or he wasn't going to give me a uniform.

"The thing that really upset me," Sid continued, "was that (freshman brother) Billy was right behind me in line on weigh-in day. He weighed 248 pounds and Coach Bryant told him that was all right. I weighed 230 and he told me I was too fat."

The frustrations mounted, and as a result Sid quit the team. "I thought it was real unfair," he said. "I was considering going to another school, but I didn't because I felt like my mother needed me at home. Bobby, my younger brother, was real sick and Momma needed my help. So I lived at home that year, held two jobs, and continued to go to school."

Sid was one of several seniors in 1958 that succumbed to the discipline of Bryant. For years it was a hard pill for him to swallow, but time has now healed the wounds.

"I understand it now," Sid said. "Time cures a lot of ills. You have to have some discipline when you rebuild. You have to have some goats, and I happened to be one of the goats. I regret that I ever quit."

Playing as a center and noseguard, the 5′11″, 250-pound Billy made All-County and All-State at Tuscaloosa County High School. Pat James, Alabama defensive line coach, recalled recruiting Billy for the Tide.

"My first impression was that Billy would never make it because he was too fat," chuckled James, who played under Bryant at Kentucky and is now owner of P.J.'s Lounge in Birmingham. "He was overweight when I first met him.

"I told him if he wanted to stay at Alabama, he'd better lose some weight. I think he finally got down to about 230."

Billy had many scholarship offers but chose Alabama "because there was no doubt where I wanted to go." He wasn't the only one that wanted to wear the Crimson in 1958—84 other freshmen and transfers also signed scholarships.

Billy had been looking forward to playing with Sid, but they never stepped on the field together. Sid exited as Billy entered.

"I strongly considered going to play somewhere else with Sid," Billy said, "but I had *always* wanted to go to Alabama. At the time he quit, Coach Bryant was trying to establish some kind of discipline at Alabama. The Whitworth years weren't very productive, and Sid had a lot of frustrations. Then Coach Bryant came and made all the changes. Sid had made a lot of sacrifices earlier (for the family), and I understood his decision to quit."

Billy's freshman class, which Bryant called "hand-delivered by (Tide assistant coaches) Jerry Claiborne and Hank Crisp," was loaded with talent. In the group were three high school All-Americans (Travis Casey, Steve Anderson, and Billy Coleman), two honorable mention All-Americans (Carl Hopson and Billy Richardson), and 23 All-Staters from Alabama, Texas, Tennessee, Arkansas, and Washington.

Players such as Tommy Brooker, Richard "Digger" O'Dell, Jimmy Sharpe, John O'Linger, Mal Moore, Pat Trammell, and Bill Oliver joined Billy in a class that Bryant later called "probably the best freshman group I ever had in terms of character and dedication."

"We didn't know what to expect (from Bryant)," Billy said. "I was not afraid of him, just apprehensive. I think to be a good football player you've got to have confidence in yourself and not worry about who the coach is. There's always that uncertainty, but I wasn't afraid.

"The first thing that impressed me most about Coach Bryant was his attitude about winning. He told us in the first meeting that if we stayed we would win the national championship in 1961. He was to the point."

Although Bryant's prediction to the freshmen was not public knowledge at the time, he fondly recalls the meeting in

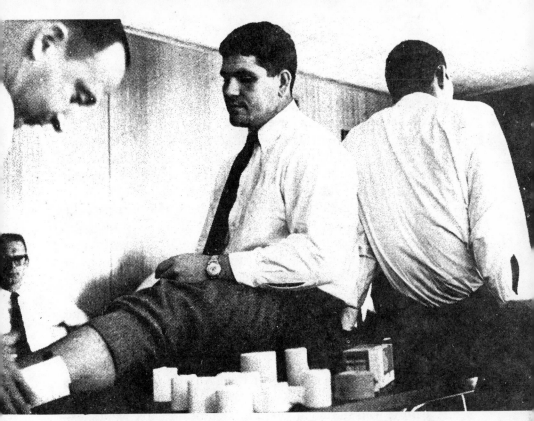

Trainer Jim Goostree prepares Billy Neighbors for another gridiron battle.

his book, *Bear.*

"In the fall, ...I met with just the freshmen," he wrote. "It was to be a regular thing from then on, those noon meetings, but that first one set the tone.

"I just sensed they were something special. I told them what football should mean to them, and what the program would be. Then I challenged them.

"I said, 'What are you doing here?' And I waited. It was so quiet in there you could hear a pin drop.

"I said, 'What are you doing here? Tell me why you're here. If you're not here to win the national championship, you're in the wrong place.'

"Then I told them what I thought it would take to do it, and they believed me. They believed every word.

"They believed it then, and they believed it all the way

through school....

"When I walked out that day I knew we were going to win the national championship with that group. Before that I had just talked about it, thought about it, and dreamed about it. This time I was sure. And every time I saw them after that I felt the same way. The pride they had. They had a goal and they never lost sight of it."

For that freshman class of 1958 the road to the national championship began with a scoreless tie against the tough Mississippi State Bullpups. Seventeen more freshmen left the team in the ensuing two weeks, but that didn't keep the Baby Tide from ripping Tulane, 25-6. In that game enthusiasm surfaced as more than 3,000 fans turned out under the lights at Denny Stadium to cheer their Tide to victory.

The Tide offense came alive against the Baby Greenies with quarterbacks Mal Moore, Pat Trammell, and Billy Coleman all completing two passes each for a total of 164 yards and three touchdowns. Ronnie Davis led the rushing attack with 62 yards in five carries.

The freshmen knocked off rival Auburn to finish with a 2-0-1 record.

Billy, who started at guard in each of the three games, explained the formula for the freshmen team's success. "We were committed to winning," he said. "Coach Bryant told us (freshmen) that when the year was over, we would be playing like juniors. I think we were. He told us to be tough, disciplined, and to play like a team, and we did."

Bryant made quite an impression on the freshmen that year. Bill Battle, a member of the 1959 freshmen group, remembers well a pep talk Billy gave a gathering of high school prospects during the 1958 season.

"When I was a prospect in 1958, I went to the Alabama-Vanderbilt game in Birmingham," recalled Battle, later Tennessee head coach and now an executive with Disco Aluminum Products and Golden Eagle Enterprises in Selma. "Back then all the prospects, along with the freshmen team, sat down on the sidelines during the game.

"I remember (Pat) Trammell, Neighbors, and Gary Phillips were all down there. I was sitting next to Neighbors, and somebody started asking him about the University and

22

about how tough Coach Bryant really was.

"Neighbors jumped up and started a recruiting pitch about 10 minutes long. He got to talking about the University of Alabama and told us how he believed in state universities and that whatever state we lived in, we ought to go to the state university because they had the advantage over the other schools.

"Then he said, 'Yea, Coach Bryant is tough, but I don't give a damn if Hitler is coaching, you still ought to go to the state university!'"

While the freshmen were rolling to a 2-0-1 slate in 1958, the varsity was making some noise of its own. Only six lettermen were lost from the 1957 team that went 2-7-1, but that didn't impress the news media. One prediction picked the Tide 12th out of the 12-team Southeastern Conference (Tulane and Georgia Tech were members then, in addition to the present-day 10 schools).

Bryant inherited a team he referred to as "the biggest collection of slow and fat people I've ever seen assembled at one university." The discipline was tough—Sid Neighbors was only one of more than 20 varsity members to quit the team. By season's end, only 46 were left.

Bryant has always credited the Tide assistant coaches for his successes on the gridiron. His first staff, composed of Hayden Riley, Phil Cutchin, Carney Laslie, Pat James, Sam Bailey, Bobby Drake Keith, Gene Stallings, Bobby Luna, Jerry Claiborne, and Jim Goostree, was the beginning of a long line of men that have gone on to become head coaches in the college and professional ranks. Zipp Newman of the *Birmingham News* called the 1958 group "one of the most brilliant young staffs (of assistants) in the history of Southern football."

With only eight seniors the 1958 varsity made a mockery out of the pre-season predictions by finishing with a 5-4-1 record. The opening game was a 13-3 loss to eventual national champion LSU.

After a scoreless tie with Vanderbilt, Bryant earned his first victory at Alabama by whipping Furman, 29-6. Next came a close loss to Tennessee in Knoxville, then the Tide upset Mississippi State and Georgia. Two weeks later Bama shocked Georgia Tech, 17-8, prompting 2,500 fans to welcome the victorious Tide back to Tuscaloosa.

The finale was against Auburn, the defending national champions and winners of 23 straight games. The Tigers prevailed, 14-8, but the mold had been set. In only one season Bryant had turned the Alabama football program around. Sportswriters and columnists across the South were praising Bryant's accomplishment, one calling him "the remaker of Crimson Tide football prestige."

The freshman class of 1958 figured to play a big part in the upcoming 1959 season. Quarterback Bobby Jackson had graduated into the professional ranks, so the quarterback spot was up for grabs among James Patton, Curtis Crenshaw, Mal Moore, Pat Trammel, Bobby Skelton, Carl Barton, Ingram Culwell, and Tommy Sewell. Trammell had a good spring, leading the Red team to a 14-3 win before 15,000 spectators in the A-Day clash. The Scottsboro youngster would become the Tide's top signal caller for the next three years.

Billy's class had dwindled in numbers to 33 players entering his sophomore year in 1959. But these players were the ones needed to eventually earn the national championship. Several sophomores—Billy, Tommy Brooker, Billy Richardson, Pat Trammell, Carl Hopson, Bill Rice, to name a few—played in every game. Billy, Brooker, Trammell, and Rice were bona-fide first-teamers, quite an accomplishment in the days of one-platoon football.

The sophomores, along with 25 juniors and only 9 seniors, blitzed to an unbelievable 7-1-2 record in only Bryant's second year. Billy started at tackle in the 17-3 opening loss to Georgia, then was switched back to guard for the next game. "Billy's more at home at guard," Bryant said about the move. "He's never been loose and relaxed at tackle. We think it'll make us a better football team."

A better football team it became. After the Georgia loss Alabama battled Vanderbilt and Tennessee to 7-7 ties. Benny Marshall of the *Birmingham News* spotted the sophomores' roles in the Tennessee game. "Traditionally," he wrote, "the Alabama-Tennessee game, patterned for rock-ribbed combat, is no place for sophomores. Most of those who worked for Bryant Saturday found themselves, surprisingly, right at home."

The seven victories came over Houston, Chattanooga,

Mississippi State, Tulane (Bryant's 100th career victory), Georgia Tech, Memphis State, and Auburn. The Houston and Georgia Tech wins were decided by Fred Sington, Jr.'s, field goals. In the Tennessee tie Sington missed a 16-yarder with nine seconds left that would have given the Tide a victory.

The Auburn game was a big one for both sides. Alabama was looking for its first win over the Tigers since 1953, and Auburn was trying to extend the dominance and preserve its high national ranking. On a muddy Legion Field the Tide whipped the favored Plainsmen, 10-0, ending the five-year drought. The victory was so big that University president Frank Rose gave all the Alabama students an extended Thanksgiving vacation by calling off Monday's classes.

Stars were plenty in the Auburn game. Trammell, Richardson, Brooker, Don Cochran, and Marlin "Scooter" Dyess were

Billy Neighbors (73) shows his All-American form as he protects Tide running back Cornell Johnson (20).

exceptional. But the most memorable play of the day belonged to Billy. Bryant cited it in *Bear*.

Late in the game and 10 points down, Auburn was driving. Alabama guard Gary Phillips put a tremendous rush on Auburn quarterback Bryant Harvard, forcing a hurried pass. Billy rose up from his defensive tackle position and intercepted. He was so surprised, he just didn't know what to do with the ball.

"I was supposed to holler 'bingo' when I intercepted it," Billy recalled. "That was what they had taught us to say when anyone intercepted a pass. It was to let the other defensive players know so they could help block.

"Anyway, I forgot what to say, so I started jumping up and down, yelling 'help, help, help!'"

Alabama's 10 points came on a 27-yard field goal by Brooker and a 39-yard touchdown pass from Bobby Skelton to Scooter Dyess. The 145-pound Dyess, hence the nickname "Scooter," was voted the game's most valuable player.

Bryant was extremely proud of his squad's effort. "Before the game we said it'd take a superhuman effort to win, and I think our boys gave it," he said. "If our team played 100 percent against Georgia Tech (in a 9-7 victory), it played 135 percent to beat Auburn."

Despite its 7-1-1 record, the Tide was ignored by all the major bowls. The Blue Grass Bowl in Lexington, Kentucky, a financial flop in 1958, offered Bama a bid, but it was turned down. The day after beating Auburn, Bryant announced that Alabama would not be accepting any invitations.

But that was before 4,000 students turned out for a rally when it was learned that Navy might decline its invitation to play in the Liberty Bowl. The students thought their Tide deserved a bowl bid, and they urged the school to accept.

The next morning a delegation of players headed by guard Bill Hannah and center Jim Blevins called on Bryant to ask that the team be allowed to play if asked. Dr. Rose polled the board of trustees, and the members gave him their permission.

A day later the news came. Alabama was offered, and accepted, a bid to play Penn State in Philadelphia's Liberty Bowl.

"We're not going North to have people forget us," Bryant remarked about the match-up with Penn State. He knew the game meant a lot for Southern football. Thirty-seven years

Captains Billy Neighbors (73) and Pat Trammell (12) huddle with teammates Tommy Brooker (81), Jack Rutledge (60), and Jimmy Wilson (64).

earlier head coach Xen Scott had taken a scrappy Tide team to Philadelphia and had upset the Pennsylvania Quakers, 9-7. Bryant wanted the same in 1959.

The trip to Philadelphia was a new experience for most of the Alabama players, Billy included. When asked by Bryant if he was excited about the trip, Billy replied, "Coach, I ain't never been north of Gadsden."

After the Tiders arrived in Philadelphia and took the field for their first workout, Bryant made an unusual request for 22 folding chairs. The Philadelphia media was puzzled. Only after they saw why Bryant used the chairs did they realize the creativeness, ingenuity, and savvy of the man called Bear.

The headlines called it a "sit-down" practice, but it was known to the Alabama coaches as a "concentration drill." Eleven players were seated in their normal starting positions across from eleven non-starters in the defensive positions. The coaches yelled out a play, and the players pointed in the direction they were supposed to move for runs, passes, and blocks.

27

Using this drill many more "plays" were run, therefore saving valuable practice time. When asked why he used the drill, Bryant responded, "It saves wear and tear on my boys." The Penn State coaches knew they had their hands full.

Alabama lost a heartbreaker in the wind and cold, 7-0. In the first half the Nittany Lions scored the game's only touchdown on a fake field goal play that had been put in the playbook only two days earlier.

Bryant had lost his first bowl game at Alabama, but he began a bowl appearance streak that has stretched to 23 and counting.

"We weren't very enthused about the Liberty Bowl," Billy said. "We had been through a long season. But the seniors wanted to go, so we went. The weather was horrible (cold) up there. We rode a train because Coach Bryant said he didn't want to fly over those mountains.

"It was the worst football game I've ever played in my life. I was a disgrace to the University."

Billy had the opportunity to line up against Charles Janerett, Penn State's 6'3", 235-pound tackle. Janerett was Penn State's only black player (and one of the country's few).

"It was the first time an Alabama team had ever played against a black," Billy said. "I remember people coming up to me after the game asking me what it was like. It was tough, that's what."

Marlin "Scooter" Dyess, now regional sales manager for Disco Aluminum Products in Montgomery, can testify that Janerett was tough. "We ran an off-tackle play (against Penn State) and I was the running back." Dyess said. "I hit the line and Janerett creamed me, almost killing me.

"When we got back to the huddle, Billy (Neighbors) patted me on the rear end and said, 'Scooter, I'm sorry, but I missed my block.'

"I said, 'Yea, I noticed.'"

Billy's class, the "super sophs," was making quite a name for itself. Billy and Tommy Brooker made the SEC All-Sophomore first team, while Bill Rice, Pat Trammell, and Billy Richardson were chosen to the second team. The cool Trammell, rapidly becoming known as a general on the field, rushed for more than 500 yards and was second in the SEC in total offense with 818 yards.

Bryant was being called a defensive genius after only two years. His first Alabama squad surrendered only 75 points, and the 1959 team held its opponents to a mere 59 points. The much-needed offensive punch was expected to improve with the addition of several outstanding running backs.

Billy sensed a special feeling going into his junior season. Lee Roy Jordan, Bill Battle, Charley Pell, Jimmy Wilson, Cotton Clark, and Mike Fracchia were a few of the sophomores in 1960 that would be counted on to continue the Tide's resurgence as a national football power.

"There was such a oneness with that team," Billy said. "Coach Bryant told us we were the people that were going to bring Alabama back to the tradition of winning."

The road to that national championship continued on September 17, 1960. In front of 44,000 fans and a nationwide television audience, the Tide ripped the Georgia Bulldogs, 21-6.

"Fran Tarkenton was a senior then," Billy said. "I was assigned to watch the draw, the screen, and rush the passer. I couldn't do anything. He scrambled and threw all over the place."

Billy may not have been impressed with his play against Georgia, but Pat Dye surely was. Dye, former Tide assistant and now Auburn head coach, was an All-American guard for Georgia in 1960. He recalls going one-on-one with Billy the whole game.

"Billy and I played right across from each other (in that game)," Dye said. "They got down to the one-yard line, and (Tide quarterback) Bobby Skelton ran a quarterback sneak. Billy knocked me way back into the end zone, allowing Skelton to score. Yes, I remember that well."

Alabama streaked to fifth in the national polls (Ole Miss was first) after the Georgia win. The Tide rallied to tie Tulane, 6-6, then whipped Vanderbilt. A trip to Knoxville proved disastrous, as Bama was trounced by the Tennessee Volunteers, 20-7.

"We probably got beat on Thursday in that game," Billy said. "The coaches got us fired up too soon. We had a lot better team than Tennessee.

"Football is 98 percent emotion. By the time you're a

junior or senior, the physical part is developed. Then it's up to the coaches to take that talent and develop it. That was one of the few games that I thought the timing was off getting us up for the game.''

The Tide defeated Houston, Mississippi State, Furman, Georgia Tech, Tampa, and Auburn to finish with an 8-1-1 mark. In the Tech game Alabama was behind, 15-0, at halftime, then came back to win, 16-15, on Richard O'Dell's field goal with time running out. It was his first-ever attempt of a field goal. The game prompted Bryant to say in *Bear* that ''if it wasn't the greatest comeback I have ever seen, it was certainly the greatest one I've been involved in.''

Billy remembers the day well. ''We were getting beat 15-0 at halftime,'' he said, ''and we were apprehensive about what Coach Bryant would say. He came in and told us we had played well. He said we needed to go back out there and play our same game, but a little better.

''He won the game at halftime by his attitude. That was the greatest coaching job I've seen in my life, not by the X's and O's, but by the mental attitude of the people involved.''

The Tide had finally gained some respect, so this time it didn't have to *hope* for a bowl bid—one was assured. Immediately after the Auburn victory, Alabama accepted an invitation to play Texas in the two-year-old Bluebonnet Bowl. The smaller, quicker Tide (the line averaged only 193 pounds) battled the Longhorns to a 3-3 tie to wrap up a successful 8-1-2 season.

Billy and halfback Leon Fuller made third-team All-SEC. For a team to go 8-1-2 and have only two players chosen for All-Anything showed the balance of this Tide squad.

After the season Bryant praised Billy's performance throughout his career. ''Neighbors,'' he said, ''has been the finest all-around lineman we've had here in two years. He's done a fine job for us, offensively and defensively.''

The road to that national championship continued as the Tide entered the 1961 season. But for the first time in three years the end was in sight; the destination almost a reality.

Eleven games later the Alabama team finally arrived. In early December of 1961 Alabama was named the best football team in all the land. Through hours, days, weeks, months, and years of blood, guts, and determination by the men in Crimson, the Tide was finally rewarded for its efforts. But—who in that freshman class of 1958 was surprised when they won the national championship? No one.

"When we were freshmen," Billy emphasized, "we said we were going to win the national championship. That's all we thought about. Nobody was going to beat us."

The undefeated 1961 campaign began with a 32-6 trouncing of Georgia and ended with a 10-3 victory over Arkansas in the Sugar Bowl. In between, the awesome Tide defeated Tulane, Vanderbilt, North Carolina State (and its quarterback Roman Gabriel), Tennessee, Houston, Mississippi State, Richmond, Georgia Tech, and Auburn. Only 25 points were scored on the Tide defense all season. Six shutouts were recorded including the last five regular season games in a row.

"In 1961 we had the best team in college football," Bryant wrote in *Bear*. "I could name so many 'favorite' players on that

Billy Neighbors (73) and Charley Pell (69) close in to tackle an Auburn runner in the 1961 contest.

team. Mike Fracchia, Billy Neighbors, Pat Trammell, Lee Roy Jordan, Jimmy Sharpe, Richard Williamson, Billy Richardson, Ray Abbruzzese, Bill Rice, Bill Battle, Charley Pell, Darwin Holt, Tommy Brooker, Cotton Clark—they played like it was a sin to give up a point.''

Following the undefeated 1961 season, Billy, Pat Trammell, and junior Lee Roy Jordan were named All-SEC (along with junior Mike Fracchia and senior Tommy Brooker). Then the trio reached the ultimate when they were named to several All-American teams, making them Alabama's first All-Americans since Ed Salem in 1950. Billy's mate at tackle on most of the All-American squads was Merlin Olsen, a 6'5",

The 1961 Alabama squad was the best in the land. Celebrating, seated from left to right, are Lee Roy Jordan, Ray Abbruzzese, John O'Linger, and Pat Trammell. Standing, from left to right, are Charley Pell, Mike Fracchia, Billy Neighbors, Tommy Brooker, Butch Wilson, and Bill Battle.

WE'RE NUMBER ONE

265-pounder from Utah State and later consensus All-Pro with the Los Angeles Rams.

Trammell, the SEC offensive king, finished fifth in the balloting for the Heisman Trophy, which was won by Syracuse's Ernie Davis, the first black to win in the award's 27-year history. Trammell passed up a professional football career to attend medical school. On December 10, 1969, in the prime of life, Dr. Pat Trammell died of cancer. He was 28 years old.

Billy won the Plitt Theatres Outstanding Defensive Award, the Birmingham Monday Morning Quarterback Club's Outstanding Lineman Award, and participated in the Coaches All-American game in which Ohio State's Woody Hayes was his head coach. He also played offensive and defensive guard in the Senior Bowl.

"Dedication" best described Billy Neighbors during his playing days at Alabama. Darwin Holt, Alabama linebacker in 1960 and 1961, spoke of Billy's dedication.

"Billy, Pat Trammell, and I had single rooms right next to each other," said Holt, now a Birmingham insurance executive. "After the tough two-a-day practices, Pat and I would be exhausted and about to fall out. I remember several times Pat and I hearing Billy in his room lifting weights. There we were, totally exhausted from a hard day's practice—and Billy was in there lifting weights. That was dedication."

The city of Northport honored Billy on "Billy Neighbors Day," and local Bama supporters presented him a 1962 Pontiac Grand Prix. Anyone else would have been excited to receive a car, but Billy had a problem. He couldn't drive. "My family couldn't afford a car, so there was no reason for me to learn how to drive," Billy said. "I had girls drive me around. I saved myself a lot of money that way.

"After I got my car, I learned how to drive and I've been driving ever since. I've had one wreck and one ticket."

Tide teammate and close friend Tommy Brooker fondly recalls Billy's inability to drive. "Billy couldn't drive a lick," Brooker chuckled.

"Several of us used to go to the picture show quite often. We would go in two or three different cars — Billy Richardson had a car and Brother (Bill) Oliver had a car called the 'tank.'

"We had it planned so that when we walked out of the show, we would all go jump in the car and leave the driver's seat vacant, because we knew Billy would be the last one there. We'd *make* him drive home.

"He got under the wheel and we'd jump all the way from the picture show to a service station across from the stadium. That's as far as he would go. He didn't want to go up by the dorm to let anybody see him driving.

"So when he heard he might get a car (from Northport)," Brooker continued, "he asked me to teach him how to drive. So I took my car and we'd go out and I would teach him how to drive. I'd act like the highway patrolman giving the drivers' test. We did that continuously for about two weeks.

"Sure enough, they gave him a car — a Pontiac Grand Prix with a stick shift. I had taught him enough to drive around the stadium, so we made it through that. But when we got to the gate, he put it in 'super' and we jumped down the road. I thought my head was going to fly off."

Another good buddy of Billy's was Billy Richardson of Jasper and now a stockbroker with Paine Webber in Birmingham. They played against each other in high school and became the best of friends during their football days at Alabama. Richardson smiles broadly when asked to recall stories about the easy-going, fun-loving Billy.

"Billy developed the name 'Steak' while we were in school," Richardson recalled. "I guess it came from the way he would devour his food. Sometimes he would pick up a big ol' T-bone and eat it without using a fork or knife. He was in a big hurry to get his food in.

"But one of the funniest things I remember about Billy happened one fall semester during finals week. We were all studying for exams, and a bunch of us back then would take No-Doz to help us stay awake at night.

"One night I had planned to stay up all night, studying for an exam. Around 11:00 Neighbors came up to my room and said he was sleepy and he needed to stay up and study. He asked me for a No-Doz, so I gave him one. I told him to take it, wash his face with cold water, and go outside (in the cold) and walk around the dorm a couple of times. I told him it would help him stay awake. He took the pill and left.

"About one-thirty or two he came in my room and said, 'Damn, Richardson! How do you turn this thing off? I'm ready to go to bed!' He was ready to hit the sack, but couldn't."

And of course Billy's size and physique were constantly topics of conversation around the dorm. "Billy used to be very self-conscious about being short and stocky and maybe even fat," said Brooker, now in the real estate and insurance business in Tuscaloosa. "He always claimed he was six feet tall, but we all knew he was 5'11" and three-quarters. But Billy wasn't really fat—his high school coach had taught him how to keep his belly sucked in.

"To kid him we'd try to pinch him in the stomach, and when we did he'd suck that stomach in and his big ol' chest would puff out. We figured out the only way to get him was to catch him at night after he had gone to sleep.

"When we knew he was asleep, we'd tiptoe down there and try to grab him on his stomach. When he realized what we were doing, he'd stick that chest out and that belly disappeared."

Billy's name and reputation made him a natural for professional football. Despite his relatively small size for a lineman (5'11", 240 pounds), he was in heavy demand. The Boston Patriots of the American Football League and the Washington Redskins of the National Football League drafted Billy in the fourth round. To make things more interesting, he was also being sought by the Edmonton Eskimos of the Canadian Football League. All the attention flattered Billy.

"During the middle of the (1961) season," Billy said, "I gained a lot of confidence in myself as a football player. I thought I could play professional football.

"The draft was held before the bowl games. I remember seeing (Arkansas end) Lance Alworth stand under the goalposts right after the Sugar Bowl and sign with the San Diego Chargers. I decided to play with Boston, and I signed with them a few days afterwards."

Before traveling to Boston, Billy married his college sweetheart of two years, Susan Kinzer of Huntsville. The couple had been introduced by two of Billy's closest friends and Tide teammates, Mike Hopper and Benny Nelson.

The first few days of practice with the Patriots still linger in Billy's mind. "Rookie camp was an experience of humiliation,"

In only his fourth year as Alabama head coach, Paul "Bear" Bryant and his 1961 team brought home the national championship. From left to right are Tommy Brooker, Pat Trammell, Lee Roy Jordan, Bryant, Mike Fracchia, and Billy Neighbors.

he said. "The veterans treated us like we were nothing. You had to prove yourself. I did well though, especially on the one-on-one drills. I was 'accepted' on the third day of practice."

Billy's rookie season started on somewhat of an unpleasant note. "In the first exhibition game," Billy recalled, "I had a hip pointer and didn't play that well. The *Boston Globe* wrote that I was slow and unimpressive. That got me fired up."

Fired up he got. As a rookie he started every game at offensive guard and quickly earned the reputation as one of the league's sharpest and hardest blockers. In 1963, Billy's second season, the Patriots won their first AFL Eastern Division championship. Billy was a consensus All-Pro and was considered one of the main reasons for the Patriots' improvement.

Backs Larry Garron and Ron Burton and quarterback Babe Parilli were but three of Billy's teammates that praised his talents. Garron, who held most of the Patriot rushing records in the sixties, said after the 1963 season that "Billy is the kind of guard every back dreams of running behind."

Burton echoed Garron. "Billy pulls and blocks better than any guard I've ever run behind," he said. "He's amazing. Looking at him you'd never think that with his size he could ever beat the halfback to the corner. But I can honestly say I have never come close to running up his heels yet."

Parilli was Paul "Bear" Bryant's All-American quarterback at Kentucky in the early fifties. He too appreciated Billy's "Patriot-ism."

"That Billy has done so well has really made me happy," Parilli said at the time. "I helped our club sign Billy and I've never regretted it. Of course, I had the feeling all along that he would be a great one.

"Any boy who plays football for Alabama coach Paul Bryant is given the best football training in the country. I only hope Bryant will send a few more like Billy up to us. I'm getting older and I can use all the help I can get." (Bryant would indeed send another lineman — John Hannah — to the Patriots. Unfortunately, Parilli had long since retired from professional football.)

Boston line coach Art Spinner was an All-Pro guard six times with the Baltimore Colts, and he really appreciated Billy's fine play. After Billy's second year with Boston, Spinney said that "Billy will be the best guard in all of football with just a little more experience. He had the best blocking record of anyone in our entire line, which is quite an achievement for a boy who has been in pro ball for just two years."

Billy repeated All-Pro honors in 1964 but was out for most of the 1965 season with a broken collarbone. He still started every game, but his injury was reflected by the team's record—it dropped to a dismal 4-8-2 in 1965 after being 9-4-1, 7-6-1, and 10-3-1 in Billy's first three years.

Billy had enjoyed his four years in Boston, but he was ready to move on. He got his wish and was sent in the 1966 expansion draft to the Miami Dolphins. "I'm glad to be getting out of there (Boston)," he told *Miami Herald* sportswriter Edwin Pope after his arrival in Miami. "I wanted to come south and I'm about as far south now as you can get in pro football."

Miami head coach George Wilson, who had starred for Washington against Alabama in the 1926 Rose Bowl, was counting on Billy as one of the key men to build his offensive line around. After one week of practice, Wilson was sold on Billy. "Billy tears those defensive men up in one-on-one drills," he said. "That's where you tell who the football players are."

Billy started in all but one game for the Dolphins from 1966 to 1969. His prematurely gray hair and stubby appearance at 5'11" and 260 pounds earned him the label of "2,000-year-old man" among his teammates. Many of those same teammates—Dick Anderson, Mercury Morris, Jim Kiick, Larry Csonka, Bob Griese, Larry Little, Bill Stanfill, Manny Fernandez, Nick Buoniconti, and Howard Twilley, among others—would become Super Bowl champions in 1972 and 1973.

Billy retired from professional football following the 1969 season. He had been a model of consistency, a true "iron man." During his eight years he played in 111 games, 91 of them in succession before a deep shin laceration kept him out of a 1968 meeting with San Diego. Billy was elected the Dolphin co-captain in 1968 and was voted the Most Unsung Player Award. He also served as Miami's player representative.

Billy never experienced a winning season with the young Dolphin club, but he played a big role in laying the foundation for the championship years ahead. The announcement of Billy's retirement prompted Joseph Robbie, managing general partner, to remark, "Billy has been at the heart of this club from the outset—a courageous leader and a real class performer. He'll be sorely missed around here."

Billy has no regrets about retiring when he did. "After my third year (with the Dolphins)," Billy said, "I knew they were going to have a good team for the future. I believe I could have stayed and played at Miami two or three more years. But I had been injured some and saw myself slipping, and I didn't want to make that a habit. Instead of trying to hang on, I decided to retire. If I had stayed on, I would have had a chance to be on a Super Bowl team.

"But," he stated, "that's second-guessing yourself, and you should never do that. I'm not doing it now."

Billy has done little second-guessing since he retired from

Billy Neighbors played on the Miami Dolphins' first team in 1966.

football. Even as a player he was a stockbroker in the off-season, and the business interested him enough to make a career of it. He is currently vice president and branch manager of Thomson & McKinnon Securities in Huntsville, where he resides with wife Susan and children Wes (2-28-64), Claire (7-23-67), and Keith (11-29-69).

Wes, a consensus football All-Stater in 1981 at Huntsville High School, is hoping to spread even further the Neighbors family tradition at Alabama. The 6'2", 235-pound center-linebacker is entering the Alabama program as a freshman in the fall of 1982.

Billy and Wes will make up the first father-son duo to have both played football at Alabama under Paul Bryant. Although Wes could have played football anywhere in the nation, Billy wasn't shy about where he wanted Wes to attend college. "Yes, I wanted Wes to go to Alabama," Billy stated, "and I told him so. If not, I wanted him to go to Harvard or Brown, not to play football, but to study. Anybody who has a chance to do so should go to Alabama and play for and learn from Coach Bryant."

Sid resides in Shalimar, Florida, a small community outside Fort Walton. From the time of his graduation in 1959 Sid spent 11 years coaching high school football and 6 years at the B.F. Goodrich plant in Tuscaloosa, and since 1975 he has been dean of students of the Bay Area Vo-Tech School in Fort Walton. He is married to the former Charlotte Wynne of Pulaski, Tennessee, and they have two children, Sidney III, and Nancy.

Another brother, Bobby, was perhaps the biggest Alabama fan of all. Crippled since birth, Bobby missed only four Alabama games at Bryant-Denny Stadium since Coach Bryant came "back home" in 1958. He was not expected to live 24 hours, much less 40 years. After 33 operations and tons of courage, Bobby died in December of 1981.

As Coach Paul Bryant has said many times, the freshman class of 1958 occupies a special place in his heart. "There were a lot of boys who made the 1961 national championship possible," he said. "But it was that first group that was with us from the start, when things didn't look so good.

"They were the ones who said they came to win and stuck with it all the way. They were the nucleus and the backbone. It was very fitting that they played on a national championship team in their senior year."

Billy's praise of his hero never ceases. "Coach Bryant has been like a father to me," he said. "He's been good, kind, and understanding. He's always responded when I've called.

"He taught us to believe in ourselves, set some goals for ourselves, and to monitor ourselves on those goals. I've never met anybody that could touch him as an individual. He's the greatest person I've ever known in my whole life."

STEPHENS

Gerald • Charlie • Bruce

Charlie Stephens, even in his wildest dreams, never considered "pulling" for Auburn—in anything. After all, the Thomasville, Alabama, youngster had played his collegiate football with the University of Alabama (from 1960 to 1964) and went on to earn master's and law degrees at Alabama. Charlie's older brother, Gerald, had also played at Alabama, as did younger brothers Bruce and Benny Ray. For Charlie, Alabama's Crimson Tide was a family pedigree.

But, from January of 1977 until October of 1980, Charlie swapped his Crimson and White of Alabama for the Orange and Blue of Auburn University. Charlie Stephens became an attorney for Alabama's arch-rival, prompting a lot of good-natured family kidding.

The Stephens family was a name quite familiar to Alabama fans throughout the sixties. All three Stephenses that lettered — Gerald, Charlie, and Bruce — won national championships during their playing days at Alabama, making them the first of two "Triple Crown" families in Alabama football history. (Tim Davis, Steve Davis, and Bill Davis won national championships in 1961, 1965, and 1973, respectively.)

The Herbert Stephens family of Thomasville is no small gathering — Charlie was the second of seven brothers.

"Daddy worked at a local lumber company and mother at a local shirt factory," Charlie said. "They are hard working people. We grew up working — we had to. I think the values we learned were good for us. Now, I'm grateful for it, and I think I'm a better person to have grown up where we were expected to work and carry out certain responsibilities.

"As early as I can remember, we had odd jobs, went to school, and played whatever sport was in season. There were enough boys in our family to form our own team, whether it was football, baseball, basketball, or whatever. I think all of us played all three major sports. We played rough and were very competitive.

"(Older brother) Gerald set the stage for sports in our family. I kinda followed in his footsteps, and then it just passed on down to the others."

Charlie had plenty of brothers to "pass it on down" to. Bruce, Larry, Benny Ray, Don, and Randy were all waiting in the wings to carry on the Stephens family tradition. However, it was Gerald that started the (foot)ball rolling.

Growing up, Gerald was the biggest of the family, and the fact he was also the oldest made it even rougher on the others when it came to butting heads on the football field. "Gerald had to go in slow motion," Charlie recalled, "because he was so much bigger and stronger than the rest of us."

Bruce, perhaps the smallest of the clan, had a solution to battling Gerald. "Anytime we wanted to get after him, it would take two or three of us to catch him," he said. "I guess that's where most of our athletic abilities came from. We were always either running from each other or chasing each other."

Gerald graduated from Thomasville High School in 1958. Friends of the family considered Gerald's graduation as a continuation of a miracle that began in early June of 1954. It was then that Gerald was struck by a car and fought for his life in a hospital.

For two days he was not expected to live. He gradually showed signs of improvement, but his future remained cloudy. Gerald, the victim of a broken back, two broken pelvic bones, two crushed hips, and numerous internal injuries, was told by doctors that if he lived, he would never walk again.

But miracles do happen, and one happened to Gerald. After two months flat on his back, Gerald began walking on crutches. Two months later a cane replaced the crutches, and after a couple more months he was home free.

Gerald's burning desire to continue his football provided the motivation for his recovery. "I wanted to be able to play football again," he said. "The first time I ran the hundred-yard dash (after the accident), I ran it in about 16 seconds. Once I was fully recuperated, I could run it in about 10.6 or 10.7 seconds.

"I thank God and all my friends and family for guiding me through it all. Without them I would have been helpless."

Because of the accident Gerald missed his sophomore year of football. But he didn't stray too far from the action—his coach, D.F. Anderson, let him be one of the team's managers. Anderson had coached Gerald's father in high school and would coach three more of the Stephens family after Gerald.

Gerald's fine performances at center and linebacker during his junior and senior years didn't go unnoticed. He was

After an All-American junior college career, Gerald Stephens transferred to Alabama in the spring of 1961.

recruited by several colleges, one of which was the University of Alabama.

Alabama had just hired a man named Paul "Bear" Bryant to coach its victory-starved football program. Bryant had coached at Maryland, Kentucky, and Texas A&M before "coming home" to the same school where he had played 23 years earlier.

Bryant was a hard-nosed, tough disciplinarian, and his uncanny abilities to get the maximum out of his players was the main reason for his successes in turning the Terrapin, Wildcat, and Aggie programs around.

Bryant brought to Tuscaloosa several members of his Texas A&M staff, one of whom was Bobby Drake Keith. Defense was Keith's specialty, and one of his first assignments was to recruit Gerald Stephens. But Gerald wasn't sure if he was ready for Alabama football, so he declined the scholarship.

Instead, Gerald signed with Southwest Mississippi Junior College in Summit, and three years later he was a junior college All-American. Prior to the 1958 season Gerald cut his foot while jogging and was forced to sit out the entire year. During his freshman (1959) and sophomore (1960) seasons, the four-year college recruiters were once again out in numbers, all wondering why he had ever declined the Alabama scholarship.

Meanwhile, Charlie became the first football player from Thomasville High School to earn an SEC scholarship when he signed with Alabama in 1960 (Gerald's sophomore year at Southwest Mississippi).

Charlie, the 6-foot, 168-pound quarterback-linebacker, had played organized football since the fifth grade, and signing with Alabama was a dream come true for him. Bobby Jackson, Bryant's first quarterback at Alabama, was a graduate assistant coach in 1960, and it was his duty to recruit Charlie.

"He saw me play against Jackson High School one night," Charlie said, "and I don't know if it was my performance during the game or the fight after the game that impressed him most.

"Jackson was our big rival. If they won, we'd fight. If we won, we'd fight. If we tied, we'd fight. We had a big fight after the game. Bobby came down on the field and after the skirmish was over, he told me that he was impressed and that somebody would be coming down later to talk to me.

"Coach (Gene) Bebes Stallings came down to Thomasville soon after that, and we talked for about 30 or 40 minutes. He asked me whether I would like to play quarterback or linebacker. I told him I liked defense better. I didn't know it at the time, but he was a defensive coach. If I had told him I liked offense better, he might not have recommended me to be signed.

"He went back and recommended me for a scholarship. After I committed, the Auburn people in town got some Auburn coaches to come talk to me, but I told them I had already committed to Alabama."

Charlie signed as a quarterback and joined about 60 others in that freshman class of 1960. At first glance the talent was surprisingly strong. "The coaches kept bragging on us, telling us how good we were," Charlie said. "We went to play Tulane in New Orleans, and even Coach Bryant came to watch us. They beat us, 24-0, or something like that. The coaches were all disgusted.

"We drove almost nonstop from New Orleans to Tuscaloosa. When we got back to campus, the coaches' attitude was much different. Coach Bryant let the varsity off, and all the coaches came out to watch us practice under the lights until about nine that night.

"That practice was unbelievable," Charlie continued. "Jimmy Dill got hit on the chin hard enough to get him sewed up in the infirmary. But they just put a Band-Aid on him and sent him back out.

"Al Lewis got hit in the head so hard that it knocked his glass eye out. He wanted to call time out, but he couldn't. He wanted to get out of the practice, but nobody got out that night.

"They found his eye—it was covered with mud, just like a little mudball. Somebody kept his eye for him while we finished practice.

"That practice probably set the tone for our group from then on. We didn't lose another (freshman) game."

A junior college All-American (such as Gerald) in the neighboring state of Mississippi just doesn't go unnoticed by major colleges, and Alabama was no exception.

"One night I was in the athletic dorm at Southwest,"

Gerald recalled, "and Coach Bryant called me. In the conversation, he said, 'Do you think you can make the team?' I said, 'No sir, I don't think I can—I *know* I can.' That must have been what he wanted to hear, because he said, 'Well, I want to see you in Tuscaloosa on Saturday.'

"I had the opportunity to go to several schools in the SEC, but I told Coach Bryant that I wanted to play at Alabama. If I couldn't play for them, then I wanted to play *against* them."

Gerald traveled to Tuscaloosa that next Saturday and signed a scholarship. Because of his redshirt year in 1958 he was able to transfer between semesters, so in the spring of 1961 Gerald joined younger brother Charlie in the Crimson Tide football program.

Rarely does the *older* brother later join the *younger* brother, but that's what happened. "I was glad to have Gerald there," Charlie said, "because (growing up) he always gave me that confidence or took up for me. When I went to Alabama, I was strictly on my own, so I was glad he came."

Likewise, Gerald took advantage of the fact that Charlie had a year of Alabama football under his belt. "Charlie was like a big brother to me," Gerald said of his younger brother. "He looked out for me, showing me the ropes and helpful hints."

Charlie had played quarterback on the freshman team but was switched to offensive end and linebacker to open up 1961 spring practice. He never really got a chance to learn the new positions.

"On the fifth day of spring practice I hurt my left knee (stretched ligaments) and missed the rest of the spring," Charlie said. "I went to Thomasville over the summer to recuperate. We didn't have any weights, so I went outside and made a little apparatus with weights on a picnic table. Every day I did leglifts to strengthen the knee. In mid-summer they checked it, and it was OK."

Charlie returned to the Capstone for his sophomore season with his mind set on playing football. Unfortunately, his knee was thinking different.

"After the second week, I had not made the progress they expected of me," Charlie said. "Coach Bryant said they would redshirt me, and I didn't think too well of it. I wanted to play right then—I knew I was able to play. We had great hopes for

47

Charlie Stephens (15) was a quarterback on the Tide's 1961 freshman team.

that season, and I wanted to be a part of it."

The "great hopes" Charlie spoke of came true. The 1961 Tide squad, led by All-Americans Pat Trammell, Billy Neighbors, and Lee Roy Jordan, recorded 11 straight victories to win the national championship. Four years earlier Bryant had told the freshmen that it would happen, and they never doubted it. The road to the top had been tough but well-deserved.

Gerald backed up Lee Roy Jordan at center and linebacker during the 1961 season. Although he played frequently, Gerald didn't receive a letter for his efforts.

"Coach Bryant probably thought that I had not contributed as much because I hadn't gone through the whole program," Gerald said. "I don't guess I was a full member of the 'family' at that time. But, he was fair and had his standards."

Gerald and Charlie were finally able to play together during the 1962 season. Both earned letters—Gerald as a center and

Charlie as a split end and rover. As a team Alabama finished 10-1, its only loss by one point to Georgia Tech, 7-6.

The season opened with a 35-0 whitewash of Georgia in Legion Field. For the first time Legion Field's new upper deck was used. The addition had been condemned on the eve of the previous year's Alabama-Tennessee game for safety reasons.

Sophomore quarterback Joe Namath came into the contest untried but with a tremendous reputation. All he did was complete 10 out of 14 passes for 179 yards and 3 touchdowns. The "Bomber from Beaver Falls" would become perhaps the most famous name associated with Alabama football, with the exception of Bryant himself.

The Georgia game was the subject of a very controversial article printed in March of 1963 by the *Saturday Evening Post* in

Charlie Stephens wore the crimson colors of Alabama, then after becoming an attorney, was asked to defend arch-rival Auburn.

which Bryant and Georgia athletic director Wally Butts were charged with "fixing" the game. Both men sued the *Post,* and on February 3, 1964, Bryant settled out of court for $300,000. Butts was awarded $460,000.

After the Georgia game, the Tide traveled to New Orleans and ripped Tulane, 44-6. Namath was once again magnificent, hitting six of seven passes for 98 yards.

Victories over Vanderbilt, Houston, Tennessee, and Tulsa boosted Bama's record to 6-0. The Tulsa game was the 24th straight without a defeat, breaking Coach Wallace Wade's record of 23, set in 1925 to 1927.

Following a 20-0 win over Mississippi State, Alabama played Miami in Tuscaloosa. For the first time in 15 games the Tide fell behind, trailing 3-0 at halftime.

"We hadn't done anything right," Charlie said. "I was terrified when we went into the dressing room. Everybody was trying to find a corner to hide in. We were expecting Coach Bryant to break the door down.

"He walked in there, clapping his hands and singing. 'It's a perfect day for football,' he said, 'just like a storybook finish. You go in there behind, you come from behind to win—that's the way to show your class.'"

The Tide listened well, scoring 5 touchdowns in 23 minutes for a 36-3 victory. Once again Namath was the star.

Alf Van Hoose of the *Birmingham News* wrote: "The darkhaired boy (Namath) from Pennsylvania pitched and ran his mates from a three-point halftime deficit to a 36-3 triumph over upset-vowing Miami with a performance that put jubilant homecomers among a record Tuscaloosa crowd of 43,000 wondering if Alabama's hallowed old home field ever saw a better 30 minutes of football—by one man, or a team."

The bubble burst the next week as Georgia Tech intercepted five Tide aerials on its way to a 7-6 upset victory. Tech head coach Bobby Dodd called it his "greatest triumph."

The Crimsons closed out the 1962 season with a 38-0 trouncing of Auburn and a 17-0 victory over Bud Wilkinson's Oklahoma Sooners in the Orange Bowl. President John F. Kennedy, who had received an honorary Alabama letter in 1961 from Bryant, was in attendance at the Orange Bowl. Kennedy gave the Alabama squad some extra incentive before the game when he failed to come by the Alabama locker room after visiting with the Oklahoma team.

Gerald started at center against Oklahoma so that Lee Roy Jordan could concentrate solely on his linebacker position. The All-American Jordan, who had finished fourth in voting for the Heisman Trophy, responded with 24 tackles against the Sooners in what he called his "best football game as a collegian."

Charlie backed up Richard Williamson at end and finished the season with five receptions for 64 yards. Williamson, halfback Cotton Clark, and Namath made All-SEC. Others who played a big part in the 10-1 campaign were linemen Charley Pell, Jimmy Sharpe, Dan Kearley, and Frankie McClendon; ends Richard O'Dell and Bill Battle; backs Butch Wilson, Benny Nelson, and Eddie Versprille; and placekicker Tim Davis.

"I think the '62 team was better than the '61 team," Charlie said. "We were more wide open and versatile offensively, and probably just as good defensively. We had the material to win the national championship again but fell short."

Gerald and Charlie were virtually inseparable during the 1962 season. "We were real close," Gerald said. "He helped me and I did what I could to help him. He was a good football player, but more than anything he was an inspiration to me. If I was down, he was always there with a word of encouragement."

By 1963 Joe Namath was making quite a name for himself. However, it wasn't necessarily Namath's actions *on* the field that gave him the headlines—it was his behavior *off* the field.

Nine days after Alabama lost, 10-8, to Auburn, Bryant suspended Namath from the team for breaking training rules. Two national television contests remained on the schedule—Miami and the Sugar Bowl against Ole Miss. Namath's absence painted a cloudy picture ahead for this Tide squad.

"Joe got caught doing something anybody on the team could have done," Charlie said. "He had been to a fraternity party just like a lot of the rest of us.

"Later that night, Joe and (team manager Jack) Hoot Owl Hicks went down to the Little Cookie, a little snack shop the players always went to. The gentleman that owned it always furnished our fruit for the road games, and we always used to eat there after the home games.

"It was real crowded, so Joe pulled his '54 Ford into this gentleman's special parking place right out front. He and Hoot Owl went in and ate. The man came in and told Joe to move his car. They got into a little discussion, and someone called the police.

"Because it was Joe, the thing was blown way out of proportion, and he got suspended."

In Namath's place enter a skinny sophomore from Cleveland, Tennessee, named Steve Sloan. Sloan and senior Jack Hurlbut quarterbacked Alabama to a 17-12 victory over Miami on national television, despite an NCAA record-breaking passing performance by Hurricane quarterback George Mira.

Sloan started at quarterback against Ole Miss in the Sugar Bowl, but it was Tim Davis' field goals of 31, 46, 22, and 48 yards that accounted for all the scoring in Bama's 12-7 victory. Nicknamed the "Snow Bowl" because of the record snowfall the night before, the game was a fierce defensive struggle from start to finish.

"I'm wearing Tim's (Davis) Sugar Bowl watch right here," Charlie chuckled. "The press was real negative toward us before the game. They were calling it a mismatch and said we weren't even in the same class with Ole Miss.

"We had enough unity and togetherness to go out there and beat them," Charlie continued. "They probably had a better team than we did, but they thought it would be an easy game. We showed them otherwise.

"Joe (Namath) didn't make the trip with the team, but he was there supporting us. Nobody on the team had any bad feelings toward Joe. I think it made us a little closer."

Charlie was on the receiving end of several Namath passes in 1963, one being a 60-yard touchdown for Bama's only points in the 10-6 loss to Florida. The game was Bryant's first defeat in Denny Stadium, and until at least the 1982 season it was also his last.

Namath and Sloan split quarterback duties during the undefeated 1964 season. The Tide lost a heartbreaker in the Orange Bowl to Texas, 21-17, but the 10-0 regular season record was enough to earn it the national championship.

Charlie Stephens (82) fights for yardage in a 1963 loss to Florida in Denny Stadium.

"We were good (in 1964) but not as good as '61 or '62," Charlie said. "We played hard and had a good, unified group. In the Orange Bowl we changed our defense to confuse Texas, and they just ate it alive. They ran down the field like nobody had ever done. We just couldn't stop them.

"We were behind, 21-7, at the half. Coach Bryant came in and told us to forget the new stuff and to play with the defense that got us there.

"We went back out," Charlie continued, "and they didn't score again. Joe got the offense going, and we scored 17 points. Near the end of the game Joe tried a quarterback sneak and didn't make it.

"The cameras showed he scored, and we felt he had scored. Coach Bryant had a very simple answer. He said that it shouldn't have been close enough to be questionable, and if it was that close we didn't deserve it."

Namath may not have scored on that sneak, but he certainly made up for it the next day when he signed an unheard-of

$400,000 contract with the New York Jets of the American Football League. He would go on to become one of the greatest passers in professional football history.

Charlie Stephens' three-year record as a team member at Alabama was 29-4, including a national championship in 1964. He was a two-year starter at split end but rarely made the headlines. His biggest asset to the team was his leadership, both on and off the field.

Steve Sloan, a teammate of Charlie's and now head coach at Ole Miss, remembers Charlie's impact on the team. "Charlie was a guy that I would categorize as a natural leader," Sloan said. "He had a lot of leadership qualities and showed them by speaking at team meetings on several occasions.

"Charlie was an 'effort' guy, a good, tough player. He not only articulated his leadership, but he gave it by example also."

Charlie had made up his mind to enter the coaching profession, so he served the Bama staff as a graduate assistant during spring training of 1965. Staying for the spring also gave Charlie

Charlie Stephens (82), along with teammates Bob Pettee (62), Gary Martin (42), Grady Elmore (37), Mike Hopper (86), and Ken Mitchell (60) escort head coach Paul "Bear" Bryant off the field following a 17-0 shutout of Oklahoma in the 1963 Orange Bowl.

the chance to see younger brother Bruce in action as a Tider. Actually, Bruce had entered the Alabama program in 1963 when Charlie was a junior. However, a strange turn of events after Bruce's freshman year kept him and Charlie from ever playing together.

Bruce came out of Thomasville High School in 1963 as a 5'8", 155-pound linebacker. Alabama saw him play only once, but that was enough to offer him a scholarship. "Since Gerald was bigger and Charlie was taller, I guess they thought I'd grow some more," Bruce chuckled, "but I fooled 'em. I never did grow very much."

Joining Bruce in that freshman class of 1963 included Kenny Stabler, Cecil Dowdy, Tom Somerville, Richard Cole, David Chatwood, Les Kelley, and Dickey Thompson. By the start of the season Bruce was up to 5'10" and 175 pounds.

"I played noseguard and was used a few times as a dummy," he recalled. "They'd put me on three-on-three drills, and I was the 'one.' Gaylon McCollough was the center, and all the guards were bigger than me. They really beat me around a lot."

Bruce was switched to offensive guard during spring practice and responded well. At the conclusion of the spring he had earned a starting position and was being counted on heavily for the upcoming 1964 season. And because Charlie was a senior-to-be, the Stephens family tradition at Alabama would continue without interruption.

In late summer of 1964 the Stephens family tradition almost ended. After only one year of college football, Bruce called it quits.

"About a week before time to report back to school," Bruce said, "I decided I wasn't going back. I got to thinking if it was all really worth it or not. Because of my size I didn't think I would be able to play the next year. I thought I would be red-shirted.

"So I left and went to New Orleans and got a job as a carpenter. I didn't tell anybody, because I would have probably been talked out of going. As soon as school started, when I knew it was too late to go back, I called to let my parents know where I was. I had made up my mind that I wasn't going back to college."

55

Charlie had the unenviable task of telling Coach Bryant about Bruce's decision. "On reporting day," Charlie recalled, "I kept looking and hoping Bruce would come back any minute, but he never showed up.

"Coach Bryant came by just before the evening meal and said, 'Charlie, I've seen everybody but ol' Bruce. Where's Bruce?' I said, 'Coach, I don't know, but I don't think he's coming back.' He looked at me and said, 'Well, I hope your daddy kicks his butt.' I said, 'Coach, if Daddy ever sees him, I'm sure he will.'"

While in New Orleans, Bruce couldn't keep himself from tuning in to Alabama football games every weekend. Hearing Charlie's name over the airwaves started making Bruce a little "schoolsick." Finally, in late October, his heart led him back home.

"About the middle of the season, I decided I would go back to school," Bruce said. "I left New Orleans and came back to Thomasville. I called Coach Bryant to see if I could get my scholarship back. I made an appointment, and he said he would talk to me.

"I went in his office scared to death," Bruce continued. "I was embarrassed because I had quit. I felt like I had let him down. I asked him for my scholarship and he said, 'No, I won't give you your scholarship back, but I'll give you the opportunity to earn it.' That's all I wanted.

"When the spring semester started I paid my way through school. After the first day of spring practice I asked Coach Bryant what I had to do to earn my scholarship back. He told me that when I wore the red jersey (signifying first-team status), I'd get my scholarship back."

Earning a scholarship after quitting the team was not an easy task for anybody, as Bruce quickly found out. "The first day, I was put at the bottom of the depth chart on *seventh* team," he said. "Actually, I was the only one in that spot—there were six teams, then me. I wore a yellow jersey, indicating that I was hurt and couldn't practice. I was the only one out there in a yellow jersey. I felt kinda low."

Bruce earned a red jersey and therefore his scholarship after only three days of practice. "I was ready then," Bruce said. "From then on I lived in Tuscaloosa every summer so that

56

Bruce Stephens followed brothers Gerald and Charlie to play football for Alabama.

I wouldn't tempt myself to leave again. But after I started that sophomore year, there was no way I was going to leave again.''

By mid-season Bruce earned a starting position on the offensive line, and for the next two and a half years the right guard spot was his. As a team in 1965 the Crimsons were 9-1-1 and won their second straight national championship.

But it didn't come easy.

In the opening game Georgia nipped the Tide, 18-17, in Athens on a controversial last-minute play. With less than three minutes to play, Alabama was leading the Bulldogs, 17-10. Georgia had the ball on its own 27-yard line. Georgia's Kirby Moore of Dothan, a seldom-used, second-string quarterback, dropped back and flipped a 10-yard pass to Pat Hodgson. The Alabama secondary converged, only to watch Hodgson lateral the ball to Bob Taylor, who fled uncontested the remaining 65 yards for the touchdown. With 2:08 left, the score was Alabama 17, Georgia 16.

Second-year Georgia head coach Vince Dooley elected to try the two-point attempt. The gamble paid off as Moore hit Hodgson for the two-point conversion to push the Bulldogs ahead, 18-17.

But the Tide wasn't dead yet. Steve Sloan and fullback Steve Bowman led the Tide down to the Georgia 26-yard line. With 14 seconds left, David Ray, the NCAA scoring champion in 1964, came in for a chance to win the game. His 32-yard field goal attempt was wide and short as bedlam broke out in Athens. The victory was Georgia's first over Alabama since 1959.

The following day, stop-action pictures taken from the game films clearly showed that Hodgson's knees were on the ground before he lateraled the ball to Taylor, therefore indicating that the play should have been called dead at that point. The game officials said they saw Hodgson's knees on the ground but agreed that "he did not have a ball long enough to rule he had control of it. A pass receiver is permitted to bat the ball in any direction, even forward, from any position, even lying on the ground."

The officials agreed that Hodgson batted the ball to Taylor rather than actually lateraling it. Alabama head coach Paul Bryant never complained or protested, simply saying that "The game is over. We have nothing to say. The score is 18-17, and that's it."

The Tide swamped Tulane the next week, then scored come-from-behind victories over Vanderbilt and Ole Miss. Bruce was seeing action only on the kickoff teams, but he remembers the Vanderbilt game as if it were yesterday.

"I learned at the Vandy game that anytime Coach Bryant is calm, then something's wrong," he said. "We were behind 7-0 at the half. He came into the dressing room and told us everything was all right. He was even whispering, more or less, saying the first half was theirs and the second half would be ours. He was real calm.

"The referee walked in the door and said we had three minutes to get on the field and five minutes before kickoff. As soon as the ref closed the door, Coach Bryant turned from a Dr. Jekyll into a Mr. Hyde. He started yelling and screaming at us—it was as different as night and day. None of us were that big, and he towered above all of us. We were even smaller after he got through with us.

"We went out and beat them, 22-7."

Alabama's hopes for a repeat of the national championship were almost gone after the Tennessee Volunteers fought the Tide to a 7-7 standoff. With less than a minute remaining and the score tied, Alabama faced a third-and-18 at the Tennessee 18-yard line. Sophomore quarterback Kenny Stabler rambled 14 yards to the four-yard line. Thinking he had made the first down, Stabler took the snap on the next play and threw the ball out of bounds to stop the clock. David Ray ran on the field to attempt a chip shot field goal but was motioned back by the officials. Stabler had thrown the ball out of bounds on fourth down, giving Tennessee the ball...and the tie.

Bruce played most of the Tennessee game, then earned a starting position the next week against Florida State. The Tide regrouped from then on, defeating Florida State, Mississippi State, LSU, South Carolina, and Auburn to finish with a 8-1-1 regular season record.

Michigan State was declared the national champion in the United Press International poll. Alabama got the break it needed when the Associated Press decided to hold its final poll until after the bowl game because eight of its top ten teams were involved in bowl action.

Alabama was ranked fourth heading into Miami to meet third-ranked and unbeaten Nebraska in the Orange Bowl. Fifth-ranked UCLA was playing top-ranked Michigan State in the Rose Bowl, and LSU was paired against second-ranked Arkansas in the Cotton Bowl.

As if Bryant had written the script himself, what had to happen did happen. UCLA bumped off Michigan State, 14-12, while LSU surprised Arkansas, 14-7. Because of those events the Orange Bowl was transformed into a winner-take-all battle for the national championship.

Nebraska outweighed the Tide by an average of 35 pounds per man but was still a one-point underdog at kickoff. "Sizewise, we probably shouldn't have been on the same field with them," Bruce said. "It was unreal how big they were and how small we were. But we were a lot quicker and more tenacious than they were. They didn't take us very seriously."

Nebraska learned the hard way that it should never underestimate a Bear Bryant-coached football team. The Crimson warriors thrashed the Cornhuskers, 39-28, to win a second straight national championship. Steve Sloan completed 20 passes for 296 yards, and Ray Perkins had 10 receptions for 159 yards and 2 touchdowns.

On offense Alabama started Dennis Homan, Jerry Duncan, John Calvert, Paul Crane, Bruce, Cecil Dowdy, and Wayne Cook on the line; and Steve Sloan, Les Kelley, Steve Bowman, and Ray Perkins in the backfield.

On defense the starting linemen were Creed Gilmer, John Sullivan, Tom Somerville, Richard Cole, and Ben McLeod. Linebackers were Jackie Sherrill, Wayne Trimble, and Tim Bates; and the defensive backs were David Ray, Bobby Johns, and John Mosley.

"That was probably the most fun I've ever had in a ball game," Bruce said. "We moved the ball almost at will. (Jerry) Duncan caught a couple of tackle-eligible passes, and we recovered a couple of onside kicks. Everything went right for us."

After the game Bryant emphasized Bruce's role in the big win. "I certainly want to emphasize this," Bryant told several reporters. "All of this—our tremendous offensive showing—wouldn't have been possible if it hadn't been for those little ol' boys in the middle. They made it possible for all those records to be set.

"Jerry Duncan, John Calvert, Paul Crane, Bruce Stephens, and Cecil Dowdy made it possible for (Steve) Bowman and (Les) Kelley to do all of that running. Sloan never would have set those records if it hadn't been for those little folks, and we certainly would not have had all of those completions."

Likewise, Sloan himself appreciated the fine protection. "Bruce played particularly well in the Orange Bowl," Sloan said. "Nebraska had a big front, and we ran the ball really well the second half. The pass protection was good the whole game.

"Bruce contributed so much to the entire season. He was not big, but he was real quick and tough."

Pat Dye, now head coach at Auburn, came to Alabama in

1965 as an assistant coach. He remembers Bruce as one of the key players in the Tide's rise to the top.

"Bruce was one of the players that came through for Alabama in 1965 and made a real outstanding offensive lineman," Dye said. "I saw Bruce go through some tough times (early in the year).

"After we lost to Georgia in the opening game, we came back. The rest of the season, we really worked hard, and maybe even pushed our players. Bruce was one of those players that grew up during that period of time, making the transition from being an average football player to being a real good football player by the time we played Nebraska."

Gerald won a national championship in 1962, Charlie won one in 1964, and in 1965 Bruce became the third member of the Stephens family to wear the national championship ring. And if justice had prevailed, he would have had another one in 1966.

But a perfect 11-0 record in 1966 wasn't good enough to convince the pollsters to declare the Tide national champs for the third straight year. Despite a 34-7 thrashing of Nebraska in the Sugar Bowl, Alabama finished third in both polls, behind Notre Dame and Michigan State. The Irish and Spartans had battled to a 10-10 tie late in the season, leaving Alabama with the only unblemished mark.

Many believe the 1966 team was perhaps the best Tide squad ever. The offense piled up 301 points while allowing only 44. Six games were shutouts, including four of the last five.

In his book, *Bear,* Bryant said, "The 1966 Alabama team was the best I ever had and got done in by the ballot box....The final vote went to Notre Dame, but I wish we could have played either them or Michigan State that year."

Bruce started every game during the 1966 season. "We were a much better football team in 1966 than in 1965," he said. "The only person we graduated off the offensive line that year was (center) Paul Crane, but Jimmy Carroll came in and was able to do the job.

"We were convinced that if we walloped Nebraska in the Sugar Bowl, we would be national champs. But they proved us wrong."

The disappointment spread into the 1967 season, Bruce's senior year. An opening game 37-37 tie with Florida State was

The 1966 Tide offensive line gave quarterback Kenny Stabler (12) all the protection he needed. From top to bottom is John David Reitz (48), Cecil Dowdy (70), Bruce Stephens (68), Jimmy Carroll (53), Johnny Calvert (62), Jerry Duncan (77), and Wayne Cook (83). Also blocking for Stabler is David Chatwood (31).

the beginning of a four-year slide that saw Alabama finish 8-2-1 in 1967, 8-3 in 1968, 6-5 in 1969, and 6-5-1 in 1970.

Bruce was the only returning starter on the offensive line. "We had a complete rebuilding year on offense," he said. "The defense had lost a lot, too."

The Tide lost to Tennessee in mid-season and owned a 7-1-1 record going into the season finale against Auburn. In a cold, rainy, muddy, and sloppy defensive struggle, Alabama came out on top, 7-3. Senior quarterback Kenny Stabler waded 47 yards for Alabama's only score with 11:29 left in the game.

"Stabler really earned his nickname of 'Snake' on that run," Bruce said. "Until that game I had never seen mud cleats before. We put them on at the half. The water on the field was up to almost the tops of our shoes."

The next day on his television show Auburn head coach

Shug Jordan accused Alabama tight end Dennis Dixon of holding Tiger linebacker Gusty Yearout on Stabler's touchdown run through the mud. "I wonder if No. 84 (Dixon) thought he was on defense, because he made one of the finest tackles on Yearout that I have ever seen," Jordan said.

The complaints were ignored...but according to Bruce, Jordan may have been telling the truth. "When I got to the sidelines after Stabler's touchdown," Bruce said, "Dennis (Dixon) was sitting on the bench with his head in his hands. Everybody was going crazy on the sidelines because we had scored—except for Dennis. He looked real sad and dejected.

"I walked over to him and said, 'Hey, what's wrong? What's the matter? We just scored the touchdown that's going to win the game for us!'

"He looked up and said, 'I held him (Yearout) on that play.' On that particular play the tight end's job was to come down and block the linebacker, and that's exactly what he did. He blocked him, then held him by the foot. He was almost ready to cry because he had done it."

Bruce closed out his career against Texas A&M in the Cotton Bowl. The Aggies' head coach was none other than Gene "Bebes" Stallings, the former Tide assistant that had traveled to Thomasville in 1960 to sign Charlie to a scholarship. Stallings left the A&M post in 1971 to become defensive backfield coach for the Dallas Cowboys.

The Aggies were outrushed and outpassed, but they weren't outscored. The Tide fell, 20-16, making Stallings the first Bryant "pupil" to ever defeat Bryant, the "teacher." The loss must have been a sign of things to come, because Alabama would not win another bowl game for eight years.

Bruce's efforts and abilities earned him All-SEC honors in 1967. The 5'10", 185-pound senior had truly come a long way from being an apprentice carpenter in New Orleans.

Jackie Sherrill, a teammate of Bruce's in 1965 and now head coach at Texas A&M, recalls fond memories of Bruce's abilities. "Bruce was kinda short, but very quick and tough," Sherrill said. "He played extremely well. We were all amazed at what he accomplished with his size. He was a real tough football player."

Bruce played a vital role on the small, quick teams of the

Bruce Stephens (68), Jimmy Fuller (73), Cecil Dowdy (70), Jimmy Carroll (53), and Jerry Duncan take a breather during a 34-7 rout of Nebraska in the 1967 Sugar Bowl.

mid-sixties. Tom Somerville, now with South Central Bell in Montgomery, was another one of those "little" linemen, and a close friend of Bruce's. Known as "Stumpy," Somerville played defense his sophomore season, then was switched to offense midway through his junior year.

"Bruce was the kind of player Coach Bryant liked to recruit and build his program around," Somerville said. "He was very quick and tough. He was the kind of guy you could count on."

Bryant counted on Bruce enough to ask him to stay on as a graduate assistant coach for the 1968 season. A year later Bruce joined the army and served for two years, one of which was in Vietnam. In 1971 he and the former Sammie Ryan, his wife of three years, moved to Newnan, Georgia, where he coached for three years. He left Newnan in 1974 and went to Briarcliff High School in DeKalb County where he was an assistant under former Tider Dickie Bean. Bruce became Briarcliff's head coach in 1975 and remained there until 1980.

A new high school was being formed in Gwinnett County, Georgia, and a coach was needed to start the school's football program. Bruce accepted the challenge and in 1982 is in his first varsity season as head coach at Brookwood High. Bruce, Sammie, and children David (11-16-69) and Mandy (8-6-74) reside in Stone Mountain, Georgia.

Gerald graduated from the University in 1963 and after receiving his master's degree, he began a high school coaching career that would extend until 1976 when he decided to "administrate" instead of coach. He served one year each as an assistant at Tuscaloosa High School and Gadsden High School, then was head coach at Gadsden from 1965 to 1971.

He went "back home" to Thomasville in 1972 and coached at Grove Hill Academy for one year, then moved to coach at Clarke County High School from 1973 to 1975. In 1976 Gerald left coaching and became principal of Clarke County High, where he is today. Gerald, his wife Jo Ann, and children Brent (5-7-62) and Kerry (5-6-64) reside in Thomasville.

Of the three Stephens brothers, Charlie has perhaps the most interesting story to tell. After high school coaching jobs at Opp High School, Hardaway High School in Columbus, Georgia, and Livingston High School, he graduated into the college coaching ranks. In 1969 and 1970 he was an assistant on the Southern Mississippi staff under P.W. Underwood.

"During all this time," Charlie said, "I was trying to decide if coaching was what I really wanted to do. I had to make some plans for the future. Coaching was a great profession—a lot of rewards other than monetary. Working with young people in athletics—that's where my heart and life had been.

"I was happy," Charlie continued, "but at the same time I was looking beyond. I kept thinking about the coaches that had been fired at one time or another—Charlie Bradshaw, Jerry Clairborne, Phil Cutchin, Bebes Stallings. I had feelings for all these men. I know what traumas their families went through. I had moved five times, and it was tough. I finally made the decision to get out of coaching."

Charlie might still be coaching today if he had not taken an interest in entering law school. "I was always fascinated by law but had committed myself to education," he said. "I thought it would be a waste of time to take the LSAT (Law School Admissions Test). A good friend of mine convinced me that the law school's way to review applicants was not based on background as much as the LSAT. So I took it anyway."

Charlie was accepted and entered the University of Alabama Law School in 1971. After graduating in 1974, he moved to Jasper, where he became a partner in the law firm of Bankhead, Savage, and Stephens. In early 1977 the firm accepted a request from Auburn University to represent the institution against the National Collegiate Athletic Association (NCAA).

"Switching" sides to represent Auburn was no problem for Charlie. He had coached at Southern Mississippi with Doug Barfield and P.W. Underwood, later Auburn coaches. One of his law partners, Morris Savage, was on Auburn's 1957 national championship team and is a member of the Auburn University Board of Trustees. Charlie had numerous Auburn friends and even had another brother, Larry, play football for the Tigers in the late sixties.

"I enjoyed representing Auburn," Charlie said. "It gave me another connection with college athletics, which I still enjoy so much. Representing Auburn was something I really appreciated having the opportunity to do."

Larry Stephens was not the only brother to play college football after Gerald, Charlie, and Bruce. Benny Ray, an All-State guard at Thomasville High School, entered the Alabama program in the fall of 1968.

"Benny Ray was a great football player," Charlie said. "He played regularly as a freshman, but he had an inner-ear problem which caused a loss of balance. He dropped out after a year and transferred to Troy State. He suffered the same injury there and had to give up football or risk permanent impairment."

Two more younger brothers (there were seven in all), Don and Randy, were not able to play football because of childhood injuries.

In August of 1982 Charlie left the law firm of Bankhead,

66

Savage, and Stephens to open up a practice of his own. He and his wife, the former Susan Holloman of Tuscaloosa, reside in Jasper with children Charles, Jr. (8-14-68) and Rachel (4-26-71).

Whenever the Stephens family congregates in Thomasville for a family reunion, they have a lot of fun, eat a lot of food, share old and new experiences, and just plain relax.

And with national championship rings on the fingers of Gerald, Charlie, and Bruce, this Tide trio has something special to talk about.

FORD

Mike • Steve

As a youngster Steve Ford wanted to play football so bad that he even broke the rules to do so. No, he didn't cheat—he just sort of stretched the truth a little bit.

"I first tried to get in the little league program when I was nine or ten," Steve recalled. "There was a weight minimum of 70 pounds, and I weighed 68 pounds on the first day of practice. They wouldn't let me play because I didn't weigh enough.

"That was in the morning, and that afternoon I ate some bananas and drank some milkshakes and tried to eat anything I could. I even put on a pair of shorts and stuffed them with penny and nickel rolls, then I put another pair of shorts over those. I wanted to make sure I was over the weight limit.

"I was almost sick from eating, and I went down to practice (that afternoon) and the coach said if I wanted to play *that* bad, then he wouldn't even weigh me. So I got to play after all."

Many people believe Steve should have saved the milkshakes, bananas, and money rolls for his college football career. The younger brother of former All-SEC defensive end Mike Ford, Steve was a bite-sized, 148-pound defensive back for the Crimson Tide in 1973 and 1974. But nobody told him he was small.

"Steve is one of those players that Coach Bryant uses illustrations about," Tide assistant athletic director Clem Gryska said. "They're not big enough or good enough to play—it's just that they don't realize it. Steve fits in that category."

If Steve was considered "small" as a 148-pound defensive back, then older brother Mike surely shouldn't have been play-

Mike Ford is congratulated by Alabama head coach Paul "Bear" Bryant for being selected to the "Super-Sixties" all-star team.

ing defensive end at 180 pounds. But Mike did play—well enough to earn All-SEC honors in 1967 and 1968.

Mike's rise to All-SEC status didn't come easily, however. Born in Birmingham and raised in Tuscaloosa, Mike wasn't really interested in football until Paul "Bear" Bryant came back home to the University to coach. In one year's time Bryant turned a program that had only won four games in the previous three years into a successful 5-4-1 season in 1958.

"When I saw what Coach Bryant did in 1958, I was impressed," Mike said. "I was just in the sixth grade, and sometimes I went out to the old field to watch the team practice. It was amazing what he did that year. From that point on I said I really would like to be involved with it."

Mike's first official taste of organized football came a few years later when he entered Tuscaloosa High School. He played third-string quarterback his junior year, "specializing in the helicopter pass," then was switched to defensive end his senior year.

"(Assistant coach) Richard Williamson was instrumental in me ever developing as a football player," Mike said. "Anybody that plays football will tell you that there comes a time where you realize the concept of becoming aggressive. Up until that point you have basically followed the fundamentals that you've been taught. Coach Williamson was the one that introduced me to this aggressiveness."

This "aggressiveness" he referred to definitely bloomed in 1964, when Tuscaloosa High won the state championship with Mike playing defensive end. His eyes then turned toward the University of Alabama to continue his football career.

"Dad was a rabid Alabama fan," Mike said. "We went without living room furniture for three years so we could travel around and watch Alabama play. There was no doubt as to where I wanted to play football."

Vanderbilt was interested in signing Mike, but while on a recruiting trip to Nashville he received a phone call from his father telling him just what he wanted to hear.

"Dad said that Coach Bryant had just called and told him that he (Bryant) wanted me to play at Alabama, but that he couldn't give me a scholarship," Mike recalled. "But that was all I needed to hear. I took the chance in a second."

Mike convinced himself (and the Bama staff) that a walk-on had as much chance as anybody to play football at the University of Alabama, and he wasted no time in establishing himself. By the first freshman game he was starting at offensive and defensive end.

"We served as the warm bodies for the varsity offense," Mike recalled. "Their first game was against Georgia in Athens, and we helped (Steve) Sloan and those guys get ready for the game. They lost that game, 18-17. Coach Bryant called a Monday night practice, and I had never seen him lose his temper until then.

"The first team freshman defense was standing in front of the first team varsity offense," Mike continued, "and Coach Bryant started at one end of the offensive line and began jerking people around, grabbing them by the facemasks and shoulder pads.

Mike Ford (81) made things tough for opposing runners.

"I will never forget the sense of deep, abiding fear that came over me as he got closer and closer to us. He was so worked up by the time he got down to our end that he went up to (freshman linebacker) Mike Hall and grabbed him, tore his jersey completely off, and started yelling at him about not trying hard enough.

"Mike had not even played against Georgia," Mike chuckled. "He didn't even go to the game and wasn't anywhere near Athens while the game was going on.

"That's the first time that I had seen Coach Bryant angry. It was never anything abusive—just a little something to let you know that even though he didn't have pads on, he was just as tough."

Despite the varsity's loss to Georgia and a tie with Tennessee, the Tide won its third national championship in five years with a 39-28 victory over Nebraska in the Orange Bowl.

Defensive end became a permanent position for Mike during spring practice, and along with it came a full scholarship. The third-string high school quarterback of three years earlier had definitely come a long way, as he started the second half of the Tide's 34-0 win over Louisiana Tech to open the 1966

71

season. And for the next three years that defensive end spot would be his and his only.

Mississippi and Clemson were warm-ups for the Tennessee clash in Knoxville. Down 10-0 at halftime, the Tide rallied to nip the Vols, 11-10.

"I'll never forget what Coach Bryant told us at halftime," Mike said. "He knew just the right words to say to us—he was exceptionally encouraging. We were down, 10-0, and here he was telling us we could whip them.

"Near the end of the third quarter I recovered a fumble, setting us up on about the 45 or 50-yard line. We took it in for the score, and (Kenny) Stabler hit Wayne Cook for the two-point conversion to make it 10-8. Steve Davis kicked a field goal late in the game to win 11-10.

"That was the first time I had ever smoked a cigar (in the dressing room afterwards). I was coughing on my cigar but ecstatic at the same time. I was so happy that I would have eaten it if Coach Bryant had told me to.

"And that's the first time I had ever seen Coach Bryant dance. He could do a jig, all right; at least he did then."

The Tidal wave continued over Vanderbilt and Mississippi State, then the young defense *really* started playing tough. Straight shutouts over LSU, South Carolina, Southern Mississippi, and Auburn boosted Bama's record to 10-0.

An undefeated record by any other team would have earned it the national championship. Not so with the Crimson Tide. Alabama had won the top crown in 1964 and 1965, but the pollsters just wouldn't allow three in a row.

It was then that Notre Dame (9-0-1) was named national champion, even after it opted for a 10-10 tie against Michigan State. Alabama's 34-7 thrashing of Nebraska in the Sugar Bowl was not enough to warrant a poll recount.

"Coach Bryant said there were three reasons that we didn't get the national championship," Mike said. "One was that we had a letdown against Tennessee and had to come back to beat them. Second, he said our schedule might not have been tough enough. And, he said it was because we didn't have any blacks on the team.

"It's some consolation that Coach Bryant has said several times that the '66 team may have been the best that he's ever had, which is something I appreciate."

Mike's junior season (1967) opened optimistically, but after the first game it was back to the blackboard for the Tide defense. After allowing only 37 points the whole 1966 season, the Alabama defenders gave up 37 in a televised opener against Florida State. Fortunately, the Tide offense matched FSU's points with 37 of its own.

But a 37-37 tie with Florida State was nothing to be happy about. "The next day at practice, we ran the first team offense against the first team defense," Mike said. "We (defense) just killed them, and Coach Bryant hollered down off the tower and said, 'You ought to be put in prison for not doing that Saturday night!" That was the capsule summary of exactly what had happened."

Alabama struggled to victories over Southern Mississippi, Ole Miss, and Vanderbilt, then lost to Tennessee in Birmingham, 24-13. The Tide would not win another from the Vols until 1971.

Clemson fell by three points, 13-10, and according to Mike, "we then realized we weren't as good as everybody thought we were going to be, and not even as good as we thought we were going to be."

All hope was not lost, however. The Tide managed to salvage an 8-1-1 record after victories over LSU, South Carolina, and Auburn. Next up was Texas A&M in the Cotton Bowl.

The bowl magic of the previous two years ran out on the Tide as the Aggies captured a 20-16 victory. "We really should have won that game," Mike said. "Tennessee was better, and they beat us. FSU should have beaten us, but we should have beaten A&M.

"I'll never forget Dennis Homan dropping a pass from Stabler in the last quarter. It was fourth down and 14, and Homan *never* dropped a ball. This time he was wide open in the clear, and he dropped it. That symbolized the frustration we had.

"We went into the dressing room, and I'll never forget (Tide senior) Bruce Stephens saying, 'That's a hell of a way to end a career.' I knew what he was talking about, for the guys that had been on a national championship team their sophomore year in '65 and had come so close in '66. And then to go out in a losing game in '67 was bad."

Mike ended his junior season as one of the team's top tacklers. His efforts earned him All-SEC honors along with teammates Kenny Stabler, Dennis Homan, Mike Hall, Bruce Stephens, and Bobby Johns.

Mike's senior season (1968) began with the Tide ranked an unusually low 14th in the national polls and predicted to finish third in the Southeastern Conference. The passing duo of Stabler and Homan had graduated, and their replacements would come from a group of untested players.

Returnees with Mike on defense included Wayne Owen, Bob Childs, Mike Hall, Billy Scroggins, Paul Boschung, Randy Barron, and Mike Dean. The Tide coaches were counting on the senior leadership to avoid the mental lapses that occurred in the 1967 season.

The opening game against Virginia Tech offered an unusual situation for Mike and teammate Paul Boschung. Both played at Tuscaloosa High School with Virginia Tech quarterback Al Kincaid (later to become head football coach at Wyoming). Back in 1964 when Mike was anchoring Tuscaloosa High's defensive line, Kincaid was quarterbacking the Black Bears to the state championship.

Mike and Kincaid were great friends off the field and wanted to go to the same school. Both visited Vanderbilt, but Kincaid signed with VPI and Mike opted for the walk-on route with Alabama. And on a warm summer night in Birmingham, the duo was reunited.

The Tide plucked the Gobblers, 14-7, in a tough defensive battle. Donnie Sutton, Scott Hunter, and George Ranager accounted for the Tide offensive achievements while Mike led the defensive surge. His efforts were not without pain, however, as he separated his shoulder while making a tackle. The injury put a big question mark on whether or not he could continue the season.

Hunter and Ranager combined for eight aerials and 122 yards to pace Bama to a 17-14 victory over Southern Mississippi. Then, the bottom fell out for the Tide, as it lost two of its next three games.

The first heartbreaker was a 10-8 decision to Ole Miss.

74

Mike Ford (81) closes in for the tackle against Auburn.

"That was a terrible game," Mike said. "That was (Ole Miss quarterback) Archie Manning's sophomore year. He was good and had quick feet.

"I think that some of us didn't play up to our ability in that game. I know I didn't because of my shoulder, and my mind was not completely on football. I think that had some effect."

After a routine 31-7 win over Vanderbilt, Alabama lost another close one to Tennessee, 10-9. "On the first series of downs they scored, and on that touchdown play my shoulder came out (of socket)," Mike said. "A state trooper and one of the assistant coaches took me in the dressing room where one of them stood on my chest and the other pulled up on my arm.

"I would have played if they had had to cut it off and let

75

me use it as a club. There's something about Tennessee that gets Coach Bryant going. He doesn't tell this to the public, but he really wants to win.

"I went back out there and played in the second half. We were a better ball club, and we should have beaten them."

The 3-2 Tide bounced back to defeat Clemson, Mississippi State, LSU, Miami, and Auburn to finish the regular season with eight wins and two losses. Next up was Dan Devine and his Missouri Tigers in the Gator Bowl.

What was supposed to be a close game turned into a 35-10 rout of Alabama. Quarterback Terry McMillan (whom Mike knew through the Fellowship of Christian Athletes) directed the Tigers' newly installed Power-I offense that humbled the Tide defense.

"I think that the last half of that game was the beginning of the couple of 'down' years of Alabama football," Mike said. "The score was 14-7 at halftime, and we thought we had a shot at it. We went into the game overconfident, and we just got our butts beat."

Mike was named All-SEC and second team All-American. He was scheduled to play in the Senior Bowl, the All-American Bowl, and even had an invitation from the San Diego Chargers to try professional football. However, the nagging shoulder injury prevented all three.

Mike married Candace Croft of Atlanta between the Auburn game and the Gator Bowl. The couple was planning to head to Dallas after Mike graduated so he could enter the seminary, but things changed.

"The Gator Bowl had something to do with me not going to seminary," Mike said. "Up to that point everything had been successful in my life, and after that I found that success is not what really makes it. Success is not the measure of a man's strength—failure is. And it's how a man handles failure that determines if he is successful.

"Having what was a successful football career just all at once crashed after my injury kept me out. And I also had some disillusionment about some religious concepts. It was a really testing, trying time."

Mike remained in Tuscaloosa and coached at Tuscaloosa High for a year. Younger brother Steve was one of his players, as were Sylvester Croom and John Stallworth. Croom would become an All-American center (and later a coach) at Alabama while Stallworth would one day wear four Super Bowl rings as an All-Pro receiver with the Pittsburgh Steelers.

After a year of coaching, Mike taught history at Tuscaloosa Academy for two years. Upon completion of a master's degree in history he decided to follow his father's footsteps into the law field and entered the University's law school in 1972.

Returning to the University campus gave Mike the opportunity to see little brother Steve in action as a Tider. The youngster that "stretched the truth" to play football ten years earlier was now a "grown-up" 148-pound defensive back.

"Steve had a correct assessment of where his values should be placed," Mike said of his little brother. "He was a good football player, not as talented as others, but his greatest asset was his ability to think football.

"He watched me growing up, and I think he learned from a lot of mistakes I made when I was playing football. Steve had a tremendous amount of maturity for his age, and I think he did the best he could with the ability accorded him by birth.

"At the end of Steve's senior year in high school (Tuscaloosa High) my father and I went to talk to Coach Bryant about possibly offering Steve a scholarship," Mike continued. "Coach looked at my dad and said, 'He's just too little; he's going to get killed out there.'

"I made the comment that 'Well, coach, you always look for men with heart. If you want a man like that, then Steve's going to be like that.'"

Mike's confidence in his little brother convinced Coach Bryant to offer Steve a partial scholarship (residence in Bryant Hall) with the understanding that he make the team his freshman year. And once he did that he would be given the opportunity for a full scholarship.

Steve happily accepted the challenge and entered the University in the fall of 1971. Teammates in his class included future Tide stars Sylvester Croom, Mike Dubose, Randy Billingsley, and Mike Washington. Despite his size Steve played first-team defensive back for the freshman squad and helped it to a near-perfect 4-1 record.

"We won every game except Tennessee," Steve said. "We went up to Knoxville, and Condredge Holloway was their freshman quarterback. I played against him in high school and college all the way through. They beat us badly (36-13)."

The varsity complemented the freshmen by finishing 11-1, including a stunning 17-10 victory in Los Angeles over Southern California. However, any hopes of a national championship were ended when Nebraska ripped the Tiders, 38-6, in the Orange Bowl.

An unfortunate accident four days into spring training knocked Steve out of spring practice and the entire 1972 season. "(Fullback) Steve Bisceglia was leading the blocking on a counter option play," he said, "and he blocked me right below the knees. I'm sure I had been hit that way a hundred times, but this time it snapped the two bones right below my right knee.

"I was in a cast for about three months, and I didn't put on pads again until the next spring practice (in 1973). They red-shirted me for the entire 1972 season."

When the leg cracked, Steve was a bit unsure about the scholarship that he was attempting to earn. But "the man" didn't let him down. Because of his performance during his freshman year, Steve was given the scholarship after spring training.

"I signed the scholarship with my leg in a cast," he said. "I've always been very appreciative of them for that, because they didn't know how my leg was going to heal. I wanted to work exceptionally hard for them for that reason."

Steve practiced every day with the team during his redshirt season, usually acting as a decoy. "They would dress me out in pads just as a decoy in case somebody was spying on us," he said. "I would line up at an empty spot somewhere on the field and run around with the defense. That was done to disguise what we were doing. It was really fun because I got to do it with the first-team defense."

Alabama rolled to 10 straight wins, then Auburn scored on two blocked punts in the fourth quarter to nip the Tide, 17-16. The shock of defeat carried over to the Cotton Bowl, as Texas came from behind to win, 17-13.

Steve saw plenty of action the next season (1973) in a year that saw the Tide score over 40 points per game, break two

Rarely weighing more than 155 pounds, Steve Ford proved that size isn't everything in college football.

NCAA records, tie another one, and roll to an 11-0 mark. Its perfect regular season record awarded Bama both the Southeastern Conference and United Press International championships.

"I played in over 70 plays against VPI," Steve said. "I was almost dead—it was like a track meet. I was on the kickoff team in that game, and we were run to death. We kicked off 12 times (Bama won, 77-6).

"It got to the point where it was real funny. We started telling jokes in the huddle before each kickoff. The thing that got us so tired was that we would run down on the kickoffs, then stay on the field to play defense.''

The massacre over VPI was Bama's seventh victory of the year. Wins over Mississippi State and Miami preceded a big 21-7 victory over LSU in Baton Rouge. "The LSU fans pelted us with oranges during our pre-game drills," Steve said. "I was standing next to Ricky Davis, and an orange hit me right where it hurts—in a very sensitive area. It wasn't funny at all then, but we laugh about it now.''

Revenge over Auburn to the tune of 35-0 set up the classic Notre Dame-Alabama contest in the Sugar Bowl. The Tide lost a heartbreaker—and the Associated Press national championship—by one point, 24-23.

"That was the most memorable game," Steve said. "And it was the classiest game I had ever been associated with. They were good, but I'm still convinced our team was better. There were several big plays in the game, and if we had made any one of them we would have won the game.''

Steve began his junior year (it would be his last) with a trip to College Park, Maryland, to take on the Maryland Terrapins. Sophomore Calvin Culliver led the Tide to a tough 21-14 victory over Maryland and its superstar Randy White (now an All-Pro with the Dallas Cowboys).

After a 52-0 pasting of Southern Mississippi, the Tiders scored unimpressive wins over Vanderbilt (23-10), Mississippi State (35-21), and winless Florida State (8-7).

"That Florida State game was amazing," Steve recalled. "Before the game we were laughing, telling jokes, and just messing around. Some of the first teamers didn't even have their arm pads on because they just weren't expecting to play that much.

"FSU had the nation's longest losing streak, and we didn't take them seriously. Richard Todd was hurt, and Jack O'Rear and Robert Fraley were our quarterbacks and they just couldn't get the offense going. FSU had an unbalanced line, and we didn't adjust. I don't think we deserved to win—we were very lucky.''

Of the next six victories (over Tennessee, TCU, Mississippi State, LSU, Miami, and Auburn), the TCU game in Birmingham is the one that Steve will never forget. TCU lost the game, 41-3. But more tragic than losing the game was the injury suffered by

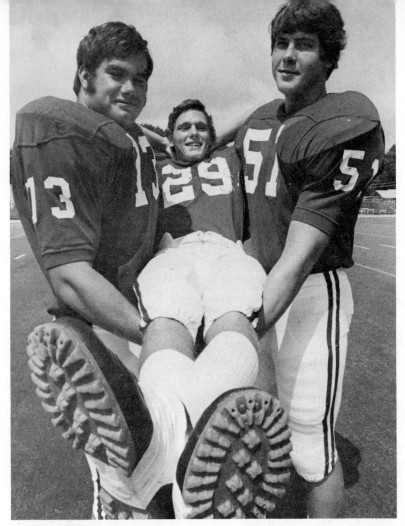

Steve Ford (29) is held by giant teammates David Gerasimchuk (73) and Charley Hannah (51).

TCU halfback Kent Waldrep. A broken neck after a tackle resulted in the youngster being paralyzed for life. Steve remembers it well.

"I was in on the play he got hurt," Steve said. "It was on a sweep, and Waldrep was carrying the ball. The guard had pulled and was leading him. I hit the guard and turned the ballcarrier inside me.

"When the guard hit me, I went down to my knees, and all I could see were Waldrep's legs. I hit them, and the other pursuit hit him at the same time. They all kind of went over him,

81

and all that weight coming down on his neck was apparently what injured him.

"Robert Fraley and I went to see him at the hospital after the game. It was a sad sight. His head was shaved and he was on a board, paralyzed from the neck down. Despite his condition he was gracious, very positive, and completely enthusiastic. It was encouraging to me to see his attitude."

Another 11-0 season, another date with Notre Dame for the national championship—and another loss. That was the summary of the 1974 season. This time the scenery was palm trees in Miami rather than Bourbon Street in New Orleans. But the results were the same—the Tide lost again to the Fighting Irish, this time by two points, 13-11 (it would lose by three points in 1976).

"Again, I think we had the much better team," Steve said. "Our offense just couldn't put the points on the board. Gary (Rutledge) had been out most of the season (with a shoulder injury), and he tried to play in that game. He just couldn't throw the ball.

"It was frustrating to watch because you knew he knew what to do—he just couldn't do it."

Near the end of that junior year Steve decided to pass up his last year of eligibility so that he could graduate with his freshman class and attend law school. Because of his redshirt year he had enough credits to graduate. It was a decision he's thankful for now, but it didn't come easy.

"I noticed that about halfway through the (junior) year, I started losing my desire as a player," he said. "After a lot of thinking, I decided that the contribution I was making to the team wasn't that significant towards whether or not we won a game.

"I was looking forward to the day I could get into law school and get out and practice with Mike and Dad. At that point I made the decision to go to law school.

"The thing that concerned me the most," Steve continued, "was what Coach Bryant would think about it. I didn't want to let him down. I didn't want to be a quitter at all. He had been real gracious to me and had extended himself to me in a lot of ways. Whenever I did something well, he always said something about it.

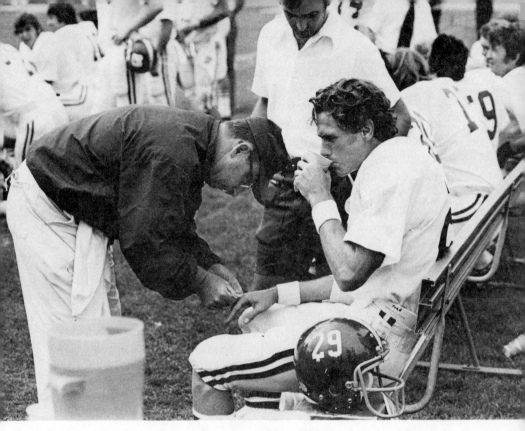

While the defense rests, trainer Jim Goostree and assistant trainer Sang Lyda tend to Steve Ford.

"I went to talk to him one morning, and I told him. My voice was quivering and I was scared to death. He was very kind and said that he respected my decision."

Steve entered law school in the fall of 1975 (Coach Bryant wrote a letter of recommendation for him) and graduated in January of 1978. He joined his father's and brother's law firm in Tuscaloosa for several months, then left with Mike to open up a practice of their own. Doug McElvy, a friend of the family, made up the third partner in the firm of Ford, McElvy, and Ford, now located in downtown Tuscaloosa.

Both Mike and Steve credit Bryant with teaching them philosophies on the field that have helped them later in life.

"The principles I learned from him and just listening to the things he's said are things I've used daily in my law practice," Steve said. "I think I win some cases I normally otherwise wouldn't because of the preparation he taught me. Coach

Bryant stresses preparation, sacrifice, discipline, and all those things that it takes to win.''

Mike, himself a very philosophical person, thinks Bryant is tops in the field. "Our society unfortunately is one that teaches young folks that they deserve something or they have a right to something," he said. "It's a society that teaches people that immediate gratification is more important than discipline.

"It's a society that emphasizes consumption rather than production. And football, as Coach Bryant teaches it, is completely opposite of that. Football teaches sacrifice of personal comfort for corporate gain. It teaches something of a willingness to see others succeed and to subject your personal success to the team concept.

"He (Bryant) is a teacher and a philosopher. Of all the teachers I've ever had, he's the best. I've written him one letter since I've been out of college, and I just told him how I felt about him. He needed to hear it, because I know his success is in the success of the men he coaches. I know he feels strongly that way."

Family life has replaced football as the top activity in both Mike's and Steve's lives.

Mike and Candace have four children—Michael, Jr., (8-11-70), Favor (3-27-73), Forrest (1-15-76), and Joanna (9-24-79).

Steve met Christine Piazza of Gadsden on a blind date and later married her during his senior year of law school. They have three children—Elise (4-23-78), Bethani (8-15-80), and Steven, Jr. (5-18-82).

Mike Ford and Steve Ford—both "too little" to play college football. But they walked on and played, and they played well.

But most important to Coach Paul "Bear" Bryant, the great philosopher, they kept playing after finishing college and are still playing today.

And they're still winning.

WADE

Tommy • Steve

The University of Alabama football team has never been short of quality athletes. Until the early sixties it was common for the players to go "both ways" with little or no rest. However, with the influx of more specialized athletes, the "both ways" concept soon faded out.

But nobody told Tommy Wade that his "both ways" talent was extinct. He did his best to continue the "both ways" tradition at Alabama. As a result, his versatility made Tommy Wade a household word for Alabama fans during the late sixties and early seventies.

After an outstanding four-sport career at Dothan High School, Tommy was recruited by schools throughout the South as a running back. But every coach knew of his defensive abilities also and considered Tommy to be a prize catch.

"I never did pick up any speed until the tenth grade," Tommy said. "I was always tall, slim, and clumsy. I played defensive end in the eighth, ninth, and tenth grades. The year after the tenth grade we got a coach that came to Dothan from Georgia. He went to Coach (Charles) McCall and suggested that I play running back.

"Coach McCall said 'no' at first, then they decided to give it a try. I guess it worked, because from then on I played safety and running back, and we went 9-1 both years after I had started running the ball. We had some real good teams then—13 signed scholarships my senior year."

The Wade family tradition would not have begun had he gone to the school he was leaning towards. "I was aiming toward Auburn," he said. "It was rough deciding where to go.

85

Tommy Wade could run with the football as well as defend against it.

Coach Bryant helped a lot in my decision. He called me about once a week to talk. Finally, he said that he would be behind me wherever I went, but that I could sure help the program at Alabama.

"He said that all he was going to promise me was that we would win some ball games. Then I got to thinking it over and decided to go play with a winner. I decided on Alabama."

Tommy entered the University in the fall of 1966. Coach Paul Bryant's promise to Tommy that they would "win some ball games" was without doubt an understatement.

Since 1961 the Tide had accumulated a record of 49-5-1 and three national championships. This remarkable record was definitely more than just "winning a few ball games," and there was no reason for anyone to think that the winning would suddenly cease.

As if he didn't have enough on his mind anyway, Tommy decided to marry his high school sweetheart, Donna Glawson, during his freshman year. "That was a rough thing to go in and ask Coach Bryant if I could get married," he chuckled. "Donna was at Auburn at the time, and I guess the love bug had hit.

"Everybody *had* to go ask him first if they could get married. He told me, 'Well, that is a big step for you and a big decision. It will make a man or a monkey out of you. You either make it or you don't.'

"In a way he discouraged me, but he went along with it," Tommy continued. "Some of my friends on the team were married. Apparently it didn't bother me that bad. All the married players had to live in the dorm anyway during the season because he liked togetherness for the team."

The team "togetherness" must have worked, because the 1966 varsity rolled to a perfect 10-0 regular season record. A total of 37 points was scored on Alabama all season, while the offense, powered by the Kenny Stabler-Dennis Homan passing combination, racked up a hefty 267 points.

Despite Alabama's unblemished 10-0 mark, Notre Dame (9-0-1) was crowned national champion at the end of the season. The Tide took its frustration out on Nebraska in the Sugar Bowl by whipping the Cornhuskers, 34-7. After the game, Bryant called this group "the greatest college team I've ever seen."

While the varsity was going undefeated, the freshman team was returning the favor. "Our freshman team was undefeated," Tommy said. "We had a good class that year—Scott Hunter, Richard Grammer, Alvin Samples, and Danny Ford were some on that team. I think they may have signed 40 or 50, and out of those about 15 played all four years."

Tommy's abilities earned him starting positions on the freshman team offense and defense. His offensive statistics were impressive, gaining 222 yards on 65 carries, catching 3 passes for 63 yards, and scoring 7 touchdowns. Bama fans were licking their chops at the thought of Tommy being a part of the next year's backfield.

The chance to show his talents never came, not that year at least. A hairline fracture of the wrist (there were other injuries later on) restricted Tommy's 1967 playing time. Nevertheless, he

87

finished his first varsity year as the team's second leading rusher with 165 yards in 55 carries.

Tommy's best game that year was against Mississippi State. He ran for 46 yards on 14 carries and scored the game's only touchdown in the 13-0 Tide homecoming win. He was also largely responsible for setting up two Steve Davis field goals.

The lone touchdown march in the State game was the highlight of Tommy's playing time thus far. With a 3-0 lead in the third quarter, the Tide had first and goal at the State nine-yard line. Tommy took a pitchout from Stabler and gained five yards. He bulled up the middle for three yards to the one, then climaxed the drive by diving over for the score.

"That's about the only game I remember," Tommy recalled. "I was so embarrassed on one play. We had the ball on about the 35-yard line, and I broke open on an off-tackle play. There was not anyone except me and this little halfback on about the 20-yard line. I said to myself that I would just run over him and ease on in. I lowered my shoulder to run into him, and he moved back out of the way. I fell flat on my face on the six- or seven-yard line.

"If he had bumped me, I could have kept my balance, but I was leaning so much. He just moved back. I got up off the ground, and he was going up the field laughing."

Bryant also recalled that run. "Tommy was running so hard he just fell down," he said after the game. "He could have walked into the end zone. I'm not being critical of Tommy, I'm just complimenting him on his effort. He was the only back that we had who ran with authority."

The victory was the Tide's tenth straight over the Bulldogs, and it upped its season record to 5-1-1. An opening game 37-37 tie with Florida State and a 24-13 loss to Tennessee in Birmingham were the team's only letdowns. The other wins came over Southern Mississippi, Ole Miss (on national television), Vanderbilt, Clemson, and LSU. The 7-6 victory over LSU in Baton Rouge practically assured the Tide of a major bowl bid.

South Carolina soon became Alabama's sixth victim with Stabler and Homan shattering two school records in the process. Stabler, who had been suspended in the off-season for training violations, broke Steve Sloan's passes-completed and passes-attempted record, while Homan erased Al Lary's mark set in 1950 for most yards by a receiver in a season.

Tommy, quickly emerging as one of Alabama's top backs (despite his injury), had 48 yards on 12 carries and scored one touchdown against the Gamecocks. The 17-0 shutout resulted in an invitation to play Texas A&M in the Cotton Bowl.

Before the Tidesmen could start thinking about boots and cowboy hats in Dallas, they needed to think about the Auburn Tigers in Birmingham. The Plainsmen had been humiliated 31-0 by the 1966 Tide squad and had a score to settle.

The pride of the Tide was at stake also. Two demerits on Bama's schedule were enough—three would have been unbearable and an embarrassment to the Alabama football program.

A fierce 25 mile-per-hour wind and rainstorm greeted the 71,200 fans in muddy Legion Field. The playing conditions were a pig's delight—mud, mud, mud, and more mud.

Auburn had somehow managed to kick a field goal for a 3-0 lead going into the fourth quarter, and it appeared that Mother Nature would keep Alabama from catching up.

Tommy Wade takes the handoff from Tide quarterback Kenny Stabler (12) in a 17-0 victory over South Carolina.

Then, with 11:29 left in the game and facing a third-and-three at the Auburn 47-yard line, quarterback Kenny "Snake" Stabler swam toward right end on an option play. A couple of key blocks sprang him down the field for the touchdown and a 7-3 victory.

Tommy, ending the game with 38 yards on 13 carries, well remembers the sloppy day. "I was the pitch man when Stabler scored the touchdown," he said. "It was cold, about 35 degrees, almost sleeting. He ran this option play and kept faking the ball to me. The films showed that when he turned upfield, I was leading cheers right behind him."

Following the victory over Auburn, the Tide took its 8-1-1 record to Dallas and the Cotton Bowl to play the Texas A&M Aggies. The Aggies came into the game unranked with a 6-4 record but were the Southwest Conference champs. Although outrushed and outpassed the Aggies prevailed, 20-16, and started Bama on an eight-year bowl skid which saw seven defeats and one tie.

A flu epidemic kept the Tiders in their motel rooms for several days, and many thought this was the reason for their sub-par performance against A&M. After the game, Tommy wished the flu had been his only problem. Whereas most players never forget their bowl games, Tommy's Cotton Bowl is one that he can't remember.

"It was right before the half, and I had been going both ways a lot," he said. "We ran an option one time, and Stabler pitched to me and I ran down the sidelines about 15 yards.

"That was the last thing I remember—me and this linebacker hit head on and I was knocked cold. I saw little stars and everything. The next thing I knew, we were coming back home."

Tommy's junior season (1968) started with the Tide in an unfamiliar position—the highest mark it earned in the preseason polls was 14th. Even more unusual than its low ranking was the fact that Bama was picked *third* in the conference behind Florida and Tennessee.

Gone was the awesome pair of Stabler and Homan. The new quarterback was expected to be chosen from a group of untested players—senior Joe Kelley, junior David Beddingfield, and sophomores Neb Hayden and Scott Hunter. Receivers returning included Conrad Fowler, George Ranager, Bobby Swafford, Donnie Sutton, Griff Langston, Rod Steakley, Dennis Dixon, Hunter Husband, and Jim Simmons.

Tommy was expected to join Ed Morgan, Pete Moore, and Larry Helm in a solid backfield, but Coach Bryant had other plans for the 6'2", 190-pound junior. Bryant had experimented with Tommy at flanker during the spring but moved him back to tailback, feeling that he wouldn't have the opportunity to run the ball enough.

Graduated from the defensive backfield were Dicky Thompson, Eddie Propst, and All-American Bobby Johns. To put it mildly, the Alabama secondary needed help. Enter Tommy Wade.

"I played tailback, defensive back, and returned punts in our first two games against Virginia Tech and Southern Miss," Tommy said. "After the Southern Miss game, Coach Bryant called me into his office and told me he was going to leave me on defense.

"He said we had a bunch of good running backs but didn't have any that could play defense. He said if they can't score, they can't win, so he wanted the best players on defense. I told him that it didn't matter, just as long as I didn't sit on the bench. From then on, I played safety."

Tommy and Donnie Sutton, who had also been switched to defense for the same reasons, led the Tide to a 14-7 victory over Virginia Tech in the opener. In that game Sutton had a 61-yard punt return, and Tommy ran back five punts for 46 yards.

Quarterback Scott Hunter and end George Ranager combined for 122 yards on eight passes in a 17-14 victory over Southern Mississippi, and then the bubble burst.

The Tide lost two games by a total of three points to knock itself out of the conference race. Ole Miss, led by quarterback Archie Manning, nipped Bama, 10-8, in Jackson; then Tennessee almost repeated the score in Knoxville with a 10-9 victory. Alabama did manage to score a win over Vanderbilt and had a 3-2 record going into the second half of the season.

Victories over Clemson, Mississippi State, LSU, and Miami greatly improved the Bama record to a respectable 7-2 before the annual Auburn clash.

In the 14-6 win over Miami, the Tide defensive secondary

had a field day in Orange Bowl Stadium by intercepting six passes. The game, attended by 43,418, including President-elect Richard Nixon, was the first-ever regular season collegiate game to be televised at night. Tommy, Mike Dean, and Wayne Owen were three of the defenders that contributed to the six interceptions.

"I intercepted two passes that (Miami) game," Tommy recalled. "I'll never forget one of them. They didn't have a good punter, so on third down he would just drop back and sling the fire out of the ball.

"One time it was third and long, and he threw a long one. I went up and intercepted it and came down in a hole and heard my ankle pop. By the time they carried me to the sidelines, it had already swelled up like a basketball.

"I worked with it for the next two weeks, trying to get it ready for the Auburn game. Right before the game Coach Bryant asked me how it felt. I said 'Pretty good.' He said 'Pretty good, hell! Can you play? Can you win?' I said 'Yes sir, yes sir.' I played with it hurt."

The secondary once again performed brilliantly against Auburn in an emotional game, intercepting five Loran Carter passes for the 24-16 Alabama victory, its fifth straight over the Plainsmen. Hunter and All-American linebacker Mike Hall were the game's heroes.

Then came Dan Devine and his Missouri Tigers in the Gator Bowl. What was supposed to be a close game turned into a 35-10 rout of Alabama. The game was one that Tommy wishes he could forget, but he remembers it well.

"They had this big guy that would run right up the middle all over us," he said. "I was playing safety and found out after the game that I had nine unassisted tackles and six assisted. When a safetyman has to do that, they're coming on through there.

"I would hit him and then holler for help. One time I gave him one of the hardest licks I've ever given anybody, and he just kept on trucking."

In 1969 Tommy accomplished a feat that probably had never been done by any college football player, nor will it ever be done again. He made Honorable Mention All-American at the end of the season—without ever playing a down.

"We were having a scrimmage on Monday before our opening game (against VPI)," he said. "I was playing safety, and they ran a draw play. I tackled the runner, and as I hit him he spun around. The front of his leg hit the side of mine, and it just popped. Of course I didn't think anything about it—I thought it was a charleyhorse, and I played several more plays. The X rays showed that I had broken the small bone in my leg.

"My leg went into a cast for several weeks, until the Vandy game, I think. That's the one where they beat us, 14-10. I tried to practice that week, but I couldn't. So I was redshirted the whole year.

"That was the most disappointing thing for me, knowing that I had gone through those two-a-day practices working so hard. Then the season came, and a fluke play like that knocked me out of it. Also, it was hard not getting to play with all the guys that I had been there three years with."

Based on past seasons Tommy sure didn't miss anything by not being able to play in 1969. The Tide finished 6-5, its worst record since 1957. The highlight of the season was a wild and wooly 33-32 victory over Ole Miss on national television. Disappointments were many—the 14-10 loss to Vandy, a 41-14 shellacking from Tennessee, a 49-26 loss to the Pat Sullivan-led Auburn Tigers, and a 47-33 defeat to Colorado in the Liberty Bowl.

After the Liberty Bowl, rumors were flying that Bryant would resign as head coach. He had been critical of himself for losing four regular season games, and after the bowl he made his intentions known to Dr. David Mathews, the new youthful president of the University.

He told Mathews to start looking for a replacement and to take an extensive look at the condition of the Alabama football program. Mathews would have none of that and announced in early 1970 that Bryant would remain as head coach.

While Tommy was nursing his leg during the 1969 season, another Wade was making himself known to the Alabama football program. Tommy's little brother, Steve, had entered Alabama that fall after an outstanding career at Dothan High School.

Tommy's athletic abilities had definitely rubbed off on Steve. During his elementary school years Steve's coaches made him play tag instead of tackle because he was so big.

"I started playing football in the third grade," Steve remembered. "I wasn't supposed to start until the fourth, but somehow the coach got me on the team. By the seventh grade I was six feet tall and almost 6'3" in the ninth grade."

Steve didn't know what playing "two ways" meant—he played "all ways." In high school he played fullback, tailback, quarterback, linebacker, safety, defensive halfback, and returned kickoffs and punts. He also lettered four years in basketball and track for his Dothan Tigers. His senior year he was All-State and All-American in basketball, and he finished third in the decathalon and first in the low hurdles at the state high school track meet.

Steve made the *Birmingham News* Super All-State first team, along with future Tide teammates John Croyle, Marvin Barron, Doug Faust, and John Hannah. In the North-South High School All Star game, he rushed for 99 yards and was named the game's most outstanding back. To say the least, his talents caught the eye of several major college coaches.

"Because of Tommy, colleges started looking at me real early," he said. "I remember one time Auburn gave me a little certificate to be a future War Eagle, but I never really looked at them. And because I was his little brother, I kinda had to face the question of whether I could play up to Tommy's abilities.

"A coach from Florida State came here one time and said that I was probably the best all-around high school running back that he had ever seen. They recruited me real heavily and wanted me to be a quarterback down there. And they said I could play basketball also, and I loved basketball. I really leaned toward them."

Steve may have leaned toward Florida State, but he signed with Alabama. "The fact that Tommy was there was one reason, but I liked their reputation," he said. "I knew that if I went there I would have a chance to be on a national championship team.

"And Coach Bryant was another reason. I had seen him a good bit when he was recruiting Tommy, so he didn't have to say much to get me to come to Alabama. Pat Dye recruited me also, and I liked him a lot."

Tommy was a mere spectator while Steve was being

recruited. "I told him to go where he wanted to, but if he didn't come to Alabama I would break his leg," Tommy chuckled. "No, not really. I told him that he was good enough to go anywhere he wanted to."

The change from high school to college is difficult for most, and Steve was certainly no exception. Not only was he entering Alabama's football program as "Tommy Wade's little brother," he was entering the University of Alabama, which meant books and classes and homework and final exams. And he was one of about 15,000 on campus, so the students didn't know Steve Wade from any other wide-eyed freshman.

"It was like a big fish going from the pond to a big lake and then becoming a little fish all over again," Steve said. "I was fine until I started to leave to go to school in August. My parents were going to take me. Then I realized just what I was doing—breaking away from the town that I loved where I was real popular and knew everyone.

"I cried all the way to Ozark. It was an emotional thing. It was a combination of the unexpected, the fear of school, and the emotional ties I had with the people in Dothan. Once I got started to school, I was all right."

Steve didn't stay all right for long, though. Besides the pressures of school and football, problems at home kept his mind occupied.

"My parents got a divorce my first year there," he said. "After that my dad didn't want to see my mom anymore, so for about six years I didn't see my dad. He would not have anything to do with me.

"And it was hard on me because I didn't have a lot of money. The other players' parents would come visit them, but my mother couldn't afford to come up to see me. I couldn't go out on a lot of dates because I didn't have the money or the clothes or the cars. I'm surprised that I finished school."

Steve's freshman season was Tommy's redshirt year. As Tommy waited for his leg to heal, Steve was being initiated into the world of college football. And it didn't take long.

"I'll never forget one of the first scrimmages we had as freshmen," Steve recalled. "We were playing against the varsity's first-team offense. They had (Johnny) Musso and (Scott) Hunter in the backfield, and I was playing defense. They were supposed to run up and down the field on us, but they weren't doing that. We were holding them, and the coaches were getting uptight. I could tell Coach Bryant didn't like it.

"Hunter threw a pass to George Ranager, and I came up and intercepted it and ran up the sidelines. A couple of big linemen came over and hit me, and I thought my head was coming off my body. That was the first big-league hit I had ever gotten. I thought I had been hit hard in high school, but it was nothing at all compared to college."

Steve's rookie year was quite impressive. He led the freshman team in rushing with 141 yards on 36 carries, caught 6 passes for 50 yards, scored one touchdown, handled all the punting with a 37.4 yard average, returned 2 kickoffs for 44 yards, and 3 punts for 13 yards.

However, more important than individual statistics was the fact that Bryant and his staff had recruited a fine class, one that would one day produce four All-Americans.

"We could tell that we had something there that was more than just a football team in that freshman class," Steve said. "We had some good, steady players—the makings of an excellent team."

As the 1970 season approached, the Alabama football team was facing one of its most difficult times yet. It had never experienced a season as bad as 1969. Bryant had considered retirement, and a murderous schedule loomed ahead, including the season opener against Southern California in Birmingham.

Steve had gone through his first year with flying colors and was looking forward to playing with big brother Tommy during the 1970 season. This was the same Tommy that he grew up with and idolized. This was the same Tommy that influenced him to come to Alabama, and this was the same Tommy that helped him through his freshman year. And regrettably, this was the same Tommy that he was having to compete against for the starting safety position. The circumstances almost wrecked him.

"During sophomore spring training I worked my way from third string up to the point where I was second team behind Lanny Norris," Steve said. "Tommy was an established first stringer at weak safety. Then Lanny got hurt, so I moved up to first-string strong safety. Coach Bryant was moving us around

Steve Wade was a three-sport letterman from Dothan High School and was one of several family" Tiders during the late sixties and early seventies.

to find the best position for us.

"Then Lanny got well, and he (Bryant) moved me to safety where Tommy was. He was number one, and I was number two. That really caused a conflict right there, because to me Tommy had always been my idol. He was an excellent player, and there we were competing for the same job.

"One day I had had enough and decided to quit the team. I went to Coach Bryant's office at the Coliseum the next morning at three o'clock and waited outside until he got there. I had already packed my bags and was ready to leave. When he came, I told him I was leaving. He said he didn't want to talk to me down there and asked me to come up to his office.

"We went up there, and he asked me for what reason was I

leaving. I really wouldn't give him a reason—I just told him I was leaving. I had been up all night long and was real tired, but I felt like I owed it to him to tell him I was leaving. He told me to go home, get some sleep, and not go to any classes because this was a very important decision that I had to make. He said to come back later when I had decided.

"So I went home and talked to Tommy about the situation. After our conversation I decided to go back to Coach Bryant and tell him I was not quitting the team. I think he realized what he had done, because he moved me from weak safety to strong safety, and I stayed there. The conflict was over."

Steve and Tommy both started in the defensive backfield against Southern California at strong safety and weak safety, respectively. The game was far from a pleasant debut for the Dothan brothers. The Trojans crushed the Tide, 42-21, making it the third consecutive game in which Alabama opponents scored 40 points or more.

"It was an exciting game, a tough one to start off with," Tommy said. "It was the first time all those sophomores had

Tommy Wade (second from left) and teammates David Bailey, Johnny Musso, and Scott Hunter pause a moment with head coach Paul "Bear" Bryant.

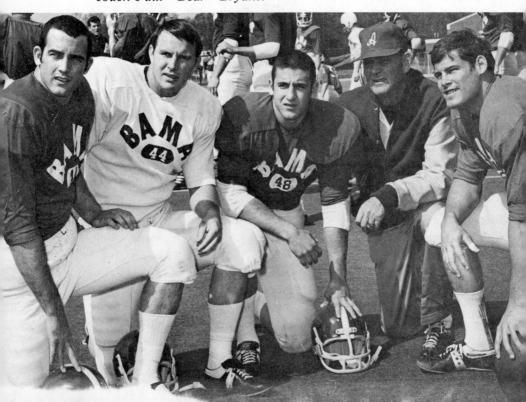

ever played in front of 72,000 people.''

Steve was one of those green sophomores, and memories of a certain Southern Cal back are still fresh on his mind. "They had big Sam Cunningham at fullback," Steve said. "He was so big and hard to tackle. One time I grabbed hold of him and he drug me five yards, and my brother Tommy hit him and he drug us both for another five or seven yards, and finally we pulled him down. He was a tremendous back.''

Alabama bounced back to whip Virginia Tech and Florida. Tommy's name went into the Alabama record books with a 72-yard punt return for a touchdown in the VPI game.

The two-game win streak didn't last long, however, as the Tide was soundly defeated by an Archie Manning-led Ole Miss team, 48-23. "Manning was a great quarterback," Steve recalled. "You could never get to him. He was so darn quick. It was as though everyone else was in slow motion and he was speeded up.

"I'll never forget watching him come out after the game—they had about four or five policemen around him, just like a national hero. People were grabbing at him like he was a big rock star. It was unbelievable.''

After a win over Vanderbilt, the Tide ran up against a big orange wall and was blanked, 24-0, by Tennessee, suffering its first shutout in 115 games. At this point the Tide was a struggling 3-3 and was headed to the Astrodome to play the Houston Cougars. In that contest junior defensive back Steve Higginbotham returned an intercepted pass 80 yards for a touchdown to lead Bama to a 30-21 upset win.

"That (Houston) game made our whole season," Steve said. "We were the big underdogs and beat a good team. That was the turning point of our season.''

Victories over Mississippi State, Miami, and a close loss to LSU upped the Tide's record to a respectable 6-4 entering the Auburn game. The 7-2 Tigers led the nation in passing and were ranked 11th best in the land.

Pat Sullivan and Terry Beasley had developed into one of the most talented duos in college football. In the 1968 Alabama-Auburn freshman game the pair led Auburn to a victory from 27 points down. The 1969 game saw Auburn fall behind early but come back to win, 49-26.

Tommy tried his best to break up that deadly scoring combination, and for a while he did just that. He literally knocked Beasley out, but the redhead came back to haunt the Tide.

"We were leading them 17-7, and Auburn was driving," Tommy said. "Sullivan threw the ball to Beasley, and as he caught it and turned around I popped him real good.

"I said, 'Come on, Terry, get up. Let's play ball.' He wasn't moving a bit. I called for help from the Auburn sideline. Blood was coming out his nose and mouth. They popped some ammonia capsules under his nose, and he still didn't move. I knew he was hurt pretty bad.

"They took him off, and he came back and beat us in the second half. He just picked us to death—he was so fast when he fired off the line. Also, we had a starting defensive back (Steve Williams) injured, and a sophomore (Bobby McKinney) started in his place."

Auburn came from 17 points down to win the game, 33-28. Beasley finished the day with 131 yards on nine receptions. Musso rushed for 221 yards and became the first Alabama back to ever rush for more than 1,000 yards in a single season.

Auburn went on to defeat Ole Miss, 35-28, in the Gator Bowl in a game that produced over 1,000 yards in total offense.

Though finishing 6-5, Alabama's rich tradition helped give it a bowl bid to the Astro-Bluebonnet Bowl in Houston, where they met the Oklahoma Sooners. Oklahoma had had an off-year also, finishing 7-4, and was rated a seven-point favorite over the Crimson Tide. Offensively the Sooners were led by quarterback Joe Wylie and the explosive back Greg Pruitt.

In one of the most exciting bowl games of the decade, the Sooners and Tide battled to a 24-24 standoff. Richard Ciemny, a junior college transfer kicker, missed a 34-yard field goal with five seconds left on the clock that would have given Alabama the victory.

"It was unbelievable to us that we got another trip to a bowl game," Steve said. "I didn't feel like we deserved it. Oklahoma was in a rebuilding stage also, so we had two teams playing with good names but not good records.

"I still feel sorry for Richard missing that kick. Everybody blamed the loss on him, and you just can't do that. I'm just glad that it wasn't me out there trying to kick it to win the game."

Tommy Wade takes a breather on the sidelines after returning a punt 71 yards for a touchdown against VPI in 1970. Alabama ripped the Gobblers, 51-18.

The game with Oklahoma was Tommy's last in a Crimson jersey. "The game was frustrating in a way for me," he said, "but we were playing such a good team. After that I went to the Senior Bowl but got my ankle hurt during the game and didn't play much. It was a privilege just to be asked."

Now it was up to Steve to carry on the Wade tradition. One would have thought Steve was content with starting several games as a sophomore. His talents had obviously been recognized by the Alabama coaching staff, but something happened after his sophomore year that almost had Steve packing has bags once again.

Actually, it was the lack of something that made him want to throw in the towel and never suit up in an Alabama uniform again. It was something so heartbreaking that he still has ill feelings about it.

After seeing action in all but one game and even starting in several, Steve was naturally expecting to earn a letter after his sophomore year. It never came.

"I don't really know why I didn't letter," Steve said. "The truth is that the coaches determine who gets a letter and who doesn't. If the coaches don't like you, you don't get a letter.

"I had hard feelings about it because I started several games that year. Later in the season Lanny Norris took my place, but he was older and better and I understood that. I played in about every game except Oklahoma. I played a lot more than a lot of guys who got letters that year."

The late sixties and early seventies were trying times for America. The Vietnam War was at its height, much to the dismay of the younger generation.

Draft cards were burned, the American flag was tortured, and the good name of the country was ridiculed. Over a half-million people turned out to a dairy farm in upstate New York for an anti-war rock concert they would later call Woodstock.

Four students were gunned down by National Guardsmen at Kent State University in Ohio, and anti-war riots and demonstrations erupted on college campuses across the nation.

The University of Alabama had its share of violence, resulting in a burned-down recreation building, 11:00 p.m. curfews, optional final exams, and the presence of the Alabama State Troopers to calm things down.

"Coach Bryant and the others were up in arms about the long hair and hippies and all the riots and stuff that went on at the University then," Steve said. "One thing they (the coaches) kinda held against me was that I had somewhat long hair. I think that was a reason I didn't letter.

"I remember one week I didn't get my four tickets to one of the games," he continued. "We had always gotten four to every game, and this time I didn't get any. I tried to find out why.

"Everyone was hush-hush, and one of the trainers said he thought it was because I had long hair and that I was not going to get the tickets until I got it cut. So I went and got my hair cut and received the tickets that afternoon."

Steve's failure to letter was not the only thing that

bothered him. He and an assistant coach had their differences, and the combination of the two had him ready to quit again.

"After my sophomore year, I was ready to quit, go home, find a job, and start all over," he said. "Then, Brother (Bill) Oliver came in and took a keen interest in the players. He talked to me and told me I was an excellent player and that I had all the potential in the world.

"Then he asked me why I had not produced. We hadn't even started the season yet! I guess he had talked to some of the coaches, and I might have gotten a reputation of being sorry or no-good.

"He said, 'Steve, you can do it, you have the potential, so let's work at it.' At that moment I was a different ballplayer. I wanted to play for that coach because he believed in me. He made the difference in my football career. From then on out I always started and was on the first team."

The positive approach that Oliver used on Steve to stay on the team may not have meant as much as the negative approach applied by Steve's mother, however.

"Another thing that kept me from leaving was the disgrace that someone would have to go through when quitting Alabama football," he said. "I would call my mother and tell her that I wanted to quit and come home. She would say that I could quit, but that I may not have a home to come to. She wanted me to grow up, and I'm glad she did. So I decided not to quit, and I'm glad I didn't."

Because of his decision to stay on the team Steve had the opportunity to be a part of the game that shocked the football world.

The place was the Los Angeles Memorial Coliseum. The time was Friday night, September 10, 1971. The opponent was the fearsome and sometimes awesome Southern California Trojans. The motive for Alabama was revenge. And the big surprise belonged to the men in Crimson and White.

It was that warm summer night that the Crimson Tide unleashed Johnny Musso and the wishbone offense on the surprised Trojans to score a 17-10 upset. The game was a sweet birthday present for Bryant, for it was his 200th career win. Only ten seasons later Bryant would become the winningest college football coach of all time by scoring a 28-17 decision over

Auburn for his 315th victory.

"I remember Southern Cal did not take us serious that year," Steve said. "But we didn't know how good we were either. Bobby McKinney took the opening kickoff and ran it for 20 or 30 yards down the field, and that got us going.

"My first impression when they came on the field was that they were the Los Angeles Rams—they were huge. By that time we were beginning to get big players at Alabama but nothing like they had. I felt like a movie star out there. The place was so big.

"They were driving one time and getting fairly close to the goal line, and I intercepted a pass intended for (future Pittsburgh Steeler All-Pro) Lynn Swann. That gave us the football and later a field goal.

"To me that game was the turning point. We knew we had something. We knew we were on our way then."

Yes, the Crimson Tide was indeed on its way back after a two-year nap. No longer were the Alabama alumni crying foul. No longer was Bryant considering leaving the game that had made him famous. And no longer would the Tide have to wonder when its next win would be. The drought was over.

The letdown that some people expected after the Southern Cal game never came. Southern Mississippi and Florida fell victims to the vicious Tide ground attack. Then, revenge game number two came at Birmingham's Legion Field against the Ole Miss Rebels. It was no contest—Alabama, 40 to 6.

"Yes, we felt like we got revenge in that one," Steve said. "I'm just sorry (the graduated) Archie Manning wasn't there to enjoy it. If we had lost that one, we would have fallen apart. I think we would have done better by getting beat by Southern Cal rather than Ole Miss."

After a 32-15 win over Tennessee, the Tide struggled to a 34-20 win over a tough Houston squad. "It was about 93 degrees and about ten to fifteen degrees hotter on the field," Steve said. "Because of the heat Coach Bryant substituted regularly, but I ended up playing all but one play.

"Houston had a great tight end, Riley Odums, and a great running back, Robert Newhouse. It was a tough game—I thought I was going to die out there. I lost 14 pounds that game. I remember Steve Higginbotham played a tremendous game. He weighed about 165 pounds, and Odums was at least 6'5" and weighed about 235. Steve manhandled him all day."

Mississippi State fell, 41-10, to set up a conference showdown in Baton Rouge against LSU. An Achilles tendon injury kept Steve from playing against the Tigers, but he made the trip anyway.

"I thought playing Georgia between the hedges was bad, but it was nothing like being in Baton Rouge," Steve said. "I remember outside our dressing room they ran sticks up and down the cage of their Bengal Tiger. Right outside the cage they had a microphone and four huge speakers set up. The noise was unbelievable—we couldn't even hear Coach Bryant give his pre-game talk.

"We came onto the field, and they threw a huge crate-size box full of popcorn all over us. One guy got hit with a Coke bottle, another with a can of beer. Oranges and apples were also thrown at us. That was not a fun place to be."

Despite the hositilities Alabama prevailed over LSU, 14-7. The victory prompted Bama fans to hurry to the newsstands to buy that week's *Sports Illustrated,* the cover of which showed quarterback Terry Davis "dazzling" LSU.

After a routine 31-3 win over Miami, revenge game number three came against the undefeated and fourth-ranked Auburn Tigers. It was a battle of the unbeatens and the last regular season game for Heisman Trophy winner Pat Sullivan and fourth-place finisher Johnny Musso.

The Tide had already accepted a bid to the Orange Bowl to play Nebraska, and Auburn was headed to the Sugar Bowl against Oklahoma. *The* most important clash in the 36-game series turned into a joke. An Alabama joke, of course—the count was Alabama 31, Auburn 7.

"We knew how good Auburn was and how they could strike at any minute," Steve recalled. "The difference in the game was that Coach Oliver knew how to play Beasley. He said to give him eight, ten, or twelve yards but don't let him catch the fifty- and sixty-yard passes. Lanny Norris and Steve Higginbotham played a great game in controlling him. They (Auburn) only scored one touchdown, and it was on a halfback pass."

Alabama took its 11-0 record and number-two national ranking to Miami to face the top-ranked and undefeated

Steve Wade (32) and Lanny Norris (40) reach high to intercept a pass thrown by VPI's Don Strock. The Tide plucked the Gobblers, 52-13.

Steve Wade (32) won this battle, but Alabama lost the war to Texas, 17-13, in the 1973 Cotton Bowl.

Nebraska Cornhuskers. The battle for the national championship ended in an embarrassment for Alabama as the Cornhuskers walloped the Tiders, 38-6.

"We just started off bad," Steve said. "We held them once or twice, but the field was wet and (Greg) Gantt bobbled the ball and they got close to our goal line and went ahead and scored. We couldn't do anything right after that.

"One thing that hurt us was that we had so many rules and regulations and restrictions," he continued. "For example, the Nebraska team went down there and went to the Playboy Hotel and saw some shows. We went out to see a Goldie Hawn movie.

"Here we were, hicks from the sticks wanting to do something exciting in the big city, and it was frustrating to hear that Nebraska was over at the Playboy Bunny Club living it up while we were watching a Goldie Hawn movie. How depressing!''

The 1972 season began with much optimism. "We believe" was becoming a common saying around the Alabama circles. Quarterback Terry Davis was back for his senior season surrounded by backs Steve Bisceglia, Ellis Beck, Joe LaBue, Wilbur Jackson, Randy Billingsley, Steve Dean, and David Knapp.

The offensive line was awesome, to say the least. All-Americans John Hannah, Jim Krapf, and Buddy Brown gave the Tide the best guard-to-guard trio in the nation. Wayne Wheeler and Dexter Wood provided much talent at the receiver position.

To no one's surprise Alabama coasted in its first five wins over Duke, Kentucky, Vanderbilt, Georgia, and Florida. Then came the miraculous comeback win over Tennessee in Knoxville. Down 10-3 with less than three minutes remaining, Alabama scored two touchdowns to win, 17-10.

"Tennessee was a good team, and we were lucky to win it," Steve said. "They had Haskell Stanback and Condredge Holloway. Next to Archie Manning, Holloway was the hardest one-on-one quarterback to tackle. He had so many moves—you couldn't get to him."

Southern Mississippi, Mississippi State, LSU, and Virginia Tech all fell to the Tide, and the Auburn Tigers were expected to be the eleventh victim.

The second-ranked Tide had already accepted an invitation to play Texas in the Cotton Bowl, but Bear Bryant wasn't thinking about Texas. A few days before the Auburn game he said, "I'd rather beat that Cow College once than beat Texas 10 times!"

If Bryant's remark made Auburn mad, it didn't show it until the fourth quarter. Trailing 16-3, the lifeless Tigers seemed to be out of the game. Alabama had dominated virtually every statistic and felt comfortable with a 13-point lead.

Then, lightning struck. Not once, but twice.

With just less than six minutes left in the game, Auburn blocked a Bama punt, picked up the ball, and scored to close the gap to 16-10. Instant replay took over from there, and the same thing happened again. The successful extra point made it Auburn 17, Alabama 16—final score.

"I was the back-up punter in that game," Steve said. "Earlier in the game I had gotten blocked and had torn the nail off my big toe. It was painful and hard for me to walk, but I continued to play.

"I was sitting on the bench, and after they blocked the first punt Coach (Pat) Dye came over and grabbed me by the shoulder. He said that Coach Bryant had told him to let me punt next time because I could get the ball off much faster than (Alabama punter Gregg) Gantt. I couldn't kick it as far, but I could definitely get it off faster.

"We couldn't move the ball and had to punt," he continued. "Coach Bryant said, 'O.K., Steve, go in there and quick kick.' So he pushes me on the field, and because my foot was hurting so bad, I kinda hobbled on. I could have kicked it. It might not have gone more than 15 yards, but it wouldn't have been blocked.

"I wanted to kick it, but about five or six yards out there he said, 'No, no, come back.' He saw the way I was hobbling and probably wondered how I could kick. And he had to make a quick decision, so he grabbed Gantt and sent him in. The kick was blocked, and we lost.

"History could have very easily been re-written."

The loss to Auburn is one that still bothers Steve. "I was literally sick for a week after that game," he said. "Even years later I dreamed about it at night. It's unbelievable how depressing it was. We should have won it. We had it and we lost it.

"I've tried to be more mature about it even now that I'm over thirty years old. I look back on it, and it still bothers me that we lost to Auburn that way."

Greg Gantt's punting, or lack of it, apparently had the coaches upset, because Steve was given the nod to punt in the Tide's 17-13 loss to Texas in the Cotton Bowl. He also intercepted two passes in the controversial game and was runner-up in MVP honors.

"The Texas game was kind of a letdown for us," Steve said. "We had the 'let's get it over with' attitude. We jumped off to a big lead, then they came back and won it. Their quarterback definitely stepped out of bounds—it was a bad call."

Behind 13-10 with less than five minutes left in the game, Texas quarterback Alan Lowry circled around left end, supposedly tightroped the sidelines, and scored to give the Longhorns the 17-13 victory.

The controversy centered around the fact that television instant replay showed that Lowry stepped out of bounds on his touchdown run. The Tide did not protest the game, however, and the 1973 Cotton Bowl was history.

Steve had seen the good and bad of Alabama football. His three-year record at the Capstone was 27-8-1, but his bowl record reflected the big goose egg—0-2-1.

Tommy's bowl record was also 0-2-1, and his career mark was 22-10-2, but he had no regrets that he played in one of the "down" eras of Alabama football.

"I was just glad that I had the privilege to play for Coach Bryant," Tommy said. "It would have been better if we had won more of our games, but a lot has to be taken into consideration. Back then it tested our fans to see how dedicated they were."

Coach Bryant greatly influenced both Tommy and Steve Wade. Though there were days when they dreaded the sound of his whistle or the low growl of his voice, he's still vivid in their

Steve Wade (32) and Lanny Norris (40) pull down a Vanderbilt runner in a 42-0 Tide win.

minds.

"He taught me that you are going to have good days and bad days," Steve said. "But on the bad days you should just try to turn them around and make them good days. Then you would eventually get where you were going."

When Tommy was a freshman in 1966, Bryant told the group of newcomers to the University's football program something that has stuck in his mind ever since.

"He went to the blackboard and wrote several things that you had to do to win," Tommy said.

"The first was 'Believe in the Good Lord.' The second thing he wrote was 'Your parents—always love and obey them.' And he told us not to forget to write them while we were there.

"The third thing was 'Your studies,' and the fourth was 'Your ballplaying.' He said that if we did the top three, then the fourth one would come natural."

Few players get to know Bryant well. Pat Trammell was probably considered to be the closest player to Bryant. Joe Namath and Kenny Stabler still seek his advice frequently. Many hesitate to talk to him, but that was not the case with Tommy.

"I would always meet him early in the morning when I needed to talk things over," he said. "One time I had some injuries, and I went up there and told him that I didn't feel like I was helping the team that much. I had been missing some tackles.

"He put me on the linebacking team. The tackling drills every day really helped me a lot.

"He builds winners," Tommy continued. "It doesn't matter who it is—from the managers to the trainers to the people that keep the equipment. He wants everybody as one group out there."

If the old adage "home is where your heart is" is true, then Tommy's and Steve's hearts are back in Dothan.

After graduating, Tommy went back to Dothan and opened a jeans store for eight years. Since 1978 he has worked at Southern Outdoor Sports in Dothan. He and Donna have two children: Tara (8-15-67) and Amy (7-7-72).

While coaching football and tennis in Orlando, Florida, Steve met and married Brenda Speight, a former professional singer from Miami. Steve, Brenda, and Heather (Brenda's daughter) lived in Florida three years before moving back to Dothan, where Steve is now assistant manager at Food World. Steve and Brenda had their first child, Jeremy, in October of 1980.

Even though Steve had his ups and downs while at Alabama, he learned something from Bryant that he will never forget.

"You learned that nothing was free," he said, "and you had to pay a price to be number one—you had to pay a price to be a winner. The same thing is true in real life—there's a price to pay, no matter what you do."

GRAMMER

Richard • Jimmy

It was to be just another duck hunting trip on the backwaters of the Tennessee River. Five young men—Joe Wright, David Smith, Kenny Wilder, Richard Grammer, and Jimmy Grammer—climbed into the 16-foot aluminum boat around 5:00 a.m. at the Decatur Boat Harbor. It was the first day of duck season (Wednesday, December 17, 1969).

The fivesome had made the trip countless times before. Joe Wright of Decatur was the Morgan County game warden. David Smith of Hartselle was a friend of the Grammers and was a frequent visitor to the Tennessee River backwaters.

Kenny Wilder of Columbiana was a senior football player at the University of Alabama, as was Richard Grammer of Hartselle. Wilder, an offensive tackle, and Richard, an offensive center, had both just completed their football careers four days earlier in a 47-33 loss to Colorado in the Liberty Bowl. Richard's younger brother, Jimmy, was a sophomore center on the Tide squad.

With the boat loaded the group departed the harbor on a glass-smooth Tennessee River. The temperature was well below freezing, and the sun had not yet risen to help them fight the cold.

The hunting gear they wore was bulky enough—for that reason their life jackets remained unworn.

A few minutes later, as the group was enjoying the fellowship, the running light on the front of the boat began flickering on and off. Richard Grammer stepped toward the front of the craft to check it, thinking there might be a short in the wire.

The weight shift was too much, and water quickly started seeping over the front. Seconds later the boat capsized, and all five occupants were thrown into the dark, icy waters. The swift current and the inability to see one another spread the group in different directions.

Joe Wright, David Smith, and Kenny Wilder struggled to shore, completely exhausted and narrowly escaping frostbite. Jimmy Grammer was picked up by another group of hunters and carried to safety.

With four of the five accounted for, their concern turned immediately to Richard's whereabouts. Even though he was an avid hunter and fisherman, Richard could not swim. But perhaps this time, they thought, he may have grabbed hold of a stray life jacket, or a log, or even the capsized boat.

They yelled for him—no reply. Despite his fatigued condi-

The center position on the 1969 Tide depth chart listed two players—Grammer and Grammer (Jimmy, left; Richard, right).

tion, Joe Wright swam back into the frigid waters to look for Richard, but the darkness and debris in the water made his gallant effort unsuccessful.

An Alabama water patrol boat arrived and joined the search. Fearing for the dangerous conditions of the four hunters, the water patrol returned them to the harbor, then continued the search for Richard.

An hour later Richard's body was found in less than six feet of water. The 5'11" senior was to have married Susan Gross of Montgomery the next Saturday, on his 22nd birthday.

Shock waves rippled through the Decatur, Hartselle, and Tuscaloosa communities. No one wanted to believe that the soft-spoken, mild-mannered Richard Grammer had met his death. It was something that people read about happening in other places—but *not* in Decatur. But it did happen, and it was hard felt by everyone.

"Jimmy (Grammer) called me around 6:15 (a.m.) from up there and told me Richard had just drowned," said Gary White, then Bryant Hall dorm director and now the Alabama athletic academic advisor. "I had to call Coach Bryant and wake him and tell him what happened. It just threw everything into total chaos around the dorm.

"Then I had to find his fiancee (Susan Gross) to tell her about Richard's accident. When I went over to her apartment, she was outside waiting on a ride to class. The minute she saw me pull up, she knew something was wrong. After I told her, she really broke down. The entire thing was a very traumatic experience.

"I really thought that Richard was one of the finest young men we had ever had in our program, and I still think that. He provided a great deal of leadership around the dorm, and I hate that we lost him at such a young age."

White had given Richard, Jimmy, and Kenny Wilder permission to go duck hunting just a few hours before they left for Decatur. "They came to see me late the night before and asked me if they could go hunting," White said. "I gave them permission to go, and they were to leave around 2:00 a.m. But at the time I didn't realize they were going so far away—I assumed they would be hunting close by. If I had realized it, I would have had some serious thoughts about letting them go so far away."

114

Teammates Danny Ford, Perry Willis, and Neb Hayden were with Gary White late that night when the three came in for permission to hunt. "We were playing Rook that night in the study room when Richard, Jimmy, and Kenny came in," said Ford, now head football coach at Clemson University.

"The players didn't have a curfew, but if you were an underclassman you had to sign out in the lobby if you wanted to stay out at night. Since Richard and Kenny were seniors, they didn't have to (sign out), but Jimmy did. They left real late, around two o'clock. I guess we were the last teammates (besides Jimmy and Kenny Wilder) to see Richard before he drowned.

"Richard was very scared of water," Ford continued. "Teammates used to kid him about it. He would be lying on a diving board by a pool in the summers, and somebody would act like they were going to push him in and he would panic. He never would get in the water.

"If he would have stood up (where he eventually drowned), he may have possibly bobbed up and down to stay alive. He just panicked with all that heavy gear on."

Richard's funeral was held in Hartselle the following Friday. Danny Ford and Kenny Wilder were two of the pallbearers—the others were Scott Hunter, Alvin Samples, Reid Drinkard, Charles Ferguson, Ken Emerson, and Steve Clay, all Alabama teammates.

Scott Hunter, record-setting Alabama quarterback and now Mobile businessman and broadcaster for WKRG Television, remembers the funeral well. "It was the toughest day I've ever spent in my lifetime," he said. "Most of the team was at the funeral. The whole event was so tragic."

All-American guard Alvin Samples played beside Richard on the offensive line for three years. Like Scott Hunter, Samples' memories of the funeral still linger. "A lot of young men our ages (back then) just didn't have a tragedy," he said. "It was hard to believe something like that had really happened. The funeral was a tough experience to go through. Most everyone there was crying."

Many of the Alabama players had planned to be in Hartselle that weekend anyway—for Richard's wedding, *not* his funeral. The tragedy touched the lives of everyone present and even changed the immediate future of one young couple.

Richard Grammer's ambition was to become a football coach.

Because of Richard's tragic death, Danny Ford and his fiancee, Deborah Anderson, made a sudden change in their wedding plans. "Deborah and I had planned to get married the next summer (1970)," Ford said. "After Richard drowned we moved our wedding date up to January. His accident made us think just how long we might live. You couldn't take time for granted. You never knew what might have happened. We didn't want to wait.

"We went home for Christmas break and talked it over with our families, then we decided to move the wedding up. We were married three weeks later (January 23, 1970)."

Richard wanted to make a career out of football as a coach. But his love of the game didn't start when he came to Alabama in 1966 or when he entered Morgan County High School in 1963. The seeds were planted early as he grew up in the Hartselle pee-wee football programs, then continued into junior high and high school.

Richard's leadership on both offense and defense at Morgan County High School (now Hartselle High) is well remembered by his coach, J. P. Cain. "We were playing Huntsville (High School) over there in 1964," Cain recalled, "and they had the ball with a 14-13 lead with less than five minutes left. Richard caused a fumble, and we got the ball and drove it into field goal range. It was fourth down and three inside the ten. I called time out to talk to our quarterback.

"I didn't know all this was going on, but Richard got them all in a huddle and he led a prayer. He said, 'Whatever the coach decides, we're going to do it. It doesn't make any difference what he says—run, pass, kick, whatever. We'll do it—full speed ahead.'

"I didn't know he had done that. We kicked a field goal and beat them, 16-14. Richard was real instrumental in that win.

"The next year (against Huntsville) Richard anchored several goal-line stands and we beat them again, 9-0."

After a 20-9-1 career record and twice being selected All-State, Richard signed a scholarship with Alabama as a defensive tackle, shunning offers from such schools as Notre Dame, Kentucky, and Ohio State. "Richard matured early in life and was well up around the 200-pound mark as a tenth grader in high school," said younger brother Jimmy. "He was larger than most kids his age. By his senior year at Alabama he was up to 215 or 220 pounds."

Coach Bryant switched Richard to offensive center for his sophomore season, and that was where he stayed. For those remaining three years, Richard became a leader on the offensive line. "Richard was a big-shouldered type guy," remarked quarterback Scott Hunter. "He was the apex of the huddle. During a tough two-hour scrimmage, people would lean on him like a streetpost."

Alabama assistant Jimmy Sharpe was Richard's offensive line coach all three years. Sharpe, later head coach at Virginia Tech and assistant at Mississippi State and Pittsburgh, recalled Richard's abilities. "Richard had real fine offensive blocking ability," Sharpe said. "He wasn't blessed with a whole lot of speed, but he was a very knowledgeable football player. What he lacked in foot speed he made up with technique and a thorough understanding of the game.

"He knew everybody's (offensive line) assignments," Sharpe stated. "He was constantly drawing up plays on the blackboard. He really understood the 'big picture' as well as anybody I've ever been associated with. He was a coach's dream as far as the offensive line is concerned. He was my coach on the field."

Tide assistant coach Clem Gryska was also impressed with Richard's capabilities. Gryska, now serving as Alabama assistant athletic director, recalled Richard's mild-manneredness. "Richard was a very quiet youngster, but a real hard worker," he said. "He played a lot different than he acted.

"In a squad meeting or group meeting, or even on the field warming up, you never did see him or hear him—until the football game started. Then he became a different person, very intense, and good at what he did."

Steve Clay of Gadsden was Richard's roommate during the 1969 season. Clay would have been the sixth participant in

Playing at a "heavy" 205 pounds, Jimmy Grammer was Alabama's first wishbone center.

Richard's tragic hunting accident, but an exam the next day kept him on campus.

"We were real close," Clay said. "I was playing defense, so we got close in that respect too, having to go against each other in practice every day.

"Richard was a real likeable person and down-to-earth. He enjoyed all sports and especially liked music. He had quite a record collection and played the guitar quite often.

"He was easygoing and had a good attitude. Of course, Richard hated the practices as bad as any of us did. I'll never forget the times I spent with him."

Richard lettered for the Tide in 1967, 1968, and 1969. His overall record of 22-10-1 came in what is today known as the "down" era of Alabama football. When Richard enrolled at the University in 1966, Alabama had captured three national championships (1961, 1964, and 1965) in the previous five years with a composite 49-5-1 record. The 8-2-1, 8-3, and 6-5 seasons that Richard experienced were quite a change.

Unlike his predecessors, Richard never won a bowl game, losing to Texas A&M in the Cotton Bowl, Missouri in the Gator Bowl, and Colorado in the Liberty Bowl. His record against rival Auburn was two wins and one loss, the defeat coming in 1969 by a 49-26 count. In that game Scott Hunter outdueled (in a losing effort) Tiger sophomore quarterback Pat Sullivan by completing 30 of 55 passes for 484 yards (all three categories are school records).

Younger brother Jimmy also played in the "down" era of Alabama football. But fortunately for Jimmy, his senior year (1971) was spent in a new era—the "wishbone" era. Little did they know it then, but the 11-1 team of 1971 would be the first of many great Alabama wishbone squads in the seventies and eighties.

Jimmy's success as center in the complicated Tide wishbone didn't come easy, however. He fought one setback after another during his rise to All SEC-status.

First he came into the Alabama program as someone's "little brother," wanting (and needing) an identity of his own. His second year he quit the team and after being reinstated was redshirted. Richard's death in late 1969 hit Jimmy very hard, and any type of mental comeback was shot down when he injured

119

his knee in the 1970 opener against Southern California. Surgery was required, and he was out for the entire year. Finally came 1971, and the Tide was back in the national spotlight.

Jimmy began his Alabama career as a 5'11", 185-pound freshman center. Another product of J.P. Cain's at Morgan County High School, Jimmy "had a conversation or two" about attending Auburn, but he knew where he wanted to go.

"When Coach Gryska offered me a scholarship (at Alabama), there was no doubt in my mind where I wanted to play," he said. "I wanted to go with a winner."

Jimmy's freshman squad finished with three wins in four attempts, the loss coming at the hands of Archie Manning and the Ole Miss Rebels.

Entering the 1968 season Jimmy was expected to compete for the center position (against Richard), but he never gave himself the chance. One week before the season opener against Virginia Tech he quit the team and headed home to Hartselle.

"The 24 hours a day of football is what got to me," Jimmy said. "To me, high school football under J. P. Cain was fun, but the pre-season practices (at Alabama) back then were anything but fun.

"I thought that if I quit everything would be fine and Mom and Dad would welcome me back with open arms. But it didn't take me long to find out that my father expected me to go back to college or go to work. It was not going to be the easy life that I had expected it to be."

Richard tried his best to talk Jimmy out of quitting, but to no avail. "He begged me to stay," Jimmy said. "He told me to wait and see if things would improve, but I didn't (wait). I had already made up my mind and thought it was best."

After numerous calls and letters from friends, talks with his family, and some soul-searching of his own, Jimmy decided to rededicate himself and return to the squad. But...he didn't know if Coach Bryant would want him back.

"I went into his office," Jimmy said, "and apologized for what I had done and asked him for the opportunity to come back. He said that he would have to talk it over with the other coaches and let me know. A week later I got a letter saying to come back to the team.

"Coach Bryant really went out on a limb for me and did

something he did not have to do," Jimmy continued, "because at that time I really was not all that important to their program. It would have been so easy for him to say 'no.'

"I went up to him and told him how much I appreciated what he had done. He said something to the effect that he was glad I found out early that I had made a mistake. A lot of people don't find out that quick. I think I would have some very bad regrets if I had not come back."

Because of his late return and missed practices Jimmy was redshirted. Meanwhile the Tide was having a successful 8-2 season—its two defeats were by a total of three points to Ole Miss (10-8) and Tennessee (10-9). Missouri overwhelmed Bama in the Gator Bowl, 35-10, making it the second straight bowl loss. The Tide would not win another for six more years.

Jimmy's redshirt year put him and Richard two years apart in eligibility. The 1969 season began with the senior Grammer and the sophomore Grammer battling for the top center spot. But this was not the knock-down, drag-out affair that is characteristic of most duels for a single position. The older, experienced Grammer was the solid number one.

"Every day at practice Coach Bryant had the depth roster on the bulletin board," Jimmy recalled. "On offense he would have Grammer, Grammer. Richard and I would always kid each other about which one was first. Of course we knew.

"During a long practice he and I would alternate plays. For example, he would run three plays, and I would run three. One day I got hurt, and Coach (Jim) Goostree told me that I didn't have to practice.

"Richard didn't have a substitute," Jimmy chuckled, "and I can remember standing on the sidelines in sweats and watching him practice. He was about to die and was giving me some hard looks. He made it clear to me that I had better be able to practice the next day."

Jimmy backed up Richard at center for the 1969 season and handled all snapping on punts and extra points. After three straight wins, Bama fell to Vanderbilt, 14-10, in Nashville. The rest of the season seesawed and ended with the humiliating losses to Auburn (49-26) and to Colorado in the Liberty Bowl (47-33).

Four days after the Liberty Bowl, Richard drowned in the

Tennessee River backwaters. Once again Jimmy was faced with some big decisions. "I stayed home during the Christmas holidays," he said. "During that time I did a lot of thinking. People would ask me if I was going back to school. Really, there was never any indecision—I wanted to go back. I knew there would be a lot of good memories and a lot of bad ones."

One of the Grammer family's closest friends was their dentist, Dr. Bob Sittason of Hartselle. Sittason had played a big role in Jimmy's return to the squad after quitting and was now offering the same encouragement to Jimmy after Richard's death.

"Of all the people I've ever known," Sittason said, "I've had as much or more respect for Jimmy than anybody. He had to prove himself again (after Richard's death), and he did."

Jimmy did prove himself in spring and fall practices, but lady luck dealt him a blow in the 1970 season opener against Southern California. A knee injury in the 42-21 loss required surgery, and Jimmy was out for the season.

As a team the Tide finished the regular season with a 6-5 mark. Despite its record an invitation to play Oklahoma in the Bluebonnet Bowl was extended and accepted. Alabama and Oklahoma, two teams that would soon help make the wishbone offense famous, battled to a 24-24 standoff.

During the summer of 1971 Texas coaches Darrell Royal and Emory Bellard came to Tuscaloosa for a coaching clinic. Tide coaches Paul Bryant, Jimmy Sharpe, and Mal Moore cornered the pair for a couple of days, and out of the pow-pow came the wishbone offense. The wishbone was not entirely new—the Longhorns had used it some in 1970. But it was the kind of offense that required a certain blend of backs and a smart, quick-footed quarterback. Fortunately, Alabama met those requirements.

"You don't adapt players to your offense—you adapt the offense to your players," Jimmy said. "We had some good backs—Joe LaBue, Johnny Musso, Ellis Beck, Steve Bisceglia, Wilbur Jackson, and a good quarterback in Terry Davis. Coach Bryant decided that the wishbone would be our offense.

"We had a team meeting, and he told us to forget anything we had ever learned about our offense. He drew the wishbone on the blackboard, we watched some films of it, and the very

On a warm summer night in September of 1971, the Alabama wishbone was unveiled against the Southern California Trojans. Jimmy Grammer (55) and Buddy Brown (65) carry head coach Paul "Bear" Bryant off the field after the 17-10 Tide victory.

next day we started practicing it.''

The best-kept secret in college football was let out of the bag on September 10, 1971, in Los Angeles against Southern California. Alabama whipped the Trojans, 17-10. "The wishbone was a total surprise to Southern Cal," Jimmy said. "On the first play we lined up in the old split back offense. The next time we lined up in the wishbone and really surprised them.

"They didn't have any idea how to defense the triple option. I think they took a short course in it at halftime, but it was too late then."

During the 1971 season the Tide offensive line became one of the most feared in the country. Jimmy, now at a "heavy" 205 pounds, anchored the center position. Surrounding him, at one time or another, were All-Americans John Hannah, Buddy Brown, and Jim Krapf.

No team threatened Alabama during that season—the closest score was 14-7 over LSU in Baton Rouge. The sweetest win, according to Jimmy, was the 31-7 revenge victory over

Auburn.

"I have never seen our football team get more fired up before a game than in the Auburn one," Jimmy said. "There were a lot of things that got us fired up. (Auburn quarterback) Pat Sullivan had just won the Heisman Trophy the week before, and of course we were all prejudiced—we felt Johnny Musso should have won it.

"Also, there were several billboards up in Tuscaloosa that said Alabama would never beat Auburn as long as Sullivan and (Auburn receiver Terry) Beasley were there. And Auburn had beaten us the year before (33-28), so we had revenge on our minds."

Revenge they got—and with it came a number-two national ranking and an invitation to play top-ranked Nebraska in the Orange Bowl. The battle for the national championship ended (and started) in disaster for the Tide, however, as the Cornhuskers scalped the Crimsons, 38-6.

In that game Jimmy had the task of blocking Nebraska All-American noseguard Rich Glover, and according to him it was no contest. "Glover was probably the best football player I ever came up against," he said. "I'm not saying that just because he whipped me so bad that night—I'm saying it honestly.

"He was quick as a cat. On the snap of the ball he was gone. It was not a question of whether I could block him or not—it's just that he was so fast he wasn't there to block. I couldn't even make contact with him. It was embarrassing."

Jimmy's performance during the 1971 season earned him All-SEC honors, but that wasn't the most important thing he wanted. "With all the honors I got, I would have rather beaten Nebraska and won the national championship more than anything," he said. "Making All-SEC was a big surprise because I was considered a very small lineman. It was quite an honor."

Jimmy had bounced back from quitting the team, Richard's tragic death, and a serious knee injury to earn All-SEC status. His comeback was heroic—the kind you read about but never really believe.

Today Jimmy is fulfilling his late brother's dream—coaching. After two years of graduate school at Auburn, Jimmy took his physical education/biology double major and went to work for the Joe Wheeler Wildlife Refuge in Decatur.

Football was still in his blood, however, and in 1975 Jimmy accepted a coaching job at Decatur High School under (now retired) Coach Earl Webb. He remains there today but still resides in nearby Hartselle with his wife, the former Sharon Livingston of Danville. They have two children—Jami (2-5-79) and Preston (2-3-82).

Although he has been out of college football since early 1972, the philosophies taught by Coach Bryant are evident in Jimmy's coaching.

"I think it's evident that I use his philosophies," Jimmy said. "I think a coach is doing a bad disservice to kids if he doesn't teach them something that will help them later in life. If he teaches them just football, like how to block and tackle, he hasn't helped them very much. They can't do that all their lives.

"That's what sets Coach Bryant apart from a lot of other coaches these days. He genuinely tries to help people for later on in life. And I try to do that at Decatur."

Jimmy's mother, Mrs. Ruth Grammer, still lives in Hartselle. His father, Henry Grammer, died of a heart attack in late 1978 while working in his garden.

The Grammers (including older brothers Scotty and Bob and older sister Janice) have recovered from Richard's shocking accident of 1969. And so have people such as Gary White, Danny Ford, Scott Hunter, Alvin Samples, J. P. Cain, Jimmy Sharpe, Clem Gryska, Steve Clay, and Bob Sittason. But the memories of Richard still linger in their minds.

Paul "Bear" Bryant was so touched by Richard's death that he wrote a dedication to Richard in the 1970 *Corolla,* the University yearbook.

"Richard was one of the finest young men I have ever been associated with," Bryant wrote. "He had his entire life in front of him. I had just had a wonderful visit with him the day before the accident, and he was telling me about his plans for the future.

"Richard didn't say much in meetings or on the field, but he got things done with his dedication and pride. We probably were playing him out of position at center, but that was the kind of young man he was, he wanted to play where he would be of the most value to his teammates.

"When you have been in coaching as long as I have, you get a kick out of watching young men go out into the business or professional world and do well. Richard wanted to be a coach, and I'm sure he would have been a good one. He had a great feeling for others. I wish my vocabulary was such that I could adequately tell you what is in my heart, but let me just say that we have lost a young man who stood for all the good and honorable things that intercollegiate athletics are all about."

From the pee-wee fields of Hartselle to the big bowl games while playing at the University of Alabama, Richard and Jimmy made their marks in the sport of football. Unfortunately, only Jimmy will be able to pass on to youngsters what he has learned from men like J. P. Cain and Paul Bryant.

And when Jimmy decided to take up his late brother's ambition, it was Coach Cain and Coach Bryant that rested easier, because they knew the young men he was coaching were in good hands.

HOBSON

Clell • Butch

Clell Lavern Hobson, Jr., has a label he will carry forever. He's known as the "third baseman that played quarterback for the Bear," but that doesn't bother him. Better known as Butch, he earned the "quarterback" status from 1969 to 1971 as a member of Coach Paul "Bear" Bryant's Alabama football squad.

Butch's father, Clell Hobson, had the same honor under coach Harold "Red" Drew from 1949 to 1952, making the pair the only father-son quarterback combination in Alabama football history.

However, it was baseball that made Butch Hobson famous. Following a record-breaking career as a Tide third baseman in 1970, 1972, and 1973, Butch fulfilled his dream of playing professional baseball when he was drafted by the Boston Red Sox. After eight years with the Red Sox organization, he spent one season with the California Angels and is now wearing the pinstripes of the New York Yankees, which he says "is a dream come true."

He may still carry the "quarterback" label, but to fans in the Boston, Anaheim, and New York areas Butch is known as a hard-nosed, durable youngster that has fought injury after injury to become one of professional baseball's top young third basemen.

Butch was born on August 17, 1951, just before Clell's junior football season with the Crimson Tide. Clell also had a dream to play professional baseball, and his dream was fulfilled in early 1953 when he signed with the Cleveland Indians organization.

127

Five of the first seven years of Butch's life were spent on the road with his family while Clell was touring with the Indians. Idolizing his father as a professional, Butch picked up his first ball, bat, and glove at a very early age. Growing up, football was a distant second to baseball—until his freshman year at Aliceville (Alabama) High School.

"Up until the ninth grade I concentrated on playing baseball," Butch said. "I enjoyed football and played pee-wee and junior high, but baseball was my favorite. Then I fell in love with football and just kind of let baseball go."

The Hobsons moved to Bessemer in 1967 after Clell accepted the head football coaching job at Bessemer High School (now Jess Lanier High). Butch played football and baseball his junior and senior years at Bessemer, and in the spring of 1969 he signed a football scholarship with the University of Alabama.

The talent in Butch's 1969 freshman football class was spectacular, despite its 3-2 record. Wayne Wheeler, Dexter Wood, Wayne Hall, Jeff Rouzie, John Croyle, John Hannah, Buddy Brown, Steve Wade, Ellis Beck, Joe LaBue, and Jim Krapf were just a few of the 39 signees that year.

Butch played defensive back and quarterback, sharing the latter with Billy Sexton and Johnny Sharpless. He finished as the team's fourth leading rusher with 113 yards on 38 carries and one touchdown. Meanwhile the varsity was suffering through its worst season (6-5) since 1958. Included in the five defeats was an embarrassing 14-10 loss to Vanderbilt.

Although he signed a football scholarship, Butch also wanted to play baseball, and Bryant gave him that opportunity. "Coach Bryant told me I could play baseball," Butch said, "but he said I would be behind in football because I would have to miss spring practice. (Head baseball) Coach (Hayden) Riley wanted me to play also, so I did."

Butch started at third base for the Tide, hitting three homeruns and batting .230. In Riley's first season after succeeding Hall of Famer Joe Sewell, the young Tide finished with 10 wins and 22 losses. Better baseball days lay ahead for Butch.

The 1970 football season began with Scott Hunter in the top quarterback spot, followed by seven others—Sexton, Sharpless, Terry Davis, Neb Hayden, Benny Rippetoe, Ricky Pitalo...and Butch. The coaches knew of Butch's abilities at strong safety (he had played there occasionally as a freshman), so he was moved to defense.

"I was moved to strong safety before the season started," Butch said. "They were going to redshirt me that year up until our first game against Southern Cal in Birmingham. In that game Lanny Norris was the starting strong safety, and he got hurt. Steve Wade played in Lanny's place, and I was moved up to back-up strong safety.

"The next week I made the trip to Birmingham and played almost the whole game against VPI. I played in a couple more games that year, so I was not able to be redshirted."

Alabama lost the Southern Cal game, 42-21, but bounced back to defeat VPI, 51-18. The remainder of the season saw the Tide lose four more and finish with a 6-5 record, then battle Oklahoma to a 24-24 standoff in the Bluebonnet Bowl.

Scott Hunter, who still holds most of Alabama's passing records, graduated after the 1970 season, leaving the top quarterback position up for grabs. If Butch was to be a contender, then sacrifices would have to be made. And he was willing to make them.

"I went to coach Bryant early in the (1971) spring and told him I wanted to play quarterback," Butch recalled. "He said O.K. but that I would have to go through spring training and therefore miss baseball season. I was willing to give up baseball that year to be given a shot at quarterback. So Coach Riley redshirted me for that baseball season, and I went through football spring training.

"I was the number-six quarterback and got the hell beat out of me. Out of the 20 practices, I ran the offensive scout team in 19 of them. I did, however, get to play one quarter of the A-Day game."

It was during the summer of 1971 that Paul Bryant, Jimmy Sharpe, and Mal Moore huddled with Texas coaches Darrell Royal and Emory Bellard to learn the wishbone offense. Bryant, the coach that had lived and died by the forward pass, was having a change of heart. He knew he didn't have any great passers among the half-dozen quarterbacks battling for the job. But he did have some exceptional runners, and Butch happened to be one of them.

So at the beginning of fall practice, Bryant and his aides

Butch Hobson played quarterback and defensive back for the Tide in 1970 and 1971.

told the Tide troops to forget their old offense and to sink or swim with the new wishbone.

Swim they did; the splash began against Southern California with a shocking 17-10 victory. Because of his running abilities Butch moved ahead of the passing quarterbacks into the back-up role behind junior Terry Davis.

Davis executed the wishbone to near perfection, with help from an All-American offensive line (Jim Krapf, John Hannah, Buddy Brown) and a multitude of running backs (Johnny Musso, Steve Bisceglia, Ellis Beck, Wilbur Jackson, and Joe LaBue, to name a few.) Butch played in 9 games, gaining 154 yards on 25 rushes and 2 touchdowns, and completing 2 of 8 passes for 29 yards.

The 1972 Orange Bowl game between Alabama and Nebraska was billed as the "College Super Bowl" and the "Game of the Decade." It was for all the marbles—the big number one.

Because of the game's importance Butch was expected to be a mere sideline spectator. The only way he would play was if the game was a rout, or if Terry Davis was injured and unable to play.

Well, the game *was* a rout, Davis *was* injured, and Butch stepped in to lead the Tide. Unfortunately for Alabama, though, it was Nebraska administering the rout. When Davis went out with bruised ribs early in the fourth quarter, the score was Nebraska 31, Alabama 6. And it got worse—the final count was 38-6.

Butch directed the Alabama wishbone 60 yards on the final 10 plays of the game. A potential scoring drive fizzled on the

Although out of football since 1971, Butch (17) Hobson is still referred to as "the third baseman that played quarterback for the Bear."

Nebraska 12-yard line as the game ended.

"They (Nebraska) just beat us to a pulp," Butch recalled. "I didn't run a single offensive play during the week of practice before the game. We could carry only a certain number of guys (to Miami), and the coaches had to put some of us on defense. So I ran the defensive scout team all week. I wasn't expecting to play in the game."

The 38-6 defeat to Nebraska was the worst ever suffered by an Alabama bowl team and the worst defeat under Bryant. Alabama finished fourth in the final polls behind a Big Eight Conference one-two-three sweep by Nebraska, Oklahoma, and Colorado, respectively.

With football over, Butch traded his helmet and pads for a bat and a glove and began his second Tide baseball season. From a record of 10-22 in Butch's freshman season (1970), the Tide steadily improved to 18-26 in 1971 and 21-14 in Butch's sophomore season (1972). Butch played shortstop, batted .240, and hit two homeruns.

With two baseball and three football seasons under his belt, Butch faced an important decision in the summer of 1972. He had entered Alabama in 1969 excelling in both baseball and football and had been given the opportunity to play both. But he realized that if he was to ever achieve his lifelong dream of playing sports, then he must choose between the pair.

Of the two sports, he knew he had a better shot at playing professional baseball, but he also felt he could challenge Terry Davis the upcoming fall for the starting quarterback position. Then he could still give professional baseball a chance once football season was over.

"I went to a (professional baseball) tryout camp that summer," Butch said, "and one of the coaches told me that if I wanted to play baseball, then I needed to concentrate on baseball. He said it was tough for anybody to play two sports.

"I thought about it a lot over the summer and decided that I would give up football so I could spend more time on baseball. I went to Coach Bryant and told him how I felt. He said that if I didn't make it in baseball, then I could come back if I wanted to. He was kind enough to let me keep my football scholarship."

Despite his playing time during the 1971 football season,

132

Butch did not earn a letter. He didn't understand why at the time, and even today he feels he should have received one.

"I don't really know why I didn't letter," he said. "I never confronted Coach Bryant with it, either. The answer I got from one of the assistant coaches was that Coach Bryant only lettered two quarterbacks at a time. Of course Terry (Davis) lettered, and because Benny (Rippetoe) was a senior, he received the other letter. The seniors almost always earned letters. I was sure that I had enough playing time, but I still didn't letter.

"I was very disappointed. The only guys that received the SEC championship rings (in 1971) were the ones that had lettered. At that point I was really considering leaving football, but I had not decided for sure. Then during the summer I decided to devote full time to baseball."

While his former football teammates were rolling to a 10-2 season in the fall of 1972, Butch was practicing baseball, weather permitting. When the weather was bad, he would take a bat and several hundred tennis balls to the racquetball courts beneath Memorial Coliseum. For hours he would hit the balls to keep his timing sharp. To say he was dedicated would be an understatement.

Few people now question Butch's decision to leave football for baseball. His junior season (1973) with the Tide was spectacular. He led the team in at-bats (120), hits (38), RBI (37), and homeruns (13). He tied for most doubles (6), triples (1), and runs (20). His 13 homeruns that year is a school record and was an SEC record until 1979.

As a team the Tide finished 22-14, won the SEC Western Division, and finished second in the conference behind Vanderbilt.

Butch's performance during the 1973 season caught the attention of several major league scouts. To no one's surprise he was drafted in the eighth round by the Boston Red Sox. His dream was now a reality, but he wasn't sure if he wanted it so soon. He still had another year of college eligibility left and felt that another year's experience might help him. But deep down he knew what he wanted.

"I decided it would be best for me to go ahead and sign with Boston," Butch said. "I would have had to have an extra-good senior year, better than my junior year, in order to get any more money at all. So I signed in August and reported to Winston-Salem, North Carolina.''

Butch joined the class A Winston-Salem team near the end of the season and played in 17 games. After the season he and his wife, the former Allen Jones of Birmingham, moved back to Bessemer. In January of 1974 they had their first child, Allene.

Butch played outfield, first base, and third base for Winston-Salem during the next (1974) season. His batting average soared to .284 with 14 homers.

Double A ball in Bristol, Connecticut, was Butch's next stop for all but two games of the 1975 season. He batted .265, banged 15 homeruns, and tied for tops in the league by playing in 138 games. When the Red Sox expanded their big-league roster near the end of the season, Butch was called up for the final two games of the year.

"I felt very good about being called up," Butch said. "I had a real good year in Bristol, and we won the Eastern League championship. The Red Sox expanded their roster to 40 players and brought up some youngsters. It was more or less a reward for having a good year.''

The roster was trimmed back to 25 players when the playoffs started, so Butch headed home after the season was over. The Red Sox advanced to the World Series against the Cincinnati Reds and lost in seven games in one of the most exciting championship series in professional baseball history.

Butch began the 1976 season in Triple A ball at Pawtucket, Rhode Island. Ninety games later, on June 28, he was called up to the Red Sox after veteran third baseman Rico Petrocelli was injured.

In his first official game as a major leaguer, Butch hit a two-run inside-the-park homer in Boston off Baltimore's Rudy May. With that shot Butch had finally made it in the big leagues. Players he had idolized such as Fred Lynn, Carlton Fisk, Rick Burleson, Jim Rice, and Carl Yastrzemski were now his teammates. The former quarterback for Bear Bryant had found a home, and he was there to stay.

Over the next four years Butch became one of the league's top young third basemen, despite battles with numerous injuries. In 1977, his first full season with Boston, he hit 30 homeruns and 112 RBI, both club records for a third baseman.

During that year he had a career-high 18-game hitting streak and led the team with 18 homers on the road. One of Boston's toughest critics called his play "heavenly."

Butch's enthusiasm earned him the Man of the Year Award by the Red Sox for his contribution to the success of the team and for his involvement in community endeavors.

At the end of the 1977 season Butch began experiencing elbow problems, the result of chips suffered from banging the hard astro-turf while quarterbacking at Alabama. By spring training of 1978 the elbow required constant treatment but improved enough for him to start the season.

Two weeks before the All-Star break Butch pulled a hamstring that kept him out of action for three weeks. Before the injury he had hit 15 homers.

"When I came back (after three weeks), my arm was never the same," he said. "The three weeks that I didn't do anything caused my elbow to get worse. It just never got well that year."

The injury affected Butch's throwing more than his batting. He still managed to hit .250 for the season, but his 43 (mostly throwing) errors led the American League. As a team the Red Sox lost a one-game playoff to the New York Yankees to finish the year with 99 wins and 64 losses, its best record since 1946.

Surgery to remove the bothersome chips was performed the day after the season ended by team physician Dr. Arthur Pappas. Recovery took longer than expected—Butch's next action was 13 games into the 1979 season.

But the wait was worth it—he finished the year with 28 homeruns, most in the league for third basemen. He hit .261, had 93 RBI, and led the team in triples with 7. During a September series with the Yankees he homered off Ron Guidry, Luis Tiant, and Tommy John in three consecutive nights.

The 1980 season was another frustrating one for Butch. In Cleveland in mid-May he separated his left shoulder while diving for a ground ball. He was twice placed on the disabled list, missing 69 games. He finished with a .228 batting average and 11 homers, mostly as a designated hitter.

Butch's heroic efforts reaped praise from Boston manager Don Zimmer. "Butch has as much guts as anybody who ever played this game," Zimmer said following the 1980 season. "He plays 'hurt' with problems that many guys wouldn't even think of playing with.

"He gives you 125 percent. This has been a crippling (1980) year for him, but I'll never forget his first three years. In those three years he was maybe our best clutch hitter. He knocked in more big runs that I can count.

"As an old player and with 30 years in baseball, I respect Butch Hobson to the fullest."

Since after the 1979 season, Butch had heard rumors that he may be traded. At that time he had been put on the trading block by Red Sox management, despite Zimmer's objections. And after the 1980 season, several teams showed interest in obtaining the youngster from Alabama.

Finally, in December of 1980 Butch became a California Angel in a five-player deal between the two teams. Fellow infielder Rick Burleson also became an Angel, prompting Angel owner Gene Autry to exclaim, "We feel really good about this (trade). It gives us one of the best infields in baseball."

Like father, like son. Clell (left) played five years of professional baseball in the minors. His dreams of playing in the big leagues were fulfilled when son Butch (right) was drafted by The Boston Red Sox in 1973. Butch played for the California Angels in 1981 and is now a New York Yankee.

Butch's stay in Anaheim with the Angels lasted only one year until March of 1982 when he was traded to the New York Yankees. His season with California was interrupted for more than two months by a players' strike, the results of which severely hampered Butch's play.

"I was hitting pretty good (.295) until the strike," Butch said. "The strike got my timing off, and I hurt my shoulder again. I ended up hitting .235.

"At (1982) spring training the Angels treated me like a scrub player. I saw the handwriting on the wall, especially when they traded to get (veteran third baseman) Doug DeCinces. Then, about two weeks before the season started, I was traded to the Yankees."

Butch's move to the tradition-rich Yankee team was a dream come true. "It's everybody's dream to play for the Yankees, and here I am," he exclaimed after the trade. "This is a top-of-the-line organization. I appreciate the chance to be here, and I look forward to someday playing in the World Series. We have the talent to get there—we just need to get it all together."

Butch's first meeting with outspoken and controversial Yankee owner George Steinbrenner was one he will never forget. "When I arrived in New York, Mr. Steinbrenner called me into his office," Butch said. "He told me what the Yankees expected of me. He said I would back up (All-Star Graig) Nettles at third base, start when he needed a rest, take some turns as a designated hitter, and play some first base if needed.

"Then he asked me if that was agreeable. I told him, 'Sure, Mr. Steinbrenner, those are acceptable goals for me in my first year with the Yankees.'"

The switch to first base came sooner than expected. While moving from Anaheim, Butch aggravated his elbow and was put on the 15-day disabled list. He came back and on April 22, 1982, he made his Yankee debut as a first baseman. He played only one inning but banged a double for his first hit.

"I was almost as nervous as my first time at bat with Boston," Butch remembered. "Dave Winfield and Graig Nettles had struck out before me, but I got a good pitch and drilled the ball off the (center field) wall.

"The reaction was wonderful. The fans gave me a nice

137

ovation. I guess they remembered me from some of the good games I had in Yankee Stadium when I was playing with Boston. I also got a nice reception in the dugout. Finally I felt like a member of the Yankees."

Steinbrenner continues to swap managers or players almost daily, but Butch thinks he's doing the best thing for the team. "I like George—he deals straight," Butch said. "All the moving around he does goes on all the time. We have a lot of talent, and I guess he's trying to find the right combination. As for me, I plan to play the game my way, 100 percent every day.

"George told me two reasons why he wanted me as a Yankee. He said he liked the way I had played against them when I was with the Red Sox and the Angels.

"And," Butch concluded, "he said he liked me because I was one of 'Bear's boys.' He just loves Bear Bryant."

Butch's following during his 10 years of pro baseball has extended much further than the Boston, Anaheim, and New York areas. He's still talked about by Alabama fans around the country, and he's practically a hero back home in the Aliceville and Carrollton communities of Pickens County, Alabama.

"I fell in love with this area when we lived down here," Butch said. "These people don't care whether I'm a baseball player or not. They're good people and they treat you good. They'll do anything for you.

"That's why we live here in the off-season. I love to hunt, and when I want to go hunting I can just walk out my back door. One day (after baseball) I want to buy some land and try my hand at farming. I think this area is God's country, and I'd like to try farming."

Butch, Allen, and children Allene (1-24-74), Elizabeth (8-12-77), and Polly (7-22-80) officially reside on five acres of land in Union Chapel, Alabama, a community with only a church and one paved road. Butch thoroughly loves living in "God's country," and to say the least "God's country" loves having Butch as one of its own.

While Butch was with Boston, WAQT radio in Carrollton began carrying all the Red Sox games. In November of 1979 "Butch Hobson Day in Pickens County" was declared by the county commission, and hundreds turned out for a parade and a picnic.

138

Butch's greatest fan, though, lives at 1422 Clarendon Avenue in Bessemer. His name is Clell Lavern Hobson, Sr., and he's playing professional baseball right along with son Butch. Well, almost.

"I guess I'm living through Butch my major league career that I never made myself," Clell said. "My daddy did the same thing—he was living his sports life through me. He had to quit school in the fifth grade (to help raise the family) but always loved sports. He worked with me and gave me the opportunity to play sports."

Because there were no organized youth leagues in his hometown of Tuscaloosa, Clell grew up playing football in the nearest cow pasture or playground. If he wasn't doing that, he could usually be found with a bat, ball, and glove looking for the nearest baseball game. Or he might have been found peeking through the bushes to watch the Alabama football team toil through another practice.

"We kinda looked up to all those (Alabama football) guys," Clell said. "They had guys like Harry Gilmer, Norwood Hodges, Lowell Tew, Herb Hannah, Pat O'Sullivan, George Albright, and Gordon Pettus. They took care of us Tuscaloosa youngsters. One time Gordon Pettus gave me a pair of football pants to practice in at high school, and I was thrilled to death.

"We would always go to the stadium on game day and usher. That gave us the chance to get in free and watch them play. There was only one place that I was going to school, and that was Alabama."

Clell entered the University on a football scholarship in January of 1949 after an outstanding three-letter career at Tuscaloosa High School. He also played baseball (shortstop) as a freshman under Coach Tilden "Happy" Campbell, helping the Tide to a 14-8 overall record.

Even after one semester of college and a full season of baseball, Clell was still allowed during the summer of 1949 to play in the All-American High School Football Classic in Corpus Christi, Texas, and the Alabama High School Football All-Star Game in Tuscaloosa. The games presented a new offensive twist for Clell—in high school he had played left halfback in the old Notre Dame box offensive formation. In the two all-star games he was moved to quarterback in the T-formation, and in

Clell Hobson was an outstanding three-letter athlete at Tuscaloosa High School.

the Alabama all-star game he responded by leading the South team to a 7-6 victory over a North squad led by future Tide great Bobby Marlow.

Marlow and Clell, who shared MVP honors in the all-star game, helped lead the baby Tiders to an undefeated freshman football season in 1949. The varsity lost its first two games that year, then didn't taste defeat again until Auburn prevailed, 14-13.

The 6-3-1 record in 1949 greatly improved in 1950, Clell's sophomore season. All-American Ed Salem ran and passed for 1,252 yards total offense, leading the Tide to a 9-2 record, its best in five years.

"We were using the Notre Dame Box formation in 1950, and I was playing (second team) left halfback," Clell recalled. "Occasionally we would run the T-formation with (quarterback) Butch Avinger under the center, but mostly it was the

Notre Dame Box.

"About four or five weeks into the season Butch Avinger's back-up quarterback broke his finger in practice. Coach (Harold 'Red') Drew knew I had played quarterback in the all-star games, so he moved me to quarterback. Everytime we got ahead by a comfortable margin I got to play. I had the opportunity to play in about five games that year."

Despite its 9-2 record Alabama was ignored when bowl season rolled around. "To be honest we all felt that they did not have anybody they thought could beat Alabama that year," Clell said. "I think the 1950 team was one of the best ball clubs Alabama had ever had.

"We had a lot of players coming back for the 1951 season, and we were expecting to have a good football team. But we started off bad and wound up with a losing record."

No one dreamed that Alabama would have a losing (5-6) record in 1951, especially after the opening game against Delta State. The Crimsons chewed, swallowed, and digested Delta by a score of 89-0, the third most lopsided win in Alabama football history.

In that game Selma senior Jack Brown was given the starting nod at quarterback over junior Clell. A week later Brown started against LSU, but Clell was called on to begin the second half. He never relinquished that spot until an ankle injury kept him from starting in the season finale 25-7 win over Auburn.

After the Delta State victory, the Tide hit a slide, losing four straight to LSU, Vanderbilt, Villanova, and Tennessee, its longest losing streak since 1910. Clell showed signs of greatness at the quarterback position but never had much success in putting many points on the board.

Finally the dry spell was broken with a 7-0 shutout of Mississippi State. Victories over Georgia, Southern Mississippi, and Auburn and defeats to Georgia Tech and Florida finished the Tide season with a disappointing 5-6 mark.

If there was a highlight of the 1951 season, it was the 25-7 victory over Auburn, spoiling Tiger head coach Ralph "Shug" Jordan's coaching debut against the Crimson Tide. Bobby Marlow exploded for three touchdowns and gained 233 yards, the most single-game yardage ever gained by a Tide player. Only Johnny Musso (against Auburn in 1970) has ever threatened

141

Marlow's total.

Clell's statistics for the 1951 season were quite impressive. He finished second in the nation in pass completion percentage, connecting on 66 of 114 attempts (57.9%). He became the fourth back in Alabama football history (behind Dixie Howell, Harry Gilmer, and Ed Salem) to exceed the 1,000-yard mark in total offense, finishing with 1,087.

As the new year rolled around, Clell's attention turned to his senior baseball season. His sophomore and junior years had

Clell Hobson in 1951 became the fourth back in Alabama football history to exceed the 1,000-yard mark in total offense.

been very productive—the Tide's 16-9 record in 1950 earned it the SEC championship. After a 17-5 record in Clell's junior year (1951), the squad finished 13-11 in 1952.

Clell's and Marlow's senior leadership helped pace the 1952 Tide football team to an impressive 10-2 record.

After a routine win over Southern Mississippi to open the season, the Crimsons traveled to Baton Rouge to visit the Bayou Bengals of LSU. As usual the Tigers attempted to intimidate the Tide with their pre-game harassments. This time it almost worked.

Alabama won, 21-20, but was behind 20-14 in the fourth quarter. "They went ahead of us late in the game," Clell recalled. "We drove down and were near the goal line.

"I felt like they would figure that I would hand the ball to Bobby Marlow. Bobby Luna was the left halfback, and I looked at him and told him I was going to let him run the ball. I told him if he didn't make it, then he couldn't run anymore.

"I gave it to him, and he went in for the score. We kicked the extra point and won, 21-20. It was quite an exciting game for us."

Big wins over Miami and Virginia Tech boosted the Tide's record to 4-0 as it headed to Knoxville for a big clash with Tennessee. General Bob Neyland and his Volunteers proved too much for Red Drew's Tide—the final count was Tennessee 20, Alabama 0. It was the first time in 42 games the Tide had failed to score.

Bama lost only once more that season, a 7-3 decision to Georgia Tech. In a 27-7 victory over Maryland, Clell's outstanding rushing performance earned him the Associated Press National Back of the Week award. Following the game the Tide was extended an Orange Bowl invitation to play either Navy or Syracuse.

Auburn fell to the Tide, 21-0, then the Crimsons traveled to Miami to meet Syracuse in the Orange Bowl. Alabama was rated a 13-point favorite over the pride of Eastern football.

In the most lopsided bowl game ever, Alabama crushed the Orangemen, 61-6. Clell completed 14 of 22 passes in the rout. Seven different Tide players scored touchdowns, and even a freshman from Montgomery named Bryan Bartlett Starr got to join in the fun by tossing a 22-yard touchdown pass to Joe

Clell Hobson (on right without helmet), Joe Curtis (left), and Alabama head coach Harold "Red" Drew celebrate the Tide's 61-6 Orange Bowl victory over Syracuse on January 1, 1953

Cummings.

Following the debacle, *Birmingham News* sports editor Zipp Newman wrote, "Come the years and Alabama supporters will take their grandchildren on their knees and tell them about the time Alabama beat Syracuse in the 1953 Orange Bowl— smashing 12 records in the most record-breaking bowl game in history."

"We seemed to do everything right that game," Clell said. "It was the first time the fans could see all four major bowls on television on the same day, and some of them left the game early so they could watch it on TV. We had never seen a television camera before, and they took close-ups of all the players. It was quite an experience."

Although Clell's football talents had earned him the headlines, baseball would be his livelihood for the next five years.

In January of 1953 Clell was drafted twice by Cleveland—once by the Indians to play baseball and once by the Browns to play football. "But all my life," he remarked, "I wanted to play baseball. I really didn't have any desire to give football a try."

Clell signed with the Cleveland Indians organization as a third baseman. Stops in Sherbrooke, Quebec (one year); Reading, Pennsylvania; Spartanburg, South Carolina, (one year); and back to Reading (three years) proved enough for

144

Clell, and in 1957 he settled back in Alabama to begin a successful football coaching career.

"After five years (in pro baseball), I had not made it," Clell said. "I had three kids (Butch, Mike, and Linka), and I felt that it was time for me to come back and do something that I was going to do in the future."

Even though five years out of college, Clell had not finished his degree, so back to Tuscaloosa he headed. A visit with Tide assistant football coach Hank Crisp resulted in an offer to be director of Friedman Hall, the athletic dorm. With his mind set on finishing his physical education degree, Clell happily took the scholarship and moved his family into the dorm. Baseball coach Happy Campbell also took advantage of Clell's presence by utilizing him as a volunteer assistant coach.

Then in December of that year Paul "Bear" Bryant was "called back home" to coach his alma mater. Everyone knew changes would be made, and unfortunately Clell was one of those changes.

"Coach Bryant wrote me a letter and told me he wanted his own people directing the dorm," Clell said. "Coach (Sam) Bailey came by the dorm, and we showed him around. We got along just super—there were no hard feelings. I stayed on scholarship until I finished my degree at the end of the spring (of 1958)."

Over the years hundreds of nervous athletes and coaches have made the journey to Bryant's office to discuss football matters. Clell just happened to be one of the first, and he remembers it like it was yesterday.

"I went into his office to talk to him about a (football) coaching job," Clell said. "He said he would love to have me, but that they were very limited because of a tight budget.

"He looked at me straight in the eye and told me he would hire me if he could. He was real honest with me, and I admired him for that."

Clell is one of the few that witnessed Bryant's first spring practice in 1958. "The greatest coaching job that I have ever witnessed was when Coach Bryant came back to Alabama," he said. "He had about 100 athletes in the spring, and the next fall I think he wound up with 38 boys playing both ways.

"They were 5-4-1 that year, and Auburn and LSU had to

come from behind to beat them. Bryant was always out on the field coaching, right down there with them.

"I saw him make some men out of some boys."

With degree in hand and the Tide coaching staff filled, Clell headed down Highway 82 to Centreville and Bibb County High School. After only one year as assistant football coach, he took over the head coaching duties and compiled a five-year winning record of 34-13-3.

"Going to Centreville was a good opportunity for me," Clell said. "It not only gave me a job, but it gave me something that I loved—the association with high school youngsters. Also it was close to Tuscaloosa, and I was able to work on my master's during the summers.

"And it gave my parents a lot of time to spend with their grandkids," Clell continued. "My daddy had more to do with Butch and Mike playing sports than I did because I was gone a lot playing baseball. He deserves a lot more credit for their development in sports than I do."

Clell decided to move on, and in 1964 he accepted the head coaching job at Aliceville High School, leading the Yellow Jackets to 5-4-1, 8-2, and 10-0 records (including an 18-game winning streak).

In 1967 the Hobsons moved to Bessemer, and Clell became head coach at Bessemer High (now Jess Lanier). Seven years later, after both Butch and Mike had finished their high school careers, Clell retired from coaching and became assistant principal at Jess Lanier.

"I had had 15 years of coaching, and it was always in the back of my mind to be a high school principal," Clell said. "I took the opportunity and have not regretted it a bit."

Clell has very little to regret. He's thankful for the way life has treated him, and he credits "God; my parents; my wife and children; and all my former teammates, coaches, and players" for his successes in athletics.

With Butch's family in nearby Pickens County for six months a year (in the off-season), Clell and his wife Polly feel fortunate to have them so close by. Mike and Linka are more spread out, however.

Mike now lives in Tampa, Florida. He walked on at Jacksonville State in 1972 and earned a scholarship playing

Butch Hobson saw a dream come true in 1982 when he became a New York Yankee.

under Coach Charley Pell (and later Clarkie Mayfield) in 1973, 1974, and 1975. Linka, now residing in Franklin, Tennessee, was a cheerleader at Jax State for two years, then in 1977 graduated from the University of Alabama in Birmingham.

Several times during Butch's major league career Clell has had the opportunity to turn on the television and hear the announcers talk about Butch Hobson, the Alabama quarterback turned professional third baseman, and that makes him very proud.

"In my case it's a fulfillment," Clell said. "There he is, playing in the majors. It makes me feel very, very proud. I just pray that he can have some influence on young people."

As long as Butch plays professional baseball, people will

confront him with questions about "the Bear." And no matter how Butch performs on the baseball diamond, he will always be remembered as the "third baseman that played quarterback for the Bear."

But then, that's not such a bad way to be remembered.

HANNAH

Herb • Bill • John • Charley • David

Herb Hannah really started something big when he donned his first Crimson Tide football uniform in the fall of 1947. Playing as a 27-year-old freshman, Herb was so foreign to the game of football that he "didn't even know how to put on a uniform properly."

How Herb put the uniform on didn't make any difference when compared to what he did once it was on.

Herb was a devastating Tide tackle for the next four years. And, to boot, he began an Alabama dynasty that will live forever in the Crimson minds of Tide families.

In June of 1949, following his sophomore year, Herb married Geneva Watkins of Ball Ground, Georgia. In April of 1951 their first son, John Allen Hannah, was born. Charles Alvin Hannah followed in July of 1955, and only 17 months later William David Hannah came into the world.

What this family would accomplish over the next three decades is one of the greatest stories in collegiate football history.

From Herb's playing days as one of the "old men" of college football, to his brother Bill's outstanding leadership on Paul "Bear" Bryant's first team, to the national championship quests and professional careers of John, Charley, and David, the Hannahs are indisputably the most celebrated family of Alabama football.

Go back in time to July 21, 1921.

"I was born in Lawrence County, Tennessee," said Herb, the fourth in a family of nine children. "We were poor sharecroppers and didn't have a chance to play many sports.

The Hannahs, left to right, John, Herb, Geneva, David, and Charley.

Cotton and corn were our main crops, with cotton being the money crop. We were a typical depression days family, with everyone having to work in order to survive."

The Hannahs moved to Athens, Alabama, when Herb was a ninth grader. He enrolled at West Limestone County High School in nearby Salem and soon discovered football.

"My senior year we played what is called six-man football," Herb recalled. "Two ends, three backs, and a center made up each team. The field was 60 yards wide and 110 yards long. I was injured and didn't get to play much, but I still enjoyed the competition."

Rough times for his large family caused Herb to fall behind in school. As a result he was 20 years old when he finished high school. "That sounds like I was a dummy and I flunked a grade," Herb said, "but I didn't. I just didn't have the opportunities to go to school like the other kids."

Four days after graduating, Herb left for the United States Navy and World War II. First stop was Athens, Georgia, for pre-flight school. There in the heart of Bulldog country the future Alabama patriarch experienced his first taste of full-force, full-team football.

While playing in the navy intramural leagues, Herb's talents were spotted by the varsity coaches, one of which was Alabama's Hank Crisp. Herb's size (6'3", 227 pounds) and quickness impressed the coaches enough to start him at tackle. An elbow injury cut his first season short, but Herb had shown some potential.

After five years in the navy (42 months at sea), Herb set his sights on getting an education. "Yes, I wanted to go on to college," he said. "People in the navy would always be talking about the colleges they had attended. All I had to talk about was West Limestone County High School.

"I wanted to prove myself by going on to school. It was sort of a competitive challenge that I had."

The only way Herb could go to college was on a football scholarship—he couldn't afford it otherwise. As an alternative he planned a career in the navy. But he longed for a college education, an opportunity to go into business for himself, and the chance to stay near his home.

Because of a naval acquaintance, Clemson was his first choice.

"In the navy I became good friends with a fellow named Rock McCants, and he wanted me to play football at Clemson," Herb said. "So I went to talk to (Clemson head coach) Frank Howard about a scholarship. He didn't have a space for me, so I went back to Athens and got my high school principal to call Coach Red Drew at Alabama. Coach Drew had just started coaching there, and he said he would give me a chance."

Drew, possibly not knowing of Herb's inexperience, offered him a scholarship. To say the least, Herb had a lot to learn about the game of football.

"I really didn't know what was going on," he chuckled. "I didn't know how to act." His naval intramural experience differed from big-time college football.

"I went out on the field, and I'll never forget Vaughn Mancha. His arms came down below his knees. He stuck that big ol' paw out there to me and said 'Big man, we're sure glad to

Herb Hannah in 1947 started the Hannah family tradition at the age of 27. He would later play one year of professional football as the oldest rookie in NFL history.

have you with us!' That broke the ice and made me feel so good.

"Here I was, an old man, not knowing how I would compete with all these young boys and their experience. It was a new environment—I didn't know what to expect."

Herb spent most of his freshman year on the B-team, which was composed of freshmen, redshirts, and walk-ons. He traveled with the varsity to the Sugar Bowl and played five minutes in a 27-7 loss to Texas. That was truly a memorable event for the freshman, but not as memorable as the Southern Misissippi game.

"We were playing Southern Miss in the first game of the season," Herb recalled. "I wasn't expecting to get in the ball game, so I had my headgear under the bench. Coach Drew hollered at me to go in.

"I got so excited, and after finally finding my headgear I put it on and went running out on the field. When I got out there, everybody was laughing because I had it on backwards. That really embarrassed me.

"Then I got down in front of the line and made a tackle and sorta got knocked goofy," he continued. "I lined back up and a guy said, 'Hannah, get ready for the play.' I told him I was ready. Well, I was lined up against my own team. They grabbed me and pulled me back over to their side."

The 1947 Tide edition finished with an impressive 8-2 regular season record, the only losses being on the road to Tulane and Vanderbilt. The 27-7 loss to Texas in the Cotton Bowl was at that time the worst bowl defeat ever for a Crimson Tide squad.

The upcoming 1948 season would be a rebuilding year. Gone were the much-loved "war babies," the group that had started as freshmen in 1944 for Coach Frank Thomas. People such as Harry Gilmer, Norwood Hodges, Lowell Tew, Hugh Morrow, John Wozniak, and Vaughn Mancha would be hard to replace.

Herb was one of the players that would be counted on to take up the slack. With a year of stage fright behind him, he alternated with senior Dick Flowers for the first seven games of the 1948 campaign, then became a starter for the remaining four games. The Tide finished with a 6-4-1 record, but things would get better. Future All-American Ed Salem, dubbed by many as the "successor to Harry Gilmer," was impressive as a sophomore during the 1948 season, and his best days were yet to come.

Herb's mind may have been on football the following spring, but his heart was in Ball Ground, Georgia, home of his fiancee Geneva Watkins. He had met the University of Georgia coed in Athens while in pre-flight school. The couple was married on June 8, 1949, and it didn't take Geneva long to switch allegiance. "The last time I yelled for Georgia," she said, "was Herb's freshman year. Since then it's been Roll Tide Roll."

Herb was a bona-fide starter at tackle for the 1949 (6-3-1) and 1950 (9-2) seasons. Herb, Larry Lauer, and Mike Mizerany paved the way for Ed Salem to run and pass for over 1,000 yards during the 1950 season as the Tide rolled to its best record since

1945.

Salem, Lauer, quarterback Butch Avinger, and Herb were invited to Mobile to play in the second annual Senior Bowl. The game's first home was Jacksonville, Florida, then was moved to Mobile where it has remained since. At the game, the 29-year-old Herb impressed a number of scouts and coaches but none more than South head coach Steve Owens of the New York Giants.

"After the Senior Bowl, Coach Owens of the Giants said he would draft me," Herb said. "He said I should have put a different age down on the questionnaire because I was so old. I told him, 'Well, coach, I'd rather play like a 25 year old and be 30 rather than say I'm 25 and play like I'm a 30 year old.' He drafted me, took me up to New York, and was real good to me."

By the time Herb reported for practice, he was not only the oldest Giant but also the oldest rookie in the National Football League. And to this day he is still regarded as the oldest rookie to ever play in the NFL.

"Yes, I was the oldest...and probably one of the lightest linemen in the league also," he said. "I only weighed 208. I lost so much weight because I was so tense, trying so hard. I wanted to make it so bad that I just worked my fanny off. In fact, Coach Owens tried to put me on an ale diet, but it didn't work. I finally gained back up to 218 pounds by the middle of the season."

Herb signed a one-year contract for $6,000 and was immediately thrust into the starting tackle position. "The Good Lord put me at the right place at the right time," he continued. "I was real fortunate—they needed a tackle, and I happened to be available. We had some great athletes on that team—Tom Landry, Kyle Rote, Travis Tidwell, Tex Coulter, and Al Derogatis, to name a few. We lost to Cleveland in the playoffs but still had a good year."

Herb's rookie season in the Big Apple was an eye-opener. "We lived on the 14th floor of a big high-rise overlooking New York City," he recalled fondly. "We were only two blocks from Yankee Stadium. I felt like a king. I would have gone up and played for the Giants just to live in the motel."

The Giants offered Herb $8,500 to play a second season,

154

but he elected to give up the bright lights and gridiron action of New York City. Herb's age had caught up with him, John was eight months old, and Ron, Geneva's son by a previous marriage, was ten years old. With no other choice, family matters came first.

"I knew I had four mouths to feed," Herb said. "I was afraid I would get hurt and not be able to take care of my family. I had to start planning for my family's future, so I decided to come back home."

Herb coached high school football in Georgia for four years—three in Canton and one in Cedartown. Charles was born prior to Herb's season in Cedartown, and another youngster to feed and clothe made Herb reconsider staying in coaching.

Bill Bradshaw offered, and Herb accepted, a job in agri-business, selling medication and vitamins for the poultry industry. After 18 months at Bradshaw Supply, Herb joined two others in starting an agri-business company. He bought them out, and in July of 1962 Herb, Geneva, Ron, John, Charley, and six-year old David moved to Albertville, Alabama. Herb's business, Dixie Poultry Supply, would become Hannah Supply in the early seventies.

And now the real story begins.

Albertville is a community of about 13,000 people located on Sand Mountain in northeast Alabama. Agriculture (broilers, eggs, cattle, soybeans, hogs, and milk) is the main industry. The people are hard working—many have lived and died by the successes or failures of the products of God's green earth.

One such family is the Hannahs. To the home folk the Hannahs are some of the many "good people" on Sand Mountain. They're the kind that would do anything for anybody, anyplace, anytime.

But to an outsider the Hannahs are best known for their exploits on the football field. Few families in America can match the "playing experience" of the Hannahs. When the Hannah name is mentioned, one immediately thinks of Herb, John, Charley, or David. Rightly so, but few people know about Bill Hannah, Herb's youngest brother.

Bill came to Alabama as a freshman in 1952. The Tide had tumbled to a disappointing 5-6 record the year before, so the

155

1952 season couldn't be much worse. After being redshirted his freshman year Bill became discontent and joined the marines until 1957. Then he had a decision to make.

"After he got out (of the marines)," Herb said, "he called me and asked me if I thought he should stay and live in California or come back to play football at Alabama. I said, 'Just because the Alabama team is down (record-wise), I don't think you should desert them. They gave you a chance.'

"So he came back and played for Coach (J.B. 'Ears') Whitworth for a year at 240 pounds. Coach Bryant came in the next year and said to him, 'If you expect a uniform next year you'll be below 200 pounds.' He went home that summer and lost over 40 pounds. He came back weighing around 190. Coach Bryant really admired him for that.

"Bill's lifelong ambition," Herb said, "was to become an assistant coach under Bryant."

That ambition never happened. On October 23, 1971, Bill and three others were killed in a plane crash in California's Sierra Madre Mountains. At the time, Bill was an assistant coach at Cal-State Fullerton and was traveling with two other assistants to San Luis Obispo to scout Cal-Poly, their upcoming opponent in the conference championship game. Few people knew it at the time, but Bill had accepted an assistant's position beginning the next season at the University of Southern California.

"Coach Bryant told me after the crash that he had made a mistake by not getting Bill back to Alabama on the (coaching) staff," Herb said. "He thought enough of Bill that he brought him back here one summer to lecture at a coaching clinic. Bill was scared to death. He didn't want to get up in front of his master and make a mistake."

For the better known of the Hannahs—John, Charles, and David—most of their football started on the pee-wee fields of Albertville.

"There never was any pressure to play football, but he (Herb) made sure the availability of football was there," David said.

"He (Herb) never pushed us into anything, but he did encourage us to do our best," Charley said.

"Our lives didn't revolve around football (when growing

156

Bill Hannah's lifelong ambition was to become an assistant under Coach Paul "Bear" Bryant.

A victory over Auburn in 1959 is sweet as Bill Hannah (66) receives a congratulatory handshake from Tide quarterback Pat Trammell. It was Alabama's first win over the Plainsmen since 1953.

up), but we were taught that if you're ever going to do anything, do it all out—be the best you can at it," John said.

With encouragement like that the young Hannahs started into football at an early age. "The first thing I remember," David said, "was when Dad bought us some uniforms when I was five years old. We all used to go out and play in the front yard."

John's younger-day football rememberances are not so pleasant. "They wouldn't even let me play pee-wee football," he chuckled. "I was too big. In Georgia they had a team for

157

sixth, seventh, and eighth graders. They let me play on that team when I was in the *fourth* grade. When we moved to Alabama (going into the sixth grade), they had a silly rule that you couldn't play if you weighed over 120 pounds. Yet we were the ones that were going to play football in the end. I never could understand the rule—I think it was for the mommas that had little wimpy sons.''

John, to say the least, was a big little boy. Just ask his mother.

"I had to buy husky jeans for John when he was in the first grade," Geneva said. "When he was in the eighth grade, we went to Whitten's in Albertville to look for some clothes.

"Mr. Whitten said, 'Maybe I can fit him. Let me measure him.' He measured him and his thighs were 33 inches around! Mr. Whitten told John that one of his legs was bigger than most boys' waists ever get to be. There was no way he could fit John. So we've had his clothes tailored since high school.''

The Hannah boys were no different growing up than any other set of brothers. "They weren't really mean—they were just full of devilment," Herb said. "They'd fight each other and they probably snuck around and smoked and did things like that. But they were good kids.''

All three attended Baylor School for Boys in Chattanooga, Tennessee. "I felt that besides getting an outstanding academic and athletic background at Baylor, they would also get a lot of social training," Herb said. "This type training was a great opportunity and the Good Lord had blessed me enough to be able to send them. It was an excellent investment.''

Whereas Charley and David spent four years each at Baylor, John decided to spend his senior year at Albertville High School. His girlfriend, Page Pickens, was back in Albertville and as he says, "puppy love had set in." The icing on the cake, however, was when he had a run-in with the commandant during his junior year at Baylor.

"It all started when we were hazing some younger kids, making them shine shoes or something," John said. "They went and told the commandant and he got mad at me. He backed me in a corner and called me a coward and a chicken. I told him I would meet him anywhere at anytime and we'd see how big of a coward I was. I told him I would

158

whip his butt, and he got mad. I guess he felt a victory when I left.''

Richard Cole, former Tide All-American in the mid-sixties, was John's head coach at Albertville. "I felt very fortunate to have John back in Albertville and on our team," Cole said. "Ability-wise, he was head and shoulders above everybody else. No one came close to playing him one-on-one.

"He weighed about 245 pounds, and I wanted him to get down to about 230. That was until I saw him move out. Believe me, speed wasn't a problem for John. I let him stay at any weight he wanted to.''

John's size and ability to blow his opponent off the line opened the eyes of the college scouts. "But," he said, "I really wasn't that widely recruited. Other than the SEC schools, Notre Dame and Southern Cal were the only other big ones.''

Alabama was naturally in the chase for John's talents, and at the time, it probably needed him more than most schools. "We felt the trend was going toward the big men," said Clem Gryska, now Alabama assistant athletic director, "particularly after the (1969) Liberty Bowl when Colorado jumped on us. We thought we had a fine football team, but they just manhandled us. We realized we were going to have to go to bigger people. John Hannah was where we started.''

At 6'2" and 255 pounds John was definitely the largest signee in that freshman class of 1969, but he didn't particularly care for all the "big man" publicity he was receiving.

"The smaller, offensive line upperclassmen were jealous of the press," John said. "I had a lot of trouble with some of them. They busted our butts with an A-Club paddle after we (the freshman team) got beat by Mississippi State. Of course they (the varsity) weren't having the best of seasons either. When they got beat by Vanderbilt, we tacked a note on the bulletin board telling them to line up outside our rooms for paddlings. They didn't like that too much.''

In wrestling, John was undefeated as a freshman but later switched his springtime efforts to track and field since teammate Jim Krapf was also an outstanding wrestler. Krapf won the SEC heavyweight division in 1970, 1971, 1972, and 1973, while John won the Southeastern Intercollegiate championship in 1970.

John came to Alabama as an offensive lineman, but as is

the case with most freshmen he played some defensive snaps also. Offensive line is where he preferred—he knew his future was there.

John says he was "too fat and slow" to play defense. And to this day even John himself doesn't know how close he came to making the switch.

"John Hannah was destined to play defense at Alabama," said Jimmy Sharpe, John's offensive line coach for three years. "At that particular time we were going through some tough times. We didn't have a very good defense, and every day Coach Bryant kept talking about putting the best athletes on defense. And John was one of those 'best athletes' he was talking about.

"At the same time, Coach Bryant was calling Johnny Musso the greatest running back in America and saying that he ought to gain a thousand yards that season. Well, something had to give.

"I went to Coach Bryant and begged him to keep John on offense," Sharpe continued. "The fact was that Musso was indeed one of the finest running backs in the country. And it was a shame that he would never be able to gain his potential at Alabama and help us win because he would not have the athletes of John's caliber to run behind. I told him that Musso would forever be running behind folks of less ability. They had the heart and fight, but they weren't big and strong and didn't have everything going for them like John had.

"Coach Bryant went home and prayed about it. The next day in the staff meeting he told (defensive coach) Ken Donahue and the whole staff that John Hannah was an offensive player. From that day on he played offense."

Sharpe, whom John calls "a person who really cared about his players," coached many fine offensive linemen in his years at Alabama, Virginia Tech, Mississippi State, and Pittsburgh. But none measured up to John's ability.

"John is the best offensive lineman I've ever seen," stated Sharpe, now a Gadsden businessman. "With John as the bellcow and Jim Krapf and Buddy Brown on each side, that was the best offensive line I've ever been around."

Krapf, now involved in construction and real estate in Wilmington, Delaware, was one of John's closest friends while

At 6'3" and nearly 300 pounds, John Hannah was the 1972 Southeastern Conference champion in the indoor shot (59'8½"), outdoor shot (60'1"), and discus (175'9½").

at Alabama. "John was born good and made himself great," Krapf said. "I saw him go through a lot of hard times to make himself great. Because of his great size, strength, and speed people thought it was easy for him, but it wasn't. He really worked hard for what he did."

John's awards and honors piled up during his three years at Alabama. He was All-American as a junior on several teams and was a consensus choice as a senior on 10 different squads, including Walter Camp, Kodak, NEA, *Football News,* Associated Press, United Press International, *Gridiron Magazine, Time Magazine, Sporting News Magazine,* and Universal Sports.

161

He was a three-time All-Southeastern Conference choice, winner of the Jacobs Blocking Award, a finalist for the Outland Trophy and Vince Lombardi Award, and Offensive Lineman of the Year (1972) by the touchdown clubs of Birmingham, Atlanta, Miami, Washington, D.C., and Columbus, Ohio. In a 1971 game against Florida, John was named National Lineman of the Week for his blocking, the first offensive lineman to win the award since the days of one-platoon football.

John earned football letters in 1970, 1971, and 1972. The 1970 squad (6-5-1) and the 1971 team (11-1) were as different as night and day, thanks mainly to the new wishbone offense. Mal Moore, Alabama offensive coordinator, credits John with helping the turnaround.

"It was unbelievable what a lineman like John Hannah did for any offense, especially the wishbone," Moore said. "You strive to have the strength of your offensive line at the center and two guards. With the triple option that's where it starts.

"John was one of the most overpowering linemen I've ever seen in college. He had the size, quickness, and height. He had the agility and technique to make the wishbone work for us."

Pat Dye, Alabama linebacker coach from 1965 to 1973 and now Auburn head coach, had to put his linebackers against John every day in practice. "I remember when our linebackers would go one-on-one with the offensive linemen," Dye recalled. "We had some big, strong linebackers then—Wayne Hall, Jeff Rouzie, Woodrow Lowe, Chuck Strickland. I know they hated going against John because he was so big, strong, and quick. He hurt you when he hit you."

Alabama head coach Paul "Bear" Bryant stated that he had coached hundreds of players but none were better on the offensive line than John. "John Hannah is the finest offensive lineman I've been around in over 30 years as a coach," Bryant said in 1972. "He has all the physical tools of greatness, plus has a burning desire to excel. I've seen him do some things on the football field I couldn't believe, especially for a man who stands 6'3" and weighs over 260. Even as great as he is, he has never gone backwards. He is always working, even after practice, to improve."

As if football wasn't enough, John also earned three letters in track and field, where he was the SEC shotput and discus champion. In the 1972 SEC outdoor meet he was the leading individual scorer. His best marks in track and field were 61 '5 " in the shot and 177 '9 " in the discus, both school records at the time.

With all the awards, honors, and recognition one would think that John "had it made" as a football player. "No worries, no pains, no heartaches," they would say, knowing that John's career as a player would one day make him a rich man.

But life was not all roses for the big man from Albertville.

In the summer after his sophomore year John married Page Pickens, his high school sweetheart. Less than two years later they were separated, heartbroken, and confused. "Both of us were so selfish that we couldn't see the other one," John said. "But there was a love there all the time."

John had always been on the "wild side" in college, and during his pre-Page years he was a frequent visitor to bars and nightclubs. The late sixties and early seventies were times of change for all of society, especially the college generation. The drug scene was growing at an alarming rate, and even John was not spared from its effects.

"I was involved in the drug scene a little bit (at Alabama)," John said, "but I haven't used drugs since then. Drugs are just a psychological confidence builder—I don't think they actually help anyone's performance."

John's wild times increased dramatically after he and Page separated. Perhaps the person hurt the most by the separation was John's father, Herb.

"It was probably the most frustrating time I've ever gone through," Herb said. "John wouldn't take any advice whatsoever. I was afraid that if I was too strong I would ruin him completely. I don't think he was on marijuana, but he was about to get into it because of the guys he was running around with.

"I told him that I would rather him take a pistol and shoot me than him go off and get involved in all of that. I don't think I could stand to see my boy a dope addict."

John's attitude towards school and getting an education was less than desirable. "I never did enjoy college as far as schoolwork is concerned," he said. "I approached football different from the other guys. Football *was* my school. Other people were training to be a banker, doctor, lawyer, or whatever.

"I was going to college to learn to be a football player. I never got my diploma—maybe I should have. But I got my diploma in what I went after, and that was football."

If that's the case, then John "graduated" at the top of his class. Pro scouts were drooling over his blocking talents, size, and speed (weighing 305 pounds he once ran a 4.85 40-yard dash—after a tough track workout). Because of his wishbone background John's pass blocking was questionable, but the pros were sure he could make the transition.

The New England Patriots selected John fourth in the first round of the NFL draft, but oddly enough he was not the first offensive lineman picked. That honor went to Texas tackle Jerry Sisemore, drafted by the Philadelphia Eagles. Defensive tackle John Matuszak was chosen first by Houston, followed by LSU quarterback Bert Jones to the Baltimore Colts.

"The first time I ever heard of the New England Patriots," John recalled, "was when they called and said they had drafted me. I never had heard of them before that. I even had to ask them where New England was."

Before traveling north to the Boston area John took seriously some words of wisdom from his father. "Dad gave me the greatest piece of advice that I had ever heard in my life," he said. "Even though I was going through that independent, rebellious stage I listened to him. He said, 'John, when you go up there, remember this. Everybody else up there is an All-American. Everybody up there has made All-conference. You're just going to be another one of the boys when you go up there.' And that's exactly what I was."

It didn't take long for John to get initiated into the NFL. "I got my tail kicked that rookie year," he said. "I started, but I didn't deserve to. They threw me to the lions—they were going to make me or break me. I took some beatings that were unbelievable."

One such beating was by Buck Buchanan of the Kansas City Chiefs. "It was the second game of my rookie year," John said. "He's from Bessemer and he told me he was going to 'welcome me to the NFL.' One time he actually picked me up and threw me. No one had ever done that before."

Another beating—this one mental—subsided when he and

164

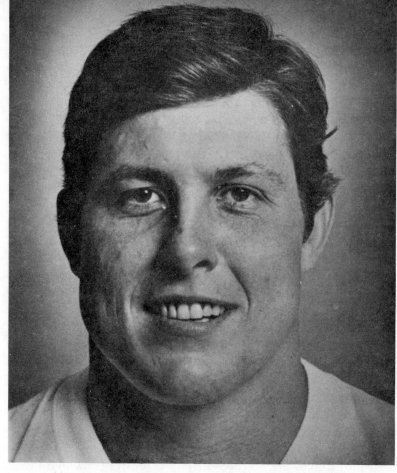

John Hannah with the New England Patriots.

Page reunited early in his rookie year. "I had been thinking a lot about her since I left Alabama," John said. "During that time Page had accepted Christ into her life. But I put the word to her right when we got back together. I said, 'Page, I'm the man of this house, and things are going to be my way or else you can pack your bags now and go on home.' She said, 'Fine, I'll do whatever you say.' That shocked me.

"She was willing to subject herself to me, knowing that's what love really was. Through her being submissive to me, she won my love even more than she ever had. Used to, I blamed on her everything I did wrong. After that I couldn't say things were her fault. I had to say, 'John, it's your fault.'"

After his rookie season John accepted Christ into his life, and he's been a different man ever since. "I had been putting on a big show so everybody would like me," he said, "but deep down inside I wasn't liking myself.

"Page never preached to me about Christ, but I knew I needed something. Her actions spoke louder than words, strictly by the life she lived. She read me a Bible verse, and it started me thinking. That's when I accepted Christ into my life."

John credits his acceptance of Christ for his successes in professional football. To say the least his accomplishments have been incredible.

Paul Zimmerman of *Sports Illustrated* put John on the front cover of the August 3, 1981, issue and called him the "Best Offensive Lineman of All Time." "And (Hannah) probably hasn't even reached his peak yet," Zimmerman wrote. "His brains, brawn, and speed make him the best."

Praises for John never end. Former Oakland Raiders head coach John Madden said that if he was given the opportunity to start a new franchise, he would build it around John. "You start building a team with an offensive line," he said in an interview with the *Boston Globe*, "so you take the best offensive lineman. Before you can build a quarterback, you have to put people in front of him to give him time to be a quarterback. To do this you have to build the line, and I'd want to build it around the best guy. And that guy is John Hannah."

Jim Ringo, the Patriots' former offensive coordinator and 10-time All-Pro center with the Green Bay Packers, played alongside Packer greats Fuzzy Thurston and Jerry Kramer. He can make an honest comparison.

"Hannah is 20 pounds heavier than Jerry and Fuzzy were," Ringo said, "yet he has far better pulling speed. Physically there's never been one like him."

John, nicknamed "Hog" (because, according to Coach Red Miller he "roots them out—just like an ol' hog") made his first AFC-NFC Pro Bowl in 1976. In 1977 he and teammate Leon Gray walked out of camp, feeling betrayed by Patriots management. At the time the All-Pro guard was making $46,000 per year. Three years earlier, in 1974, the Patriots had told him his salary would be upgraded if he ranked with the top linemen in the league.

"I was," John told Paul Zimmerman of *Sports Illustrated,* "a dumb, immature, rednecked idiot, and they stuck it to me."

John's first Pro Bowl was a nightmare—off the field. "Leon (Gray) and I went out to the Pro Bowl and started asking around about salaries," he said. "It was unbelievable. We were the lowest paid guys out there. I don't mean *kinda* low—I mean about half of what other guys were making. There were rookies that weren't even starting making more than me."

The Patriots refused to honor their promises, so John and Gray walked out at the beginning of the 1977 season. "They told me I was paid better than any offensive lineman on the team," John said. "That man lied through his teeth."

After missing the first two games, John and Gray were ordered back to work by the NFL Player Club Relations Committee. "The only thing we lost were the checks from the games we missed," John said. "The committee told the owners that unless they reached terms with us by the next season, then they would have to trade us. The Sullivans (owners) pulled every dirty punch they could. They slandered us in the newspapers unbelievably. The next year we signed for a lot more money."

The Patriots traded Gray to the Houston Oilers after the 1978 season, prompting John at the time to say, "There goes our Super Bowl down the drain. We had worked so hard to build up such a reputation to try to be the best guard-tackle combination in the NFL. And we were approaching it—we were right at it. And strictly on revenge and greed, the owners decided to tear it down."

In 1981 John signed a three-year contract with the Patriots that finally put him among the highest paid offensive linemen in the league. But he still has scars from the way he was mistreated by the Patriots. "I had always thought that the ultimate goal in football was to win," he said, "but when I went into the pros I found out otherwise. Their goal is to make money. I hold on to that dream of winning instead of trying to reduce my standards to the goal of making dollars and cents."

John was not invited to the 1977 Pro Bowl (where players are determined by the coaches) because of his "bad boy" image. Nevertheless, the NFL players still voted him the best offensive lineman in the game. "The coaches didn't recognize that at all," John said. "They said it was a union award."

John made the Pro Bowl in 1978, 1979, 1980, and 1981

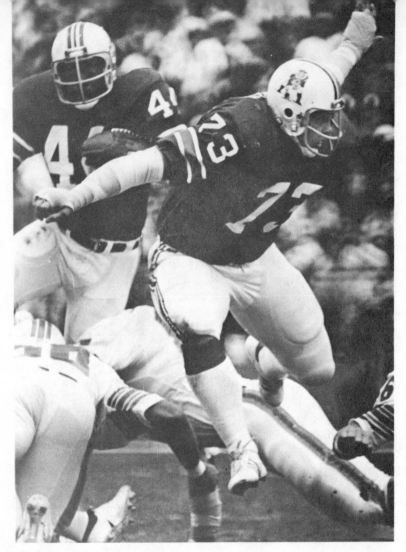

John Hannah takes to the air to show why he is the most feared lineman in pro football.

and has for all of those years been voted by the players as the NFL's best offensive lineman. During the 1978 season he was a mainstay in the offensive line that helped pave the way for the Patriots' record-setting pace of 3,165 rushing yards, an NFL single-season record.

During John's first three years with the Patriots the team never finished better than .500. After a 3-11 record in 1975, they made a complete turnaround and finished 11-3 in 1976, losing to Oakland in the AFC playoff. From 1976 until 1981 the Patriots were always playoff contenders.

Until the 1981 season, that is. A 10-6 record in 1980 plunged to 2-14 in 1981, the worst record in the franchise's 21-year history. "The toughest part (about the losing 1981 season) is the constant war inside of your mind," John said during the nightmare. "One side says you've got to give everything you have, no matter how bad the team is playing; you've got to prepare even harder to try to overcome the losing than you would if you were winning.

"But the other side of your mind says, 'Hey, whoa, what's the use? You've been busting your butt all year, and what have you gotten for it? Nothing. What's the use?' This is the hard part—finding a way to overcome this type of negativism."

Few professional football players have had to face a two-win season. John was one—and younger brother Charley was another. But Charley's 2-12 season in 1977 with the Tampa Bay Buccaneers was a marked contrast compared to John's 2-14 season in 1981. John's team was one that had a solid, 20-year history, and scores of great athletes. Charley's team was just out of the cradle, barely walking—but learning real fast.

Charley's rise to professional football is a success story in itself. Growing up in Albertville, Charley, like John, had his share of troubles. But Charley's problems were confined strictly to the football field.

"When the junior high coach at Baylor heard that John Hannah's little brother was coming, he was real excited," Charley said. "But I was having problems with my weight, and after my ninth grade year he was really disappointed in me. I had grown six inches without gaining any weight, and all of a sudden I was 6'2" and still only 140 pounds. I was really un-coordinated—pigeon-toed, knock-kneed, tall, and skinny. I remember some of the guys jumping around in line to try to go against me."

Because of the abuse Charley decided to quit Baylor after his ninth grade year. He enrolled in Albertville High School and began fall practice with the Aggies, but he wasn't happy there either. At that point in his athletic career he decided to quit football forever.

Herb remembers the emotional time. "One night Charles came in crying and woke us up," he recalled. "He asked

169

if it would be all right if he quit football. I told him 'yes,' if that's what he wanted. He said he wanted to go back to Baylor and just get a good education, not to play football. I told him, 'Charles, you're not playing for me, you're playing for yourself. If that's what you want, then I'm behind you a hundred percent.'

"The coach at Albertville had recommended that Charles not play any more football," Herb continued. "He said Charles was getting beat up out there and that he would never be able to play. But he was trying to compare Charles with John, and gosh—they're so different. Anyway, we called and got Charles enrolled back in Baylor."

With no intentions to play football Charley returned to Baylor for his tenth grade year. His athletic interests didn't go to waste, however, as he wrestled and threw the shot and discus during the spring.

Finally Charley began growing out instead of up, and head football coach Red Etter asked Charley to come back out for football his junior year. "I told him I would think about it," Charley said. "I told him I wasn't going to give up track, something I was good at at the time. Over the summer I decided to give football a try again, so I reported for camp in the fall."

Charley played defensive end and center at 190 pounds his junior season then remained only at defensive end for his senior year. By season's end, he stood 6'5" and was a heavier 215 pounds. The skinny, knock-kneed, pigeon-toed kid of three years earlier had transformed into a bona-fide All-State performer.

"I never thought about being good enough to play college football until the spring before my senior season," Charley said. "My coach told me that if I played as well my senior year as I had my junior year, then I might be able to get a scholarship. That fired me up.

"I told him I wasn't interested in anybody but Alabama and Tennessee, and I didn't care to hear from anybody else," he continued. "Then I committed to Alabama, partly because I didn't feel some of the Tennessee recruiters had treated me right. After I committed (to Alabama), I told them I would sign the next time I was in Albertville.

"Some Tennessee recruiters said that if I had committed to

Tennessee, they would have run down in a second to sign me. They tried to convince me that Alabama didn't want me that bad. And they said because I had not yet signed (with Alabama) I was leading Tennessee on. I got upset and told them I thought Tennessee had led me on a lot more than I had led them on.

"Anyway, I had given Alabama my word, and they had given me theirs, and that was enough for me. So I signed with Alabama the next time I went home."

Charley signed as a "lineman," which could have been a variety of positions. Once when he visited the Alabama dressing room while still in high school, an Alabama coach looked at his hands and said, "Man, I bet you could catch a ball with those things."

Charley replied, "I reckon, but I use them mostly for catching people."

Charley was open for suggestions as to exactly what position to play. "While being recruited I found that the more a school promises, the more promises they have to break," he stated. "When Alabama recruited me, they said they were going to try to teach me football then find the best position for me."

The 1973 season opened with a 66-0 slaughter of the California Golden Bears. "One of the biggest thrills I had (playing as a freshman)," Charley said, "was when I sacked (California quarterback) Vince Ferragamo. Here I was—a down lineman weighing about 215 pounds and I was 6'5". I was not a very imposing figure."

Charley made the traveling squad his freshman season, mostly snapping on punts. Granted, he was not an "imposing" figure at 6'5" and weighing 215 pounds. But he would soon become one along with several members of his freshman class, namely Bob Baumhower, Gus White, and Paul Harris.

After starting at defensive tackle against Maryland and Southern Mississippi to open up the 1974 season, Charley hurt his knee in practice and played sparingly the remainder of the year. The knee healed in time for him to start in the national championship showdown against Notre Dame in the Orange Bowl. This was the notorious date on which for the second year in a row Notre Dame nipped the Tide—this time the count being two points, 13-11 (following the Irish one-point win, 24-23, in the 1973 Sugar Bowl).

Charley Hannah was the tallest of the Hannahs at Alabama, standing 6'6".

The 1975 season (Charley's junior year) opened with a loss to Missouri on national television. Charley, playing his "worst game ever," re-injured his knee in the game, sat out the next week against Clemson, then returned to play against Vanderbilt. The next week against Ole Miss the Alabama defensive coaches finally settled on a starting defensive front five. Bob Baumhower, Gus White, and Charley made up the middle of the line that continued to earn its nickname of the "Redwood Forest."

After the Missouri loss the 1975 squad rolled to 11 straight wins. Included in the streak was a 13-6 finale over Penn State in the Sugar Bowl, the first bowl victory since the 1967 Sugar Bowl against Nebraska. Charley finished the season with 52 tackles; nine for losses totaling 31 yards.

Charley's senior season was somewhat of a disappointment compared to his first three years. For the first time since 1971 the Tide failed to win the Southeastern Conference championship, losing to Mississippi in the opening game and being blanked 21-0 by Georgia.

"We were really harassed over in Athens for that (Georgia) game," Charley recalled. "I think they had organized a horn blowing serenade for us all night long. We had to move our mattresses out in the hall just to sleep. The day of the game they threw rocks and bottles at our bus. I remember walking off the field, and one of the Georgia cheerleaders threw a firecracker and it went in the earhole of my helmet. We were really harassed and beaten soundly as a team."

A loss to Notre Dame in South Bend and a win over Auburn set up a match against UCLA in the Liberty Bowl. The underdog Tide braved a chill factor of below zero to stun the Bruins, 36-6.

"UCLA was real cocky," Charley said. "They talked about how the game was not really a big contest for them and how they were really going to move the ball against us. They said we weren't that good of a team and that they weren't excited about playing Alabama.

"It was a real knockdown, drag-out affair, and after (Barry) Krauss scored on the interception to make it 7-0, we were convinced that was all the points we needed. We had two or three goal line stands that were unbelievable."

The strong finish boosted the Tide's final record to nine wins and three losses. Charley led the team in tackles with 91 and for his efforts was named to the All-SEC first team. He joined teammates Bob Baumhower, Bucky Berrey, Calvin Culliver, and Paul Harris in the Senior Bowl, where he played defensive end and snapped center on punts.

Next up for the 6'6", 250-pound Charley was the NFL draft. "During my junior year," Charley said, "John said that if I had a good senior year I should be drafted in the first three rounds. I thought he was exaggerating. I thought I might go in the fourth or fifth rounds, maybe lower."

John hit it on the button. Charley was the first pick of the third round by the Tampa Bay Buccaneers. Wait a minute—the Tampa Bay Buccaneers? Who were they?

"They" were an NFL expansion team that went 0-14 in 1976, making them the laughingstock of the NFL.

"They" were a team coached by former Southern California head coach John McKay, who, after the dismal first year was quoted as saying, "I keep a picture of O.J. Simpson at my side at all times to remind me of the day when I knew how to coach."

And "they" now have the last laugh.

173

Tackles such as this earned Charley Hannah All-SEC status in 1976.

In below-freezing weather at the 1976 Liberty Bowl, Charley Hannah halts a UCLA runner. Alabama upset the favored Bruins, 36-6.

Through sound draft choices the Bucs built a hard-nosed team that in only six years has made the playoffs twice. The future looks bright for the young Bucs, but the past was anything but bright.

The team's 0-14 record in 1976 didn't bother Charley, though. "I was kinda happy in a way to go there," he said, "because I felt like I could help the team. I would know at the end of the season just what I had added. It would give me a little more pride."

For the first 12 games of Charley's rookie year he was still looking for that pride. Add to that the previous season, and the Bucs were winless in 26 games. They became the joke of the NFL.

"After my first year," Charley said, "people would ask me what I was doing. I told them I played for the Tampa Bay Buccaneers, and they would ask what that was. When I told them, they asked me if I started. I said 'no' and they thought it was worse to sit on the bench for Tampa than to start at Alabama. In other words, they thought I had regressed, even though I had gone up a level."

Nicknamed "Chicken Man" and "Huckleberry" by his teammates, Charley was a big hit in the Tampa area. Abe Gibron, Tampa defensive coach, thought Charley needed to gain some weight, so he took him to dinner one night to an exclusive restaurant. "I was shocked," Charley chuckled. "He was eatin' things that we wouldn't even go swimming with in Alabama—things like squid and stuff."

Charley got some laughs during his rookie year, but the laughter was confined to off the field. No one laughed about his abilities on the field.

He played frequently as a rookie at defensive end until a knee injury forced him out after nine games. The Bucs won their last two games that year to break the losing streak, finishing 2-12. After successful knee surgery in the off-season, Charley started 14 games in 1978, and the Bucs' record improved to 5-11.

Then came the big switch.

Entering the 1979 season the Bucs were short of quality offensive linemen. They drafted offensive guard Greg Roberts from Oklahoma to help things out, but there remained a missing

Charley Hannah with the Tampa Bay Buccaneers.

link. After almost a lifetime of playing defense, Charley filled
the void and was switched to offense (much to the pleasure of
John and Herb). "Charley didn't fail as a defensive player,"
head coach McKay said. "We just felt he had better potential
on offense."

"The switch made me nervous," Charley said, "but I was
kinda expecting it sometime. I was drafted as an offensive
lineman, but they kept me on defense. Also, I played some
center in my early days at Alabama. So it didn't come as a surprise.

"It was a difficult change for me," he continued. "Both
the mental and physical preparation are so different. The

techniques are different. I had a lot of defense in me, and my inclination was to hit and pursue, not strike and maintain balance, as in pass blocking.

"To play offense you have to be much more patient and disciplined. You're limited in how you can use your hands, so you really have to work hard to keep those linemen out of the backfield."

John McKay was pleased with his decision to move Charley to offense. "Ol' Charley's giving it everything, just like we knew he would," McKay said in a July 1979 interview with the *Tampa Sun*. "It's not an easy thing. It's a different game. As much as anything going for Hannah in this move is that he is not fighting it. He's accepting it. He wants it to go.

"You can't get enough Charley Hannahs on your team."

Charley, playing right offensive tackle, teamed with rookie guard Greg Roberts to finally give the Bucs the offensive line help they needed. "Those guys can mash people," said Detroit's Monte Clark of the Hannah-Roberts duo.

Mash people they did. As a matter of fact the whole Tampa *team* mashed enough opponents during the 1979 season to win the NFC Central Division, finishing with a remarkable 10-6 record. In the first playoff game against Philadelphia, Ricky Bell rushed behind the Buc offensive line for 142 yards to help defeat the Eagles in the NFC divisional playoffs. The Bucs finished nine points short of the Super Bowl when they lost a 9-0 heartbreaker to the Los Angeles Rams in the NFC championship game.

"They (Los Angeles) kicked their last field goal right at the end of the game," Charley said. "If we had scored a touchdown, I sincerely believe we would have won it by a point. It would have been the biggest Cinderella story if we had won it."

Charley started every game in both the 1980 and 1981 seasons. His switch to offense was greatly improving—in 1980 the Bucs' offensive line allowed the fewest sacks in the NFC, but key injuries were the reason their record dipped to 5-10-1.

The Bucs' mark improved to 9-7 in 1981, which was the year of "parity" in the NFL that saw two gutter teams of 1980, Cincinnati and San Francisco, battle each other in the Super Bowl. The Bucs' playoffs ended with a 38-0 drubbing by the

Wearing the same number as his brother John, Charley Hannah has been known to "mash people" on the opposing team.

Dallas Cowboys.

The fact that Charley was switched to offense in the pros indicated his abilities and knowledge of the game, and the same went for John at Alabama—he never actually made the switch from offense to defense, but he could have if needed.

David, the last of the Hannah clan, also had the abilities to play either way. He did just that at Baylor, playing tackle and center on offense, and linebacker and tackle on defense. And he did the same at Alabama, playing offense for one year, then defense for three years.

But David's switch at Alabama was not as peaceful as Charley's was at Tampa, or John's would have been at Alabama. During his change of position David went through some turbulent times, battling an identity crisis, numerous injuries, and most important—a battle with himself. David eventually found that pot of gold at the end of the rainbow, but it wasn't easy getting there. He battled many odds and won.

Naturally David was an outstanding football player in high school. As a senior in 1974 he was All-City, All-State, and All-South. His three-year record was 33-4, and his junior year Baylor was named national football champions by the National Sports News Service. And just like John and Charley, he earned letters in track and wrestling.

One would have assumed David was beating the doors down to play football at Alabama. Not necessarily so—Herb had different thoughts.

"I encouraged David to go to Auburn," Herb said. "He liked animals and was very interested in veterinary medicine. I felt like if he wanted to do that, then Auburn was the place. But he didn't want to play football against Charles, and that's what would have happened."

So why did the 6'4", 220-pound youngster end up at Alabama? (When asked that on his freshman questionnaire, he responded, "Because I wanted to eat.")

"I guess it was natural to go there," David stated. "It was something I had always dreamed of doing. I would have gone to USC, but it was too far from home. I had spent four years away from Mom and Dad, and I wanted to be able to see them.

"I never felt pressure from any of the family to go to Alabama. The pressure came from the people outside. John was telling me to go to Southern Cal, and Dad was telling me to 'go where your heart leads you.' Charles wanted me to go to Alabama, but he wouldn't have been upset if I had gone somewhere else.

"In the end, I wanted to be a champion. That's what I had heard John and Charles talk about for years. I chose Alabama to be a champion."

The road to becoming a champion started in 1975 when David joined a talented group of freshmen to open fall practice. Of the 28 signees in that freshman class, six are playing professional football today—Buddy Aydelette (Green Bay), Barry Krauss (Baltimore), Marty Lyons (New York Jets), Tony Nathan (Miami), Jeff Rutledge (Los Angeles), and Steve Whit-

It's signing time in 1974 for David Hannah as he followed brothers John and Charley, uncle Bill, and father Herb to play football at Alabama.

man (San Diego). But more important, they were a class that was the nucleus of a nationa championship team three years later.

David joined Jeff Rutledge and Tony Nathan as the only freshmen to make the varsity squad. David's and Jeff's situations were similar in that they both had a name to live up to. And that wasn't going to be easy. People became jealous of success.

"I don't think I was too popular with my freshman class," David said. "I would come in after practice and the varsity meetings and get some dirty looks from the other freshmen. Within five minutes they would all be in the other room.

"A lot of people thought the only reason I got a scholarship was because I was a Hannah."

Be it envy or jealousy or whatever, the facts were that David *did* earn a spot on the varsity squad as a freshman. Playing in the left tackle position he saw action in every game, starting in five of them. His first start was the opening game against Missouri in a 20-7 loss.

"We got our tails beat," he said. "Missouri came in there with an eight-man front, and to me it looked like a goal-line defense every time. Needless to say, I was totally embarrassed after the game. But...losing the game didn't bother me as much as being booed.

"The Alabama fans deserted us after that game. I would walk across the quad, and people would call me names because we had lost. I put up with that for two weeks, and it hurt. The next game we beat Clemson, 56-0, and the same people that had called me names were coming up, putting their arm around me, and calling me 'buddy' and 'pal.'

"That was my first taste of Alabama football fans. I said to myself, 'Forget it—I'll have no part of this.' So I became a loner."

David's troubles were just beginning. During the summer after his freshman year he bruised his shoulder playing basketball with Charley. Several days into fall practice he re-injured it, and X rays showed bone chips.

"The coaches thought I was faking," David said. "They were yelling at me about not using my shoulder, and I couldn't emphasize enough how much it was hurting. Finally, they X-rayed it, and the chips showed up."

After sitting out of practice for two weeks, David's shoulder improved, and he began practicing again. "I started back practicing about a week and a half before the (opening) Ole Miss game. I dressed for the game and was full steam ahead, ready to play. But I never got in the game.

"On the following Monday they told me I would be redshirted. Coach Bryant called me into his office and told me. I told him I would continue to work and try to do the best I could."

The redshirt decision was tough for David to cope with. He worked as hard as anybody in practice, blocking against people

181

like Charles, Bob Baumhower, and Gus White every day. But on Saturdays he was a mere spectator. The frustration changed his whole lifestyle.

"The redshirt year almost destroyed my life," David said. "I was filled with jealousy and bitterness. I felt like I could beat anybody that was playing. The only reason I went to the games in Tuscaloosa was to be with Mom and Dad.

"It was bitterness, but really and truly it was because I was crying inside. I saw them out there playing, and that's what I wanted to be doing. My ego was hurt."

During his redshirt year David sank to rock-bottom off the field. "I got introverted and didn't care about anybody," he said. "I became a big barhop and drank a lot. My grades really dropped—I could have done better, but I lost all interest in school. I didn't even go to class the last four weeks."

David's hard feelings carried over until spring practice. "I got real defiant that spring," he said. "John and I had really worked hard on a stance, and it was different than what everybody else did. It was a pro stance, fairly high and squatty over my legs. It put me off the ball different, and I didn't want to change."

If David was trying to get a message across to the coaches, it worked. Eight days before the end of spring practice he was switched to defense. "I was willing to do anything to start," he said. "I considered it my freedom (from frustration). I felt like I was emancipated. I got put on the 'headhunters' the next day and stayed there."

David got his wish and started the 1977 fall practice as first-team defensive tackle. But in his mind he still had bitter feelings.

"People were saying that I had been switched (to defense) because I couldn't beat out the other offensive players," David said. "I was still bitter, and during my sophomore and junior years I didn't just try to beat them—I tried to hurt them, humiliate them, and embarrass them.

"And they were bitter back to me. I wasn't afraid of any of them. I knew that a few of them could jack me up and tear me apart in a street fight. But I wasn't stupid. I waited until we were in pads, and then I outdid them.

"It was all to prove to the offensive coaches that I could

182

play defense, something I was totally alien from. When I was moved, I was determined that I was going to start.''

Alabama opened the 1977 season with revenge in a 34-13 victory over Ole Miss. The Tide's only loss of the season came the next week in Lincoln, Nebraska, against the Nebraska Cornhuskers. "They (Nebraska) found out I was real young and started picking on me," David said. "I got my tail beat all day long. For the first time in my life I wasn't able to do what I wanted to do. That Nebraska game was total humiliation."

David finished the season with 51 tackles, including a team-high nine sacks for minus 44 yards. After the Nebraska loss, Bama won nine straight (including a 21-20 victory over top-ranked Southern California) to finish the season with a 10-1 mark. Next was the "Bear Bryant vs. Woody Hayes" match-up in the Sugar Bowl. The final result wasn't close—Alabama 35, Ohio State 6.

Those that expected Alabama to move up in the polls (from number three) were most disappointed. Notre Dame defeated top-ranked Texas in the Cotton Bowl and jumped from fifth to first. "We were raped," David said. "I cried for days about it."

The polls weren't the only things David was crying about. He severely injured his knee in the second quarter, and except for two plays in the fourth quarter he was sidelined the rest of the game. The doctors thought he might escape surgery, but the toils of spring practice quickly settled the matter.

In April of 1978 David traveled to Tampa and underwent successful knee surgery to repair stretched ligaments. Dr. James Murphy, the Tampa Bay Buccaneers' (and Charley's) orthopedic surgeon, performed the operation.

After a successful summer-long recovery program, David re-injured his knee eight days before the 1978 opener against Nebraska. "The knee was ready," David said, "and it felt good. I just made a real sharp cut on it at practice and shattered the cartilage."

Within two weeks another operation was performed, and David had a new battle to fight. He had already been redshirted, so if he was to recover and play during the season, a monumental task lay ahead.

"My life was shattered after the second knee surgery," he

said. "For the first time in my life I realized how little it took to take a person out of football no matter how much he had put into it.

"And for the first time in my life I realized what it was to know that I had to commit my life to Christ. I had been a Christian, but I was a 'convenient' Christian, one that only portrayed what a Christian was *supposed* to act like.

"Nobody thought I would be back after my surgery," David continued. "They thought I would just sit back and relax and wait until next year. But I didn't have the time—David Hannah had too much to do. I had made a commitment to Christ—not to be the lackadaisical Christian that I had been but to be devoted and committed in every way of my life. (Teammates) Steadman Shealy and Keith Pugh jumped right in and helped all they could.

"A lot of the bitterness I had had (over the first two years) all of a sudden disappeared. The Lord provided everything I needed."

David, thought by many to be washed up for the year, battled back to play in Alabama's final two regular-season games against LSU and Auburn. He played only four plays in the Sugar Bowl against Penn State. Those four plays, however, are perhaps the most famous series of downs an Alabama defense has ever played.

Known thereafter simply as "Gut Check," the Tide defense held Penn State on four consecutive plays late in the game to preserve a 14-7 lead. After Tide defensive back Don McNeal saved a touchdown on second down by pushing the Penn State receiver out of bounds, the Tide front five stacked up Penn State back Mike Guman on third and goal from the one.

Then the clincher came. On fourth and goal from the ten-inch line Guman once again attemped a leap over the top and was met head-on by Barry Krauss with help from Rich Wingo and Murray Legg. Alabama took over and ran the clock out for a 14-7 victory, an 11-1 final record, and the Associated Press national championship.

Alabama assistant trainer Henry "Sang" Lyda remembers the plays well and believes David was one of the key performers in the series. "David had a part in the goal-line stand that never

Known simply as the "Gut Check," Penn State back Mike Guman is met head on by Murray Legg (19), Barry Krauss (77), and Rich Wingo (36). David Hannah is not visible at the bottom of the pile. The play secured a 14-7 Tide win and the 1978 national championship.

was written," Lyda said. "He had the Penn State runner by the leg, so he *had* to go up. It was David down there at the bottom of the pile that caused it."

Beating Penn State for the national championship was definitely an upturn for the battle-weary David. "I was so peaceful about it," he said. "I thought about all the years that I had struggled to be a national champion. Then, all of a sudden, we had won it."

One year later, after his senior season, David had the same feeling. The 1979 team repeated as national champion with a 11-0 regular season record and a convincing 24-9 romp over Arkansas in the Sugar Bowl. David started every game at right tackle, anchoring a defense that allowed only 67 total points, the fewest since the undefeated 1966 Tide squad.

"After the second national championship," David said, "I felt like a fine bottle of champagne that had just had its cork popped and all my flavor and all the things I had stored in me were just oozing out. It was great. I felt like there was nothing better."

Five Alabama players were invited to the Senior Bowl—David, Buddy Aydelette, Don McNeal, Dwight Stephenson, and Steve Whitman. To be asked to play in the Senior Bowl is quite an honor, but to be asked to play *both ways* is unheard of. But that's what happened to David.

"My future (in the pros) was on the offensive line," David

Arkansas back Roland Sales was no match for David Hannah (74), Jackie Cline (98), and Ricky Tucker (18). The Tide whipped the Razorbacks, 24-9, in the Sugar Bowl to end a perfect 12-0 season and claim the national championship.

said, "so (South head coach) Ray Perkins moved me to offense. I practiced there all week. It was the first time I had played offense since my redshirt year.

"I started off playing offense in the game and would have played a lot more, but one of our defensive linemen got hurt and I had to play on defense the whole second half. It was tough to play both ways against players of that caliber."

Herb knew that offense was David's natural position. "David had more offensive talent than defensive," he said. "We knew his future was on offense, and I was glad to see him play offense (in the Senior Bowl).

"In high school David had more technique on offense than either Charles or John had. He didn't have the leg strength that John had, but as far as finesse, David was the best of the three."

David anxiously anticipated the professional draft, but it never came. "Naturally I was hurt that I didn't get drafted," he said, "but I had realized that I might not be drafted because of my knees.

"I had had to play in a metal brace my whole senior year, and I had lost some quickness. It was showing up by the end of the year. I was a step behind on a lot of plays, where at the first of the season I was there.

"The pros recognized that and didn't want to take a chance. I can't blame them. I think it was the Lord's will that I didn't get drafted. I know that's a convenient excuse to say, but to me it's a convenient truth. I just don't think the Lord wanted me to play."

Even though Herb, John, and Charley all had played professional football, none was disappointed about David not being drafted. "I could certainly see the pros' position," Herb said. "I wouldn't hire a blind man to read to me, nor would I hire a football player with a chronic knee.

"David had to accept that, and I think he has. I felt bad about him getting hurt but not about him not getting drafted. And I think he made the right decision not to walk on anywhere. It wasn't worth it for him to walk on and get his knee hurt and limp for life."

After an amazing overall record at Alabama of 45 wins and only 3 losses, 4 Southeastern Conference titles, and 2 national championships, David proudly returned to Albertville in the summer of 1980 to begin his career with Hannah Supply. Since then David has been in sales covering seven Southeastern states and, according to Herb, "is doing an excellent job."

Charley, Margaret Anne, and Kimberly Anne (7-15-80) live in Tampa year around, which has given Charley the chance to finish his marketing degree at the University of South Florida. He is also one of the most demanded speakers on the Buccaneers' squad and was the team's representative in the 1981 Tampa United Way campaign.

During his football career Charley has had to labor in John's shadow. He's constantly referred to as John Hannah's "little brother," but that doesn't bother Charley. He and John are very close, and he's quick to brag on his big brother.

"John is the kind of athlete that doesn't come along very often," Charley said. "If he were a running back with his abillity, he would be the most famous athlete in the world. He's the only offensive lineman in the NFL that the offense is built around.

"He is a tremendous player and a great person on top of that. He means a great deal to me. We're very close.

"But at times," Charley admits, "it has hurt being John's brother. Each of us has different talents. We're built differently. He's shorter and huskier than I am. He's a guard and I'm a tackle. John plays his position his way, and I play mine my way. We do different things to get our job done. It's as simple as that.

"I don't want to live up to someone else's mold. I respect John, but I don't want to be exactly like him."

During the off-season John and Page live on a 253-acre farm between Geraldine and Crossville, about 15 miles northeast of Albertville. Some of the land is for crops, but most is devoted to raising chickens (43,000 in two houses) and cattle. The big attraction is a five-year old, 1,800-pound Santa Gertrudis bull that, according to John, "is still a baby and will weigh at least 2,200 pounds when full grown."

The big attractions *inside* the Hannah's stately two-story home are Seth (1-26-78) and Mary Beth (10-25-80). Seth, John says, "is about as tall and has the same body build as I did when I was his age, but he's not as heavy—I was really obese."

John and David spend countless hours on the road speaking to groups of all kinds, especially those that are church-related. John has been an active supporter of John Croyle's Big Oak Ranch, a home located near Gadsden for unwanted youngsters. In 1974 he donated his $30,000 bonus with the Patriots to help the ranch get started.

John Croyle, the founder of the ranch, and John were anything but friends during their early days at Alabama. Croyle was the outspoken Christian, while John was the one making fun of Croyle and his Christian teammates. When Croyle heard of John's acceptance of Jesus Christ in 1974, he went to Boston to be with the man that had laughed at him. They found a strong friendship that remains strong today.

To say the least, Herb is proud of his sons, all of which will eventually end up back in Albertville at Hannah Supply. Once John and Charley retire from professional football, they will join Herb and brothers Ron and David in the business. Ron, the oldest Hannah, has been the company's accountant since 1980 after a successful private practice in Albertville.

"We've really been blessed," Herb said proudly about his family. "I haven't been able to do a lot of things that daddies and sons do, because I've had to work pretty hard in trying to get the business going.

"When the boys were growing up, I didn't have much time to spend with them. I wish I could have spent more time with them individually—fishing, hunting, etc. I guess I lost track of priorities. Coupe did a good job of bringing them along."

"Coupe" is Geneva Hannah. She picked up the nickname at age five from her father, who named her after a Model-T Ford. She's been a pillar of strength for the Hannah clan. The phrase "behind a great man stands a great woman" was meant for Coupe Hannah.

"She's always shown that she's loved us," John said. "When we were growing up, she was such a hard worker. She would help Dad with the business, then come home and cook and clean. She was very loving and supportive of all of us."

Charley's sentiments about his mother are similar. "She petted us all like we were lost puppy dogs," he said. "She's prided herself in always being there to help."

The Hannahs have been a close-knit bunch for years. Hard

work, pride, and loyalty shine brightly. Sang Lyda spoke of the Hannah togetherness.

"The thing that impressed me about the Hannahs," he said, "was the loyalty they've held. When John came to school here, he talked a lot about his Uncle Bill. When Bill was killed (during John's junior season), it was a big shock to John. They were very close.

"When Charles came, the admiration for John was there. When David got here, he talked about all the others.

"It's a remarkable family—the closeness they have and the way they pull for each other."

The Hannahs are truly a remarkable family. They are stars in their field, no matter what kind of field it may be. After all, the Hannahs' home address is Star Route, Box 33, Albertville.

Quite an address for quite a family.

RUTLEDGE

Gary • Jeff

The date was Saturday, October 20, 1973. The place was a packed Legion Field in Birmingham, Alabama. A national television audience looked on as the undefeated Tennessee Volunteers prepared to kick to the undefeated Crimson Tide.

The Vol boot sailed into the end zone for a touchback. Bama junior quarterback Gary Rutledge led his 10 teammates on the field for the game's first play. The huddle was broken, and the standard wishbone formation was set up with Wilbur Jackson and Randy Billingsley at the halfback spots and Ellis Beck at fullback.

Gary barked out the signals, took the snap, and made a superb fake to Beck. The blocking wall set up and he dropped back to pass, spotting a wide-open Wayne Wheeler streaking over the middle. Gary launched a perfect strike to Wheeler, and 80 yards later it was Alabama 7, Tennessee 0. Fourteen seconds had elapsed in the game. Alabama went on to win, 42-21.

Shift the scene to Fulton County Stadium in Atlanta, Georgia, on Sunday, October 11, 1981. The Los Angeles Rams were in town to play the Atlanta Falcons in a crucial NFC West contest. Late in the second quarter veteran Rams quarterback Pat Haden suffered a bruised left leg when he was flattened after throwing a pass. Off the field hobbled Haden, while onto the field trotted former Tide quarterback Jeff Rutledge, younger brother of Gary and a three-year performer with the Rams.

Jeff immediately resumed the leadership role, completing 11 of 20 passes for 130 yards and 2 touchdowns. In the most important series of his pro career he completed 5 passes for 54

191

yards in the winning Los Angeles drive that covered 72 yards to the Atlanta 8-yard line. Place-kicker Frank Corral came in and calmly booted a 25-yard field goal with 24 seconds left to give the Rams a 37-35 victory over the Falcons.

Gary and Jeff have had many more outstanding football games than only these against the Tennessee Vols and Atlanta Falcons, respectively.

Although Gary is perhaps best remembered for his touchdown toss to Wheeler, he is generally remembered as the skinny redhead (hence the nickname ''Rooster'') that led the early (1972, 1973, 1974) Alabama wishbone teams to national prominence. And younger brother Jeff picked up where Gary left off from 1975 to 1978 by helping Alabama stay in that national spotlight, then continued his playing days into the NFL as a quarterback for the Los Angeles Rams.

While growing up in Birmingham, neither Gary nor Jeff had to look far to find some kind of ball lying around the house. Their father, Paul E. (Jack) Rutledge, made sure of that.

Jack Rutledge was raised in Talladega and attended Alabama on a football scholarship in 1946. But the only field he ever saw was the baseball diamond, and after three years as a shortstop with the Tide baseball team he elected to pass up his senior year and turn professional.

Three years of pro ball in the minors with the Chicago Cubs and New York Yankees were enough for Jack, and in 1952 he and wife Mary settled down in Birmingham. On June 4, 1952, Gary entered the world. And no doubt it was a sports world.

"Jeff and I got involved in sports so much because of Daddy," Gary said. "We always had a ball in our hand, whether it was a baseball, basketball, or football. We never grew up hunting or fishing—just playing sports. That's where we got our start."

Even though five years apart, Gary and Jeff started playing football about the same time. Jeff was six years old when Jack paid the $10.00 registration fee to enter him in the 80-pound football league.

"I wanted to quit after the first practice," Jeff recalled. "I told Daddy that I didn't want to play anymore. He wouldn't let me quit because he had already paid the money."

Gary was an 11-year-old sixth grader when he became interested in the pigskin. After graduation to the 120-pound league his seventh-grade year, he broke an arm and sat out the entire eighth grade season. Gary's football career continued as he entered the ninth grade at Banks High School.

"I always admired Gary when we were growing up because he was not a very big guy at all," Jeff said. "In fact he was skinny when he started playing in high school. He wasn't flashy or anything, but he was a competitor, and he worked hard, and he won."

"Like father, like son" epitomized Jack's relationship with Gary and Jeff. He taught the youngsters the meaning of competition at an early age, and according to Jeff, it was sometimes a bit *too* much.

"He (Jack) pushed me at times—sometimes I thought he pushed me too hard," Jeff said. "I was scared of him sometimes when we would lose. He was an excellent coach, and he knew exactly what was needed to teach me. He always wanted me to be the best, and when I had a bad game he let me know it.

"But now as I look back at it, I'm glad he did (push me). I love him for it and respect him for it."

As Gary's and Jeff's father, Jack wasted no time in letting the boys know when they had made a mistake. "I don't think I really pushed them, but I may have been a little hard on them at times," Jack said. "They wanted to play—I didn't force them. I was harder on them than anyone else because they were my own sons. I didn't like it when they made mistakes.

"There were a lot of nights that we would come back from a (baseball) game and they had made errors or struck out or something, and I jumped on them. I didn't like it—I was tough on them."

Whatever Jack did or didn't do to his sons, it worked. Gary started at quarterback for Banks his junior and senior years, and even as a sophomore shared some quarterback duties with junior Johnny Musso, a future Tide halfback great (and now a Chicago stockbroker).

Gary made All-City, All-State, and All-American at Banks under Coach George "Shorty" White, later an Alabama assistant coach. In all he earned ten prep letters in three sports, including All-City honors in basketball.

Gary shunned scholarship offers from Georgia, Florida State, and Auburn to satisfy a boyhood dream. "Ever since I saw Namath and Sloan and Stabler play when I was growing up, I always dreamed that I would be an Alabama quarterback," Gary said. "That was the goal I wanted to reach, so I worked at it."

Worked at it he did, and Alabama it was for the skinny redhead from Banks High School. Joining Gary in the 1970 freshman class were such players as Wilbur Jackson, Mike Raines, Paul Spivey, Chuck Strickland, Bill Davis, and Greg Gantt.

Gary led the freshman team to a 5-0 record, connecting on 33 of 63 passes (52.4%) for 538 yards and three touchdowns.

Gary was expected to challenge Terry Davis for the starting quarterback spot in 1971, but it wouldn't be easy. The year before he came, Alabama signed quarterbacks Billy Sexton, Johnny Sharpless, Benny Rippetoe, and Butch Hobson, so Gary had his work cut out for him.

Despite a good spring Gary was redshirted for the 1971 season. "Coach Bryant felt that I wasn't quite ready to contribute to the varsity," he said. "He wanted me to get another year of maturity and hopefully grow some. I didn't like it, but later I was glad he redshirted me because it gave me more time to learn the new wishbone offense."

Ah, the wishbone. The offense of the seventies in collegiate football. At least for the Alabamas, Oklahomas, Texases, and any others that were fortunate enough to have the required talent.

It was during Gary's redshirt year that the Alabama wishbone was publicly displayed for the first time against the Southern California Trojans in that September 10 classic. The future Tide star found himself caught up in the Tide ecstasy as Bama rode the wishbone to the stunning 17-10 victory over the highly ranked Trojans.

"We ran a pass offense that (1971) spring," Gary said. "When we came back in the fall, everything was real hush-hush. I think Coach Bryant had gone to see Darrell Royal in Texas and decided to go with the wishbone. Terry (Davis) was obviously not a passing quarterback, so he fit well in the wishbone

Gary Rutledge ran the new Alabama wishbone to perfection.

offense. He wasn't a power runner, but very, very fast.''

Being a redshirt quarterback is no fun. To get the defense ready he has to be the ''dummy'' quarterback and run the opposing team's offense. He is a man of 12 different faces in 12 different weeks. One week he may be dressed in white, the next in gold, the next in blue. And he has to go up against the number-one defense every day in practice.

''During practice (defensive ends) Robin Parkhouse and John Mitchell would come in there and knock my head off when I was trying to pass, and (defensive) Coach (Ken) Donahue would love it,'' Gary said. ''They wouldn't give me a chance to throw.

''I got tired of all that, but it was a part of being there. There were other guys my age going through the same thing, and I think all of us together sort of laughed it off.''

Terry Davis learned the wishbone to perfection and led the Tide to a perfect 11-0 regular season record and a number-two national ranking. Hopes of a national championship were quickly ended, however, as Nebraska ripped the Crimsons, 38-6, in the Orange Bowl.

A tough conditioning program in the summer vaulted Gary into the number-two quarterback spot (behind Davis) for the 1972 season. Both quarterbacks performed the difficult wishbone admirably as the Tide streaked to an impressive 10-0 record. All that remained before a Cotton Bowl match-up against Texas was the Auburn game.

The score was Alabama 16, Auburn 3, with 9:15 remaining in the game, then the unbelievable happened. This was the setting for that unforgettable day when Auburn's Bill Newton blocked two Bama punts and David Langner scooped up both for touchdowns to lead the Tigers to the shocking 17-16 victory.

"I held for Bill Davis when he missed the extra point (early in the second quarter)," Gary said. "Terry (Davis) had hurt his finger, and I went in and held. I don't know whether it was a bad hold or Bill missed it or what. I think it was partially blocked. We sure didn't know at the time how important that miss would be."

Alabama never really recovered from the Auburn loss and took its lackadaisical attitude to the Cotton Bowl. Texas came from behind to score the winning touchdown with just over three minutes remaining for a 17-13 win.

Gary's disappointment in the season was soon forgotten, however. Wedding bells rang in that summer of 1973 for Gary and Kathy Kinney, his high school sweetheart. "The married players got what was called a 'married scholarship' of $150 a month," Gary said. "I wanted one and I asked Coach Bryant way back before spring if I could have one, because I knew I was getting married that summer.

"He said, 'Let's wait and see how you do in the spring.' He really put the pressure on me that spring. I didn't know where my money was coming from. But I had a good spring practice and got the scholarship in the fall."

Terry Davis was graduated, and the 1973 quarterbacking duties were left to Gary and a sophomore from Mobile named Richard Todd. The 1973 season turned out to be quite an interesting one for the Alabama team.

Designed primarily for a running attack, the 1973

196

wishbone offered a little bit of everything. Backfields three and four deep rushed for over 4,000 yards. Wings were sprouted, and over 1,000 yards were gained through the air. Two NCAA records were shattered, another was tied, and a total of 477 points (a 40-point per game average) was scored by the awesome Tide offense.

The massacre began on a warm September night in Birmingham against California. "Unknowns" such as quarterback Vince Ferragamo, quarterback Steve Bartkowski, halfback Chuck Muncie, and wide receiver Wesley Walker dotted the Bears' roster. At least *then* they were unknown.

Ferragamo (who later played a big part in Jeff Rutledge's future) and Bartkowski turned out to be All-Pro quarterbacks with the Los Angeles Rams and Atlanta Falcons, respectively. Muncie, after several years with New Orleans, has been churning up yardage for the San Diego Chargers for the past three years. And the fleet-footed Walker is usually on the receiving end of most of New York Jet quarterback Richard Todd's aerials. Not a bad foursome to have—it's just that the Tide didn't have any respect for who they were *then,* much less for who they would become.

"I think we are going to be a well-balanced team with nobody able to stop us," said the Bears' Ferragamo before the game. To put it mildly, Ferragamo was in for a big surprise.

Alabama trounced the Golden Bears, 66-0. Seventy-three different Tiders played, with eight different ones scoring. The 667 total yards offense (405 rushing and 262 passing) was a new school single-game record, and the 66 points were the most scored since 1961.

Gary led the Bama passing attack, completing five of eight for 189 yards. Richard Todd was the game's leading rusher with 106 yards on eight attempts. Both threw two touchdown passes each. On the other hand, Ferramago (who the next year transferred to Nebraska) completed 15 of 30 passes for 128 yards and had two interceptions.

Competition for Bama's top quarterback spot was ever increasing between Gary and Todd. Minutes after the California game Bryant said, "Both our quarterbacks played extremely well, and we had to use each of them. Todd is still the most explosive, but Rutledge has soundness and consistency. I can't say one had a better game without seeing the film.''

Bryant must have looked at the film real close, because the next day on the ''Bear Bryant Show'' he had the answer to his question. In so many words he said that Richard Todd would make people forget the most famous quarterback he had produced, Joe Namath.

''Richard Todd is still young and still makes mistakes, but if I don't miss my guess, he's going to be the best quarterback in America,'' Bryant said.

Gary Rutledge and Richard Todd (14) listen closely to Tide offensive coordinator Mal Moore.

"And that's really not a guess, because he's got everything that goes with being great.

"If he gets the little things down, he will be the greatest quarterback ever at Alabama. And he's going to get them down, or I'll choke him to death."

Alabama fans listened to Bryant's statement with interest—but nobody listened to it harder than Gary Rutledge. And nobody was affected by it as much as he was.

"My heart went down to my feet when he said that," Gary said. "I had played real well in the (California) game—I had a couple of touchdown passes and took the team in for several touchdowns. Richard had a good game, too, then Coach Bryant came out and said that.

"I thought it was just a matter of time before Coach Bryant would put him in front of me, and I wouldn't get to play any more. It really made me mad, because Richard had not proven anything. That was the first varsity game he had ever been in.

"I felt a lot of pressure from it," Gary continued. "I felt like I had to do (extra) well when I was in there because I didn't know what Coach Bryant would do. I just knew that by the end of the first quarter I might be sitting on the bench, and Richard would be in there. He (Bryant) had never before alternated like that to any great extent."

Gary didn't know it at the time, but he just happened to be the first of many quarterbacks that Bryant would alternate throughout the seventies and into the eighties. Gary alternated with Todd in 1973, Todd with Jack O'Rear in 1974, Todd with Robert Fraley in 1975, Jeff Rutledge with O'Rear in 1976, Jeff with Steadman Shealy in 1977 and 1978, Shealy with Don Jacobs in 1979, Jacobs with Walter Lewis in 1980, Lewis with Alan Gray and Ken Coley in 1981, etc. The style has become a Bryant trademark.

"It's just that he had not done it that way before," Gary said. "The first stringer was always the guy who played the most. But over the years he started alternating the linemen, the backs—everybody. I knew it would work, and how can you doubt Coach Bryant when you're winning? If we had been losing, it might have been different."

Despite Bryant's praise of Todd, Gary remained the top

quarterback. Victories over Kentucky, Vanderbilt, Georgia, and Florida preceded the Tide's exciting 42-21 victory over Tennessee.

"That touchdown to Wheeler on the first play is what I'm best known for," Gary said. "We had planned the play the whole week. Every game that season we had run the first play with the fullback straight up the middle. So we surprised them with a fake and a pass."

Two NCAA records fell and another was tied as Bama smashed hapless Virginia Tech, 77-6. The Tide accumulated 828 yards total offense; 743 of that was on the ground. Four Alabama backs—James Taylor, Wilbur Jackson, Calvin Culliver, and Richard Todd—rushed for over 100 yards. That feat tied an NCAA mark for the most players on one team to gain over 100 yards in a single game.

After wins over Mississippi State and Miami, the 9-0 Tide traveled to Baton Rouge to face the LSU Tigers. Gary had one of his finest games as a Crimson Tider, completing four of five passes for 166 yards and gaining 60 more on 13 rushes. His efforts earned him the Most Valuable Offensive Player award (the Tide's Woodrow Lowe was defensive MVP) and the front cover of *Sports Illustrated*.

Gary accomplished a childhood dream two weeks later by scoring two touchdowns against Auburn in a 35-0 shutout.

After the game, United Press International awarded Alabama the national championship for its perfect 11-0 record. But that was before Notre Dame and the Sugar Bowl.

That was the game ABC Television still calls one of the classics of college football, in which the Fighting Irish claimed number one by only one—24-23. Notre Dame led at every rest period—6-0 at the quarter, 14-10 at halftime, 21-17 after three quarters, and 24-23 at the end. But Alabama led three times at 7-6, 17-14, and 23-21.

"If you saw that game, you had to believe you were seeing football the way it ought to be played, college, pro, or whatever," Bryant said in his book *Bear*. "I understand people had heart attacks watching it, and one Alabama sportswriter (Herby Kirby of the *Birmingham Post Herald*) died in the press box right after. We sure don't ever want football to be that exciting, but the comments I heard were mostly how good the

Alabama quarterback Gary Rutledge (right) and Notre Dame quarterback Tom Clements relax on the eve of the 1973 Sugar Bowl.

game was for college football, having two fine teams with great traditions play to such a thrilling finish."

"We all cried in the dressing room after the game," Gary said. "It was something that you come to Alabama for—it's everything you want in college football and something Coach Bryant is always talking about. It was right there for the grabbing, and we blew it."

Gary's last chance to be on a post-bowl game national championship team was 1974, his senior season. He and Todd were expected to once again compete for the top quarterback spot. Unfortunately for Gary it never happened.

Gary seriously separated his shoulder in a scrimmage just one week before the season started. Surgery was required to insert a pin, and he was lost until the last two games of the season.

"I remember right then that I cried because I knew my career was over," he said. "I had already been redshirted, and all I had lived for was to play Alabama football and I knew it was out the door."

Gary was determined to get back in the lineup, and he did so in the Miami game. But the injury had made his throwing arm useless, and he played sparingly against Auburn and in the Orange Bowl against Notre Dame. After an 11-0 season the Tide fell once again to the Fighting Irish, 13-11. Another shot at the national championship had failed.

During the team's stay in Miami, Tide offensive coordinator Bud Moore was announced as the new head coach at the University of Kansas. Moore was obviously sold on the wishbone—he immediately said that it would be the Jayhawks' offense. And he was sold enough on Gary Rutledge to ask him to join his staff as quarterback coach.

"He (Moore) asked Coach Bryant what he thought about asking me to be his quarterback coach," Gary said. "Coach Bryant said that would be great.

"I had graduated that December, so I took the job. Within a week after the Orange Bowl I was in Youngstown, Ohio, recruiting high school kids to come to the University of Kansas. And I didn't know much about Kansas. It was scary."

Gary's first year at Kansas was his best—the team finished with a 7-4 record and earned a trip to the Sun Bowl against Tony Dorsett and the Pittsburgh Panthers.

Jayhawk All-American quarterback Nolan Cromwell (later a Jeff Rutledge teammate in professional football) was Gary's star pupil. Cromwell was the main cog in the Jayhawks' record in 1975, then underwent knee surgery after three games the next year. Their record dropped to 6-5.

With Cromwell graduated, disaster struck in 1977 as Kansas plunged to a 3-8 record. "It was terrible," Gary recalled. "It's so hard to recruit out there. You've got Nebraska above you, Oklahoma below you, and Missouri beside you. We just couldn't keep the good players coming in.

"Kathy and I wanted to get back here (to Alabama). I just felt like I wasn't given enough responsibility at Kansas. I didn't have much say-so on the quarterback situation."

Gary got his wish and came back to Birmingham in 1978 to

coach Homewood High School. He won one game and lost nine in his first—and last—year with the Patriots.

"I figured I wasn't cut out to be a coach, especially in high school," he said, "so I quit immediately. I just got fed up with it—I was frustrated."

"Frustrated" was an understatement—Gary didn't even finish the school year. He learned of a good job opportunity through Dr. Willam deShazo (the Alabama team physician) and in January of 1979 joined Reid-Provident Laboratories, an Atlanta-based pharmaceutical company, as a sales representative. He and wife Kathy reside in Birmingham and have two children—Lyndy (7-31-77) and Stacey (2-18-80).

Even though Gary hung up his cleats in early 1975, another Rutledge, younger brother Jeff, was coming up to continue the Rutledge family football tradition.

In Jeff's three years as Banks' quarterback he led his team to two state championships and 36 straight victories. For his junior and senior years he was selected All-American, All-South, All-State, All-Metro, All-City, All-4A, Super 11 team, and his team's most valuable player. Jeff also earned four baseball letters and two in basketball.

During his senior year 42,000 persons turned out to Legion Field to watch the showdown between Jeff and Woodlawn halfback Tony Nathan (a future Tide teammate and All-Pro with the Miami Dolphins). In his best high school game ever Jeff led his team to victory by completing nine of ten passes for 182 yards and two touchdowns.

Because of Gary it was widely assumed that Jeff would attend Alabama, but some things happened to his big brother that displeased Jeff. Some were so serious that Jeff decided against playing there and made his mind up to attend LSU.

"I came very close to signing with LSU," Jeff said. "Jerry Stovall (now LSU head coach) recruited me, and the hardest thing I ever had to do was call him on the phone and tell him that I wasn't going to LSU. I had tears in my eyes as I was talking to him.

"I think I upset him because he thought I was going to LSU, and all along I thought I was going to LSU until the last day. It was a tough decision, one that was based on my love for my parents. I knew that if I went to LSU, they couldn't see me play as much because it was such a long way to drive.

"I prayed about where God wanted me to play. I remember praying about it and having a peace about it when I talked with my parents."

Bryant's way of alternating quarterbacks at Alabama was the main reason that Jeff leaned toward LSU. He had seen Gary go through it for two years, and frankly, Jeff wanted no part of it.

"I swore I would never go to Alabama," Jeff said, "after they yanked Gary out of the Notre Dame (Sugar Bowl) game. Gary took the team over 90 yards for a touchdown to go ahead, then they took him out and put Richard in. I was so mad—I said right then that there was no way I would go to Alabama.

"It's hard for a quarterback to keep his momentum and confidence up, because if he takes the team in for a touchdown and then gets pulled out, he thinks he's done something wrong. It was very difficult for me to understand why they would do that.

"Also I wanted to go to a school that would throw the ball," he continued. "Alabama told me if I came there they would throw the ball more, which they ended up doing. But still, 12 times a game is not many times to throw the ball compared to other schools. So I considered LSU because I knew they would throw the ball, and they ran the same kind of offense that I ran in high school. I would have fit right in and probably would have played (more) as a freshman there."

So that his parents could see him play was the main reason Jeff signed with Alabama. And the Tide's winning tradition surely didn't hurt.

"That was a big thing about going to Alabama—I knew we were going to win," he said. "I had always played on a winner in high school, and I wanted to go where I thought I had the best chance to win a national championship. As it worked out, I won one.

"I have no regrets at all about going to Alabama. That was the greatest thing that I ever did."

Jeff was one of the few freshmen that made the 1975 varsity. Although the third-team quarterback behind Richard Todd and Robert Fraley, Jeff logged enough playing time to earn a letter.

"There was no pressure there when I made the varsity," Jeff said. "I knew I wasn't going to play much with Richard there. I just hoped to get enough time in to get some experience."

Jeff finished his freshman season with 29 rushes for 101 yards and completed 8 of 16 passes for 87 yards. As a team the Tide stumbled against Missouri, 20-7, in a televised opener, then won 11 straight with ease, capped off by a 13-6 victory over Penn State in the Sugar Bowl. The victory over the Nittany Lions broke an eight-year bowl losing streak.

With Todd graduated, Jeff was given the starting nod in the Tide's 1976 opener against Ole Miss in Jackson. "I did not know I was starting until I heard it over the loudspeaker," Jeff said. "Coach Bryant had not told anyone about it before the game."

Ole Miss spoiled Jeff's debut by surprising the Crimsons, 10-7. The Rebels' only touchdown came on a deflected 24-yard interception return by linebacker George Stuart.

Jeff and junior Jack O'Rear shared quarterbacking duties throughout the 1976 season. Although O'Rear started more games, Jeff came off the bench and actually had more playing time. The alternating Gary and Richard Todd experienced was now happening with Jeff and O'Rear, and it would happen later with Jeff and Steadman Shealy.

"I couldn't stand the alternating," Jeff said. "A guy can't be honest if he says he likes to be alternated with. If the guy has a hot hand, you should leave him in. The only time you should make a quarterback change is if he is not doing his job.

"I remember Jack (O'Rear) had a great game against Tennessee that season," he continued. "He rushed for over 100 yards on television and was the player of the game. I didn't play hardly at all—but that's the way I think it should be.'

After the Ole Miss loss, the Tide smashed Southern Methodist and Vanderbilt, then ran into a brick wall in Athens against Georgia. The 21-0 Bulldog victory was the first time in 69 games and only the second time in 185 games that Alabama had failed to score.

"The fans were horrible over there," Jeff recalled. "They stayed outside our motel rooms at night honking horns and yelling. We couldn't get much sleep.

205

"But Georgia was the better team. They soundly beat us—we never were in the game."

Since 1971 Alabama had won five consecutive SEC titles with a composite SEC record of 34 wins and one loss. Now, four games into the 1976 season, the Tide was 0-2 in the conference—quite a change for the men in Crimson.

"I don't remember Coach Bryant getting all that upset at us," Jeff said. "He just said we had to learn from our mistakes, and told us to keep playing, keep fighting, and not to give up."

Southern Mississippi, Tennessee, Louisville, Mississippi State, and LSU all fell to a rebuilding Tide, and next up was the Notre Dame Fighting Irish. But this time it wasn't in the Sugar Bowl or Orange Bowl—the scene was the Golden Dome in South Bend, Indiana.

"We were getting embarrassed, 21-7, at the half," Jeff recalled, "and Coach Bryant came in and said, 'We've got them where we want them. They're over there thinking they've got it, but when we come out let's go ahead of them.'"

Bryant, the old master, knew just how to get his boys fired up. His pep talk soaked in well—Alabama came out roaring in the second half.

Jeff passed to Thad Flanagan for 24, Johnny Davis rambled up the middle for 8, and Ozzie Newsome pulled in 2 grabs for 21 more. He hit Newsome again, 21 yards downfield at the goal line, but a fierce hit coughed the ball up and it was intercepted.

Bucky Berrey hit a 38-yard field goal to narrow the gap to 21-10 going into the fourth quarter. Jeff went right back to work, throwing a 30-yard strike to Newsome for the score, then back to Newsome for the 2-point conversion to make it 21-18.

The Tide defense held, and Jeff began to march his troops down the field all the way to the Irish seven-yard line. "There was plenty of time left, and we called time out," Jeff said. "Coach Bryant said he wanted to throw, and I said, "No, let's run it.' He said 'no' to that, so I threw it and it was intercepted.

"Pete Cavan was wide open on my right side, but I did not know that until after the game. I forced the ball to Thad—it was a bad throw on my part."

The fan reaction to Jeff's throw was strong. Letters and calls flooded him. Criticism was thrown at him—"Why did you throw it?" they asked. "Why didn't you ground it?"

206

Both Gary and Jeff had their problems with Notre Dame's Ross Browner. Gary's Tide team lost to the Irish, 24-23, in the 1973 Sugar Bowl, when Browner was a freshman. In 1976, Browner's senior season, Jeff and his Alabama teammates dropped a 21-18 decision in South Bend.

"I did the best I could," Jeff said. "And if a guy does that, then whatever happens just happens. When you start worrying about what other people think, it's going to be tough on you.

"It's easy to be an armchair quarterback," he said. "I can watch a game on TV and say that guy is horrible, or he should have done this or should have done that. It's easy to say that when you're watching, but it's different when you're on the field and big linemen are coming right at you."

Jeff fought off all criticism in time to throw one touchdown and rush for another as Bama pounded Auburn, 38-7. Three weeks later in 23-degree weather (the chill factor was below zero), the Tide crushed favored UCLA, 36-6, in the Liberty Bowl to end its season at a respectable (for Alabama) 9-3.

Jeff got the nod in spring practice of 1977 over O'Rear for the top quarterback spot. The duo was being billed as the top one-two quarterback punch in the nation for the upcoming season. However, the dream quarterback combination was cut in half when O'Rear injured his knee during the summer. Another injury early in the 1977 season required surgery, and O'Rear's college football was history.

Bad luck played with Jeff's fate also during that spring. A few days after the A-Day game, on the last day of spring practice, Bryant ordered the squad to Bryant-Denny Stadium for one last scrimmage. The team was already crippled from a tough spring program, but Bryant wanted one last head-knocking session to test the players' endurance.

On one play Jeff took the ball and optioned around left end. A defensive end came up and smacked Jeff's right arm, cracking the bone in his forearm. A quick trip to the hospital for X rays verified the preliminary report, and surgery to put in a plate was performed the next day. Jeff spent the summer in a cast, hoping that he would be ready for the September 10 opener against Ole Miss.

Ready he was. Jeff connected on seven of eight passes for over 200 yards as the Tide got revenge, 34-13, in the 1977 season opener against the Rebels. His efforts earned him the Southeastern Player of the Week award.

A trip to Lincoln, Nebraska, and Big Red country the next

week proved disastrous for Jeff and his teammates. The Tide lost a 31-24 heartbreaker to the Cornhuskers on national television, and Jeff's hate mail started pouring in once again. In the game he threw five interceptions (but so did Kenny Stabler and Scott Hunter in their careers) and was called every name in the book.

"I told my brother (Gary) and myself that I was not going to throw another interception the whole year," Jeff said, "and I didn't. Those five were all I threw."

Jeff's determination not to throw another interception lasted until the Missouri game of his senior year. During the span he completed 100 passes without an interception, a school record that still stands.

Mild victories over Vanderbilt and Georgia gave Bama a 3-1 record as it headed to Los Angeles to face the top-ranked Southern California Trojans. With the Tide leading 21-6 in the fourth quarter, it appeared a major upset was in the making.

However, the Trojans didn't think so. Two quick scores, paced by quarterback Rob Hertel's pinpoint passing, pulled the Trojans to within one point of the Tide, 21-20. The attempt for a two-point conversion was spoiled by Bama defensive end Wayne Hamilton and linebacker Barry Krauss, and the nation's longest winning streak was broken. The Tide had once again made waves across the nation.

Donnie Webb, a sportswriter for the *Crimson White,* aptly described the victory celebration back in Tuscaloosa. "The University celebrated Alabama's 21-20 victory over Southern California ecstatically Saturday. . . .not so much the usual go to the bar, get drunk affair. . . .it was jump in the fountain at Rose Administration, drive around the campus hanging out the window blowing your horn, and scream at the top of your vocal cords 'Roll Tide.' It was out-and-out a circus hoedown for many students."

"That (Southern Cal) win helped our confidence," Jeff said. "There were a lot of people at the airport when we got back, and that made us feel good. We were on our way then."

Jeff finished his junior year in style. With O'Rear out and sophomore Steadman Shealy still learning the wishbone, Jeff finally had his longtime wish—to be the *only* number-one quarterback at Alabama. Victories over Tennessee, Louisville,

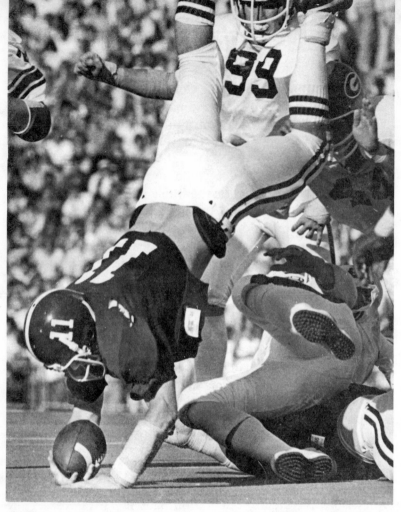

*This touchdown against Georgia in 1977 was one of Jeff's 11
rushing touchdowns during his career.*

Mississippi State, LSU, Miami, and Auburn earned the Tide the
SEC championship and vaulted it to the nation's number-three
spot. Next up was the Sugar Bowl date with Woody Hayes and
his Ohio State Buckeyes.

The game was called "the classic coaching match-up of the
century." It was old man Bear Bryant against old man Woody
Hayes. And then came the total rout—Alabama 35, Ohio State
6.

Jeff's performance in the game earned him Most Valuable
Player honors. He completed 8 of 11 passes for 109 yards, 2
touchdowns and a 2-point conversion.

In other bowl action that day, Texas and Oklahoma, the nation's top two teams, were crushed by fifth-ranked Notre Dame and sixth-ranked Arkansas, respectively. Simple mathematics would assume that when both the number-one and number-two teams fall to defeat, the highest-ranked winning team (Alabama) would move to the top.

Not so on that bowl day in early 1978. Alabama's hopes were ended the next afternoon when both major wire polls awarded their national championship to Notre Dame. Alabama was a close ("but no cigar") second, with Arkansas finishing third.

Five days after the Sugar Bowl, Jeff married his girlfriend of two years, Laura Holmes of Pensacola, Florida. "Everybody was telling me that if I had played bad in the (Sugar) bowl game, they would have known why—because I had my mind on Laura," Jeff chuckled. "I was determined to prove these people wrong, because when I'm on the football field my mind is on one thing—football. Of course I didn't want to get hurt and have to walk down the aisle on crutches or in a cast."

With revenge on its mind Alabama opened the 1978 season by soundly whipping Nebraska, 20-3. "And I did *not* throw an interception in that one," Jeff emphasized. "After their first field goal, our defense played extremely well and the offense moved the ball up and down the field.

"Beating a big power like that was a big win and a great way to start the year. Nebraska had embarrassed us the year before, and we needed to win it."

After a wild and wooly 38-20 win over Missouri, it was Southern California's turn for a little revenge. And they got it—in the form of a convincing 24-14 count. Neither team knew it at the time, but that game would be a hot topic of conversation when January rolled around.

Besides a couple of scares by Washington and Auburn, the Tide coasted to a 10-1 record against the toughest non-conference schedule in the school's history. In the 34-16 Auburn win, Jeff threw for three touchdowns, giving him 30 for his career, breaking Joe Namath's record for career touchdown passes.

Throughout the season Jeff and junior quarterback Stead-man Shealy ran the wishbone with ease. Each new year had seen a different look for the 'bone, and this diversification was credited as one of the reasons for the team's tremendous success.

The thing that Jeff had avoided somewhat in 1977 had returned in 1978— the alternating quarterback situation. This time it was between him and Shealy, who had spent all summer recovering from knee surgery.

"There was no bitterness between Steadman and me," Jeff said. "I was his biggest fan. I was the first to shake his hand when he came off the field (after scoring), not because it would look good, but because I pulled for the guy—he was my teammate. I wanted him to do well."

Shealy's words are a mirror image of Jeff's. "When I scored my first touchdown in college, he (Jeff) was the first to congratulate me," Shealy said. "That showed a lot of class and character.

"We were probably the only two people that could compete for the same position and still have a strong Christian love and still get along. The unfortunate thing was the undue pressure the fans put on us.

"After Jeff graduated and I was doing the alternating, I realized what he had been going through. It made me realize his position more. But during the whole time, I supported Jeff—I never tried to start anything between us. We were in it as a team."

The whole Alabama squad teamed well in its exciting 14-7 thriller over top-ranked Penn State in the Sugar Bowl to close the season. Jeff vividly recalls this perhaps most famous play in Alabama football history. His eyes still sparkle as he remembers the 14-7 score and 6:44 remaining in the game. On fourth-and-one from the ten-inch line, he reflects, Penn State halfback Mike Guman attempted a leap over the top and was met head on by Barry Krauss with help from Murray Legg and Rich Wingo. In a collision such as this, there is a winner and a loser.

Alabama won, Penn State lost. For its efforts the Alabama Crimson Tide was named Associated Press national champion. Southern California captured the United Press International crown.

Jeff ended his Crimson Tide career with his sweetest win ever—and a national championship ring to prove it. Against the

Jeff Rutledge listens to some words of wisdom during the 1979 Sugar Bowl victory over Penn State.

Nittany Lions he completed 8 of 15 passes for 91 yards and one touchdown, a 30-yarder to Bruce Bolton for Alabama's first score.

His four-year record at the Capstone was 42 wins and 6 losses, three conference championships, and a national championship. He passed for 3,351 yards, second best (behind Scott Hunter) in the school's history.

Jeff joined teammates Barry Krauss and Marty Lyons to play in the East-West Shrine Classic in Palo Alto, California.

"I needed to have a good (East-West) game because I had to prove to the scouts that I could throw the ball being a wishbone quarterback," Jeff said. "I had a real good week of practice and played a great deal. We were behind, 17-7, at the half and came back to win, 56-17. I threw the ball and ran well. I thought I had impressed some people."

Tony Nathan joined the trio to play in the 30th annual Senior Bowl in Mobile. Jeff was at the helm of the South squad as it blitzed to a 24-7 first-quarter lead. The final count was South 41, North 21, as Jeff ran for one touchdown, threw for another, and had a hand in scoring drives that put 31 points on the board.

"I probably threw the ball (in the Senior Bowl) as well as I've ever thrown it," he said. "After the game everybody said I helped myself tremendously with the draft and that I had proved to the scouts that I could throw the ball."

Jeff was expected to be the second or third quarterback picked in the draft, behind Clemson's Steve Fuller and possibly Morehead State's Phil Simms.

Jeff hired Irwin Wiener to be his agent and to represent him in contract talks. Wiener's clientele was quite impressive—Julius Erving, Ozzie Newsome, Walt Frazier, T.R. Dunn, and Leon Douglas, to name a few. Jeff's lifelong dream of playing professional football was here, and he was ready. But.....his dream almost never came.

"Irwin was going to be calling me after every round telling me who was going where," Jeff said. "After the first round he called and said I would probably go in the second or third rounds. He called back after the second round—no news yet.

"We were beginning to get worried. They were only going to draft six rounds that day. There were quarterbacks from small schools being drafted that I never had heard of. After the sixth round I still had not heard anything.

"Irwin couldn't believe it. We didn't know what was going on. He called and recommended for me to become a free agent if I wasn't drafted by the eighth round. That way I could go where I wanted.

"The next day came," Jeff continued, "and I didn't hear anything until the end of the ninth round. The (Los Angeles) Rams called and asked me if I was planning on going to Canada or anything. I told them 'no' and they said they were going to draft me.

"They told me that they were surprised I was still available and that I had an excellent chance to make the team because they had carried only two quarterbacks the year before. They said all I would have to do would be to come in and beat out any free agents.

"It was probably best that I went in the ninth round," Jeff said, "because my chances of making the team were much better. Here I had to come in and beat out some free agents. Somewhere else I would be competing against someone that had already been on the team.

"I believe the reason I was drafted so late was because I was a wishbone quarterback. Overall I was very disappointed that I didn't go higher because it probably didn't allow me as much money. But now as it worked out, it's probably the best thing that could have happened."

Jeff was listed as the Rams' number-six quarterback when summer camp opened, behind free agents Dan Kendra, Craig Kimball, and Jim Freitas, not to mention starter Pat Haden and his back-up, Vince Ferragamo. The Rams' promise to Jeff was kept—after beating out the three free agents he made the team as the number-three quarterback.

Even though a third stringer, Jeff was filling some big shoes from a couple of years earlier—Joe Namath had occupied that spot on the Rams' 1977 squad. Only by coincidence was one Alabama quarterback (in his first year of pro ball) succeeding another Alabama quarterback (who was retiring after 14 years). Namath won a Super Bowl in 1969; Jeff was looking for his first in 1979.

Playing quarterback for the Rams is rarely a picnic. From the time they came to Los Angeles in 1946, 30 different quarterbacks have tried to make the Rams their home. And wherever a Rams quarterback goes, there's usually controversy right behind. It began in the fifties with Bob Waterfield vs. Norm Van Brocklin and continues until today.

Haden, a local high school and college (Southern California) hero, was given the starting assignment against Oakland to open Jeff's 1979 rookie season. The Rams' 24-17 opening loss to the Raiders started a streak of mediocre play that saw them struggle to a 4-5 record. A week earlier Ferragamo broke his finger and wasn't expected back for several weeks.

Then against Seattle, Haden broke *his* finger, and young Jeff Rutledge finished the Seattle game, leading the Rams to a 24-0 shutout. The Rams' defense held Jim Zorn and the Seahawks' offense to minus seven yards total offense, an NFL record.

Because of Haden's and Ferragamo's injuries Jeff started his first NFL game the next week against the Chicago Bears. The Rams built 16-0 and 23-14 leads, but two fourth-quarter interceptions enabled the Bears to pull out a 27-23 win. Jeff ended the afternoon with 6 completions in 11 attempts for 71 yards and one touchdown, and 3 rushes for 28 yards.

"I really played well for three and a half quarters (against Chicago)," Jeff recalled, "but I threw a couple of interceptions late in the game and we lost. But that game proved to me that I could play in the league. Everybody throws interceptions—that's part of the game."

Jeff's performance may have proven to him he could play in the league, but it must not have impressed Rams head coach Ray Malavasi—Jeff didn't play another down the rest of the year. Fourteen-year veteran Bob Lee came out of retirement (much to Jeff's dismay) to save two games, then Ferragamo's finger healed in time for him to lead the Rams to the Super Bowl against the Pittsburgh Steelers. Despite its 9-7 regular season record, the Rams came within a couple of plays of beating Pittsburgh before falling, 31-19.

"The Super Bowl was not what I expected," Jeff said. "It was not as exciting as it would have been if I had played, because I really didn't feel a part of the team. But it was a thrill to be on the sidelines and watch (Pittsburgh quarterback Terry) Bradshaw play. And playing for the NFL championship the year after I had played for the college championship was exciting."

Bob Lee, the player whose selection had caused Jeff's demotion back to the third string, was not expected to return for the 1980 season. Ferragamo, deep in contract squabbles with the Rams' management, was due back along with the healed Haden.

But Lee returned, and Jeff's heart sank. If there was any consolation, Jeff wasn't at the bottom of the quarterback list this year—that spot was saved for rookie Kevin Scanlon from Arkansas.

Rarely does a professional team keep four quarterbacks, so it was obvious that two would soon be packing their bags. Scanlon was cut early—next to get the axe was either Jeff or

Lee. "It's a scary situation for me," Jeff told a *Los Angeles Times* reporter at the time. "There's no way I can compete with his (Lee's) experience and knowledge of reading defenses. But he can't play many more years, and I think they should want to keep a young guy. I feel they've got to cut one of us."

To make matters worse, Malavasi was interested only in the Haden-Ferragamo battle for the top spot. Despite their desires to compete for the third position, Jeff and Lee were mere spectators—neither one was given any practice time.

"I was beginning to wonder how they could choose between the two of us when we were not getting any work," Jeff said. "So finally I went to talk with Ray (Malavasi), and he told me not to get discouraged and that he was for the young guy. He said not to worry and everything would be all right."

Malavasi's "young guy" promise to Jeff held up—Lee was cut in late August. In the meantime Haden earned the starting spot for the Rams' 1980 opener against Detroit. In that game the Lions' rookie sensation Billy Sims ran wild, giving Detroit a convincing 41-20 win over the Rams. Lady luck (and the Lions) hit Haden hard once again, breaking another of his fingers.

One would assume Ferragamo's hopes rose because of Haden's injury. They did—but he still didn't like his measley $52,000 per year salary and said if he was going to be the top quarterback, then he ought to be paid like one (Haden was earning $200,000 plus). The Rams' management said no (for the time being), so Ferragamo walked out of practice three days before a Thursday night television clash with Tampa Bay.

For two days of practice Jeff was the *only* Ram quarterback left. The Rams' management panicked and called Bob Lee (who else?) *back* to the squad. Ferragamo decided to return the day before the game and played the entire contest in the 10-9 loss to Tampa Bay.

Haden returned to action in midseason but played very little. Lee and Jeff, once again the team's third and fourth-string quarterbacks, rarely saw any playing time. Jeff played in only one game, a 51-21 rout of Green Bay early in the season.

The Rams finished the 1980 season with an 11-5 record and second in the NFC Western Division (behind the Atlanta Falcons). The Dallas Cowboys ended the Rams' Super Bowl hopes in the first game of the playoffs.

Jeff Rutledge broke Joe Namath's touchdown passes record.

In 1981 big bucks lured Ferragamo to the Montreal Alouettes of the Canadian Football League, so the Rams' quarterback depth chart listed Haden, Jeff, Lee, and rookie Jeff Kemp as the top four quarterbacks. Just as before, one had to be cut.

This time 14-year veteran Bob Lee was axed for good, so the quarterback picture seemed clearer for those in contention. Jeff was very impressive in the pre-season games until a chest injury caused him to miss two weeks.

With only one experienced quarterback on the roster (Haden), the Rams brought in veteran Dan Pastorini, formerly of Houston and Oakland, to boost the quarterback corps. The move prompted Jeff to say, "The Rams management has confidence in me. They say they think I can play and win for the Rams. Yet they went out and hired another quarterback. Where will that leave me? I don't know and I don't understand it either."

Jeff's big chance to prove himself came in the season opener against Houston. Haden started the game but after an unimpressive performance was relieved by Jeff. The Alabama youngster completed five of eight passes for 97 yards and one interception. He rallied the Rams to a 20-20 tie with a minute left, then Oiler rookie Willie Tullis (from Troy State) ran the ensuing kickoff back 95 yards for the game-winning touchdown.

Haden was back the following week, but he was knocked out of the third game against Green Bay with a rib injury. Jeff came in and took control, completing five of ten passes for 70 yards and one touchdown, leading the Rams to a 35-23 victory.

Still the Rams management wouldn't start him, and he sat on the bench in wins over Chicago and Cleveland. In the seventh game against Atlanta, Haden was injured, and Jeff once again came to the rescue, leading the Rams to an exciting 37-35 victory.

Haden recovered the next week to play in a loss to Dallas, then was benched in a 20-13 victory over the Detroit Lions. Once again Jeff was inserted and completed 9 of 12 passes for 145 yards, directing the winning touchdown drive early in the final period.

Jeff would have finally started the next week against New

The Jeff Rutledge-to-Ozzie Newsome tandem was one of the best in Alabama football history.

Orleans, but a freak accident in the Detroit game put him out for the remainder of the 1981 season. "I was on my follow-through on a pass," Jeff said, "and my thumb hit the defensive player's helmet. The impact dislocated it, and I had surgery the next day.

"It was such a big disappointment, because Coach (Ray) Malavasi said after the game that if I had not gotten hurt I would have started the next week against New Orleans."

With Pastorini and Haden at the quarterback controls the Rams folded and lost six of their last seven games, finishing the year with a 6-10 mark, their worst season since 1965.

Jeff finished his four-game season with 30 completions in 50 attempts (60%) for 442 yards, three touchdowns, and four interceptions. But most of all he finished the season frustrated...and wondering what lay ahead for the 1982 season.

Abiding by their tradition of having a "big name" quarter-back, the Rams cut Pastorini following the 1981 season and in April of 1982 signed former LSU and Baltimore Colts quarter-

Jeff Rutledge, Gary Rutledge, and former Tide halfback Tony Nathan discuss football strategy with some youngsters at Jeff's first football camp, held in the summer of 1982 at Samford University in Birmingham.

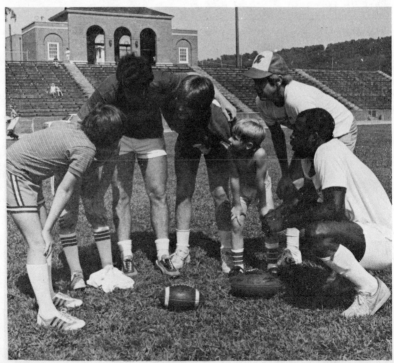

back Bert Jones. Even though Pat Haden decided to retire from football in June, more fuel was added to the fire in July when the Rams rehired Vince Ferragamo from the Canadian Football League. The acquisitions of Jones and Ferragamo naturally frustrated Jeff even further—almost to the point of asking for a trade.

"I thought about asking to be traded," Jeff said, "but I knew I wouldn't necessarily be the number-one quarterback wherever I went. I just want to play, and I'm a firm believer I'm going to play somewhere."

How about New York City? In a somewhat surprising move the Rams on September 5, 1982, traded Jeff to the New York Giants. Jeff never actually asked for the trade, but it may have been for the best. Jones and Ferragamo were in a heated battle during training camp for the Rams' top spot and Jeff's playing chances for the 1982 season were dwindling.

Jeff's move to the Giants developed after starting Giants quarterback Phil Simms was injured in a pre-season game and underwent knee surgery. After Jeff's arrival with New York (coached by former Tide All-American Ray Perkins), he was expected to battle the Giants' Scott Brunner for the starting quarterback position.

Jeff, his wife Laura, and children Brooks (8-17-79) and Christen (1-16-81) moved to New York immediately after the season began but will continue to live in Los Angeles during the off-seasons. "Career-wise, the move to New York will be good for me," Jeff said after the trade. "I think I can go in and contribute right away."

Regardless of what team he plays for, Jeff looks forward to a promising career in professional football. "I hope to play as long as the good Lord will let me," Jeff said. "I don't attach any number of years to it. I just want to play as long as I can, as well as I can."

LOWE

Woodrow • Eddie

History was made in Birmingham, Alabama, on Saturday, November 28, 1981.

For followers of Alabama and Auburn football this day will be remembered more than any other.

November 28, 1981, was the momentous day Alabama head football coach Paul "Bear" Bryant enjoyed his finest moment by becoming the winningest coach in collegiate football history. The 28-17 Alabama decision over an upset-minded Auburn squad was Bryant's 315th career victory, one more than Amos Alonzo Stagg and two more than Glenn "Pop" Warner.

Eddie Lowe, a Tide junior linebacker, was in Legion Field on this day...and he was a part of it all. Woodrow Lowe, Eddie's older brother, was in San Diego, California, on this day...and he too was a part of it all.

Woodrow was a part of it from 1972 to 1975. The Phenix City, Alabama, youngster in 1971 was told he was "too small" to play college football. All he did was become a three-time All-American linebacker for the Tide, playing in 43 of Bryant's 315 wins.

Eddie was a part of it in 1980 and 1981, playing in 19 of the immortal 315 victories. He is also having the honor of adding to the record in 1982, his third and final season with the Crimson Tide.

James "Jake" Lowe, the oldest of the Lowe family, was a linebacker in the mid-sixties for Bethune-Cookman College in Daytona Beach, Florida, then later played two years of semi-pro football. Jake was the motivator behind Woodrow's football beginning.

"I really didn't get interested in football until my brother (Jake) was playing in high school," Woodrow said. "I used to go watch him practice. I started playing (organized football) in the fifth grade and some in the sixth. But I just didn't have much talent then, so I didn't play anymore until the eighth grade."

Eddie naturally picked the game up from watching Woodrow. But if Jake, Woodrow, and Eddie had followed the wishes of their parents, the football-playing Lowe family would be just the plain ol' Lowe family.

"I really didn't want them to play football," chuckled father James Lowe, a brickmason in Phenix City. "They all started off at such an early age. They kept insisting on playing, so I said, 'Go ahead—it's your limbs that are going to get broken.' I really wanted them to play (only) baseball, but they were determined to play football."

Woodrow's "determination" to play football was very subtle and to the point. "I cried and cried when they told me I couldn't play football," he recalled. "It must have worked, because finally they let me play."

From then on it was Woodrow's opponents on the gridiron that did the crying.

Woodrow graduated from Phenix City's Central High School in 1972. Playing as a linebacker-fullback for Coach Frank Sadler, he earned All-City and Lineman of the Year honors and was captain of the football team, averaging 12 tackles per game as a senior. He also lettered two years as a baseball pitcher and earned the respect of his fellow students by being elected president of his senior class.

Because of his relatively small size (5'11", 185 pounds) Woodrow was not widely recruited as a football player. "By the middle of the season," Woodrow said, "I didn't have too many schools interested in me. My parents couldn't afford to send me to school, so the only way I could go was on a scholarship. If I didn't get one, I had already decided to join the navy. In fact I had already taken the test to get in.

"Florida State was really the only school that looked at me," Woodrow continued. "I could have gone to Bethune-Cookman where my older brother played, but it was too far from home. Coach (Frank) Sadler told me he thought I could

223

Woodrow Lowe with San Diego.

play at Alabama, so I became interested in them.''

Whereas the sixties would have welcomed a player of Woodrow's size, the seventies were different. The Neighbors, Jordans, Dowdys, and Samples of the small, quick Alabama teams of the sixties were being replaced by the much larger Hannahs, Krapfs, Browns, and Parkhouses of the seventies.

The new era was survival of the fittest—and usually the largest. At 5′11″ and 185 pounds, Woodrow was not the ideal size for a college football player, much less a linebacker.

Pat Dye, Tide linebacker coach and assistant in charge of recruiting the Phenix City area, began following Woodrow during the 1971 season but never was really sold on him until late in the year.

"We saw on the films that Woodrow had terrific speed and

224

was a great athlete," said Dye, now head coach at Auburn University. "At the time, we were running the wishbone, so we were also interested in his being a fullback. We could tell he wasn't a great fullback, but he wasn't a bad one either.

"We felt like if he grew and got big enough he could certainly be a great linebacker, and if he didn't get big enough to play linebacker then he could probably play strong safety or even in the backfield. Based on those decisions we went ahead and offered him a scholarship.

"A lot of it had to do with recommendations from Coach Sadler as far as the kind of character and the kind of kid Woodrow was. If a guy has any kind of physical limitations at all, we like to think he has all the intangibles going for him. That's the way we recruited Woodrow."

Dye was quick to tell Woodrow what lay ahead in the world of college football. "When we signed him," Dye recalled, "I said to him, 'Woodrow, you're not big enough to play linebacker in the Southeastern Conference. If you want to play linebacker in the SEC, you've got to get bigger and stronger.'"

Woodrow seriously heeded Dye's advice. "I knew the only way I was going to play was to gain weight," Woodrow said, "so I started training on those weights. I knew I was small, but I had pretty good speed. By the time I got ready to come to school I had gained about 20 pounds and was up to around 205."

Another reason Woodrow wanted to attend Alabama was because it was "fairly close to home." If Alabama was "fairly close to home," then Auburn had to be "next door." But a funny thing happened on the way to the Plains.

"A teammate of mine and I were supposed to drive over to Auburn one Saturday to visit the campus and watch them play," Woodrow recalled. "I didn't have a car, but he had an old raggedy Ford so we went in it. On the way over there, the car broke down.

"We spent most of the day hitching a ride back to Phenix City. We were supposed to meet some of the Auburn coaches after the game, but we never made it."

Woodrow reported to the University in early August ready and willing to give it his best shot. The football practices were tough, but his biggest challenge was yet to come. "The biggest problem I had," Woodrow remembered, "was registration for

225

classes. When practice started in August, there weren't too many people on campus. Then everybody came back to register. I had never seen so many people in my life. I didn't know what to do or where to go.

"I would have really been lost if it hadn't been for (academic advisor) Coach Gary White," Woodrow continued. "He got my schedule straightened out.

"I think I adjusted pretty well being a black guy from such a small town."

Athletes from "small towns" have dotted the Tide football roster since the University began its program in 1892. But in the early seventies very few black players had that distinction. Wilbur Jackson of Ozark, the first black Alabama signee, was on the freshman team in 1970. John Mitchell, a junior college All-American transfer from Eastern Arizona, became the first black to ever play in a University of Alabama varsity football game when he started at defensive end against Southern California in the 1971 opener.

Black athletes Sylvester Croom, Ralph Stokes, Mike Washington, and James Taylor were in the 1971 freshman class, so when Woodrow signed his scholarship, there were only six blacks on the entire team. He joined Tyrone King, George Pugh, and Willie Shelby as the black members of the 1972 freshman class.

"It didn't bother me at all," Woodrow remarked about being one of the squad's few blacks. "I had gone to Central High School for two years due to integration, and that helped me a lot. At Central it wasn't a big adjustment because I think I was raised pretty good.

"It wasn't a problem for me at Alabama. In fact I became pretty close to (white teammates) Wayne Hall and Chuck Strickland.

"Being a minority in that situation kinda motivated me to do a little better and be a little more outstanding than I normally would. It was that added boost that made me want to do better."

The 1972 freshman class was impressive. Besides King, Pugh, and Shelby, others such as Leroy Cook, Bucky Berrey, Conley Duncan, Larry Ruffin, Richard Todd, Dave Gerasimchuk, Greg Montgomery, Buddy Pope, Wayne Rhodes, Mike

Stock, Alan Pizzitola (walk-on), and Mike Davis (yes, another kicking Davis) were signed.

As a team the freshmen were 4-1 with victories over Vanderbilt, Tennessee, Tulane, and Auburn. Woodrow never played in a game for the freshmen—he had better things to do. His abilities and attitude earned him a spot on the varsity in 1972, the first time (except for World War II and Korean War seasons) freshmen were allowed to do such.

Besides Woodrow, six newcomers—King (defensive back), Pugh (tight end), Cook (defensive end), Montgomery (offensive guard), Pope (offensive tackle), and Rhodes (defensive back) took advantage of the new rule and immediately contributed to the varsity. Montgomery, playing as a guard but switched to linebacker after his freshman year, started every game. King, Pugh, Cook, and Woodrow didn't start, but all played nearly as much as starters.

In his first game, a 35-12 victory over Duke, Woodrow became an immediate favorite of the Alabama fans for his bruising tackles as a member of the kickoff team. "I was so nervous," Woodrow said of his opener against Duke, "I didn't know what to do. I had never seen that many people (70,000 plus) in one gathering in my life. I was so hyperactive. Once the game started I tried to phase everybody out and get real serious about it."

Head coach Paul "Bear" Bryant was so impressed with Woodrow's "seriousness" against Duke that he named the freshman captain of the specialty teams for the next week's bout with Kentucky. The defense, headed by the "Redwood Forest" of Mike Raines (6'6", 236 pounds), Skip Kubelius (6'3", 248 pounds), John Mitchell (6'3", 230 pounds), and John Croyle (6'6", 212 pounds) blanked the Wildcats, 35-0, for only its third shutout since 1967.

Linebacker Jeff Rouzie, the Tide's top tackler in 1971, was redshirted in 1972 after an off-season automobile accident, so this gave Woodrow the chance to display his linebacking abilities in addition to being a feared member of the speciality teams. Playing behind upperclassmen Chuck Strickland, Wayne Hall, Mike Dubose, Andy Cross, and Jeff Blitz, Woodrow finished the year with 46 tackles, caused one fumble, recovered one fumble, intercepted a pass, and broke up three passes. His finest single performance was against Southern Mississippi when he once again captained the speciality teams. He was in on 13 tackles as the Tide swamped the Golden Eagles, 48-11.

But it was the Tennessee game in Knoxville where Woodrow earned his spurs. Down 10-3 with less than three minutes remaining in the game, Alabama scored 14 points in a 36-second span to defeat the Volunteers, 17-10. It was Woodrow's and Dubose's crunching fumble-causing tackle on quarterback Condredge Holloway that set up the winning touchdown sprint by Alabama quarterback Terry Davis.

After blazing to a 10-0 record, the Tide dropped its last two games to Auburn, 17-16, and Texas in the Cotton Bowl, 17-13. Despite the team's poor finish Woodrow had made his mark as a freshman. "Woodrow never played like a freshman," stated linebacker coach Pat Dye. "He was a football player the first day he took to the field. He was a man—mentally and physically. A lot of players may be tough mentally and not tough physically. Others may be all physical and no mental. Woodrow was both."

Woodrow was expected to be a top performer as a sophomore in 1973, but not until late August did the fans know just how good Bryant expected him to be. "Woodrow Lowe might be as good as Lee Roy Jordan before the season is over, and he's bigger and faster," Bryant said optimistically. Woodrow was only eight years old when Jordan finished his All-American linebacking at Alabama in 1962, and he didn't remember who Jordan was.

"I didn't know what was going on," Woodrow said. "Everyone was calling me 'Lee Roy,' and I didn't even know which Lee Roy they were talking about. But I did a little research and found out he was a good one at Alabama. In fact he was still playing (professional ball) at Dallas then, and I knew he was a great one.

"I didn't know what to say when I saw the papers and read what Coach Bryant had said. It was quite an honor being compared to Lee Roy Jordan."

Lee Roy, or Woodrow rather, lived up to all his pre-season billing. In the 66-0 opener over California he made 12 tackles, caused a fumble, and intercepted a pass thrown by Bear quarterback and later NFL great Vince Ferragamo. "I

228

remember that game well," Woodrow beamed. "I got all over a guy that's a (San Diego Charger) teammate of mine right now—Chuck Muncie. He played in the backfield for California. I still give him a hard time about that."

An explosive offense averaging more than 40 points per game and a stingy defense allowing only eight points per outing gave the Tide in 1973 a perfect 11-0 regular season record and a United Press International national championship.

Woodrow, now up to 210 pounds, was spectacular in his linebacker position, finishing with 86 individual tackles, more than twice as many as any other Tider, and assisting on 48 others, also tops for an unbelievable 134 total. He caused two fumbles, recovered one fumble, broke up a pass, had three interceptions (one was that of Ferragamo's) which he returned for 20 yards, and blocked a field goal attempt.

He was named Associated Press Southeastern Lineman of the Week twice (against California and LSU), United Press International Southeastern Defensive Player of the Week once (against LSU), and ABC-TV's Most Valuable Defensive Player

Woodrow Lowe (47) makes one of his incredible 134 tackles in 1973, this one in a 28-14 Alabama victory over Georgia.

in both the Tennessee and LSU games (Tide quarterback Gary Rutledge was the offensive MVP against LSU).

Woodrow saved his best regular season performance for last when he collared Auburn runners for 20 tackles in a 35-0 rout. "I found out my freshman year that we just weren't supposed to lose to Auburn," Woodrow said. "When they beat us 17-16, it was like the end of the world, and with my home being there right by Auburn, I heard a lot about it. So there was plenty incentive to beat Auburn my sophomore year."

Alabama carried its top ranking to New Orleans and the Sugar Bowl. Woodrow will never forget that first-ever meeting against the Fighting Irish of Notre Dame when the Tide lost the heartbreaker, 24-23.

"I cried in the locker room after that game," Woodrow sadly recalled. "I'll never forget (Notre Dame end) Dave Casper catching all those passes against us. I'm very familiar with him now, too, after playing against him for so long when he was with Oakland and now Houston. He's still making those catches."

Woodrow's honors poured in at the conclusion of his sophomore season. He was named first-team Associated Press, United Press International All-SEC, and Churchman's National Defensive Sophomore of the Year. Four All-American teams recognized him—NEA (first team), *Football News* (second team), Associated Press (third team), and United Press International (honorable mention). The NEA squad was composed of 19 seniors, two juniors...and Woodrow. Ed "Too Tall" Jones and Randy Gradishar (now with Dallas and Denver professional teams, respectively) were two of the other players named to the NEA team.

All of Woodrow's awards, honors, and praises were rightly deserved, but if he had followed through with his pre-season desires, Woodrow's freshman year would have been his first...and last season with the Crimson Tide.

In preparation for his All-American 1973 season, Woodrow began having second thoughts about playing football. He went to Pat Dye with the idea of giving it up to go into the ministry. "I thought about it seriously," Woodrow stated. "I didn't know I'd be playing much in 1973, and I just wasn't sure I was doing what I wanted to do.

Woodrow Lowe (47) takes in a few words of advice from Alabama head coach Paul "Bear" Bryant and assistant coach Louis Campbell.

"I received Christ as my savior in high school, but I really didn't begin to understand what it was all about and what my purpose was until I got in college. I got to asking myself if I was living my life for the Lord or for me. I read the Bible a lot, and God revealed to me that He is the greatest. I thought seriously about living my life preaching His word."

Pat Dye vividly recalls the scenario. "It started on a Wednesday afternoon," he said. "Woodrow came in and told me he was giving up football. He told me he had felt God had called him to preach.

"I told him that I wouldn't let him quit without him going to practice that afternoon. I knew the longer I kept him out there, the less chance there was for him quitting.

"Wednesday night," Dye continued, "Woodrow came over to my house, and (Tide linebacker) Wayne Hall was there. Wayne was very active in the Fellowship of Christian Athletes

(FCA) at that time. Wayne, Woodrow, and myself sat down and talked for a long time, then went to an FCA meeting. I felt good about our talk. I felt like everything was taken care of.

"Thursday afternoon I was getting ready to go to practice, and I looked down there and Woodrow was walking up in front of the Coliseum. He comes and says, 'Coach, I just can't practice.' He said he was quitting the team again."

Dye made a call for help to the Reverend Sylvester Croom, father of Tide center Sylvester, Jr., and former football player at Alabama A&M. The Reverend Croom was close to all the team's black players, especially Woodrow. His mission in this case was to convince Woodrow that football and God's work could go hand in hand. The mission was accomplished.

"I went to the dorm that night and had a long talk with Lowe," said the Reverend Croom, now minister at College Hill Missionary Baptist Church in Tuscaloosa. "I told him that in the Bible, Paul often talked about athletes running the race of patience and that being an athlete had nothing to do with his religion.

"I told him that he could be an athlete and still preach. It would be an opportunity for him to be on national TV and testify for God because a lot of kids would look up to him. He could use his position there to witness for God.

"Through the grace of God I convinced Lowe that he would be in a better position to serve the Lord by staying on the team. So he said he would go back."

Woodrow was glad he went back, and so was Alabama. His outstanding performance during the 1973 season ranks among the greatest in Alabama football history. Bryant's evaluation before the season comparing Woodrow to Lee Roy Jordan proved correct, and going into his (1974) junior season Woodrow was expected to continue his All-American play and anchor a solid Tide defense.

The defense was indeed solid in 1974...but Woodrow wasn't. Injuries, personal problems, and financial worries hit Woodrow so hard that he slipped to fourth on the team in tackles (behind Leroy Cook, Ronny Robertson, and Greg Montgomery).

He reached such a low point that he even considered quitting football again, and only a re-dedication of his life and a

232

warm, personal relationship with new linebacker coach Paul Crane saved him.

Crane, an All-American center-linebacker for the Tide in 1963-1965, had filled the spot vacated when Pat Dye left Alabama to become head coach at East Carolina University.

In the summer before his junior year Woodrow married his girlfriend of two years, Linda Jean Wilson of Birmingham. Woodrow and Linda struggled to make ends meet, certainly not an uncommon task for any newly married couple. To make matters worse, Linda was often in bad health, a condition which later required surgery. Also Pat Dye, Woodrow's best "coaching" friend, had left, leaving him with no one to turn to for help and guidance.

Enter Paul Crane, the ex-Alabama and New York Jets great and a very active worker in the FCA. Woodrow later said his prayers were answered when Paul Crane offered his help.

"Coach Crane had a big impact on my life," Woodrow stated. "At the time, I didn't have any coach I could talk to. I was sad when Coach Dye left. I never told him this, but I really didn't want him to go. Coach Crane was new, and I didn't know if I could talk to him.

"But he came to me first. It wasn't like he was prying into my business. He came easy; he gave a part of himself to me which made me open up to him. He helped me realize that football wasn't the most important thing in the world and that life was going to continue and the sun was still going to shine."

Crane, later an assistant coach at Ole Miss and now a Mobile businessman, treated Woodrow like one of his own. "It was hard on a young man his age," Crane commented about Woodrow's difficulties. "He was trying to play to the best of his abilities, yet he was facing the problems of injury (pinched nerve in his neck) and a new marriage complicated by his wife being sick, which led to some financial problems. He had a lot on his mind that people didn't know about."

Woodrow's 68 tackles in 1974 were almost half of his 1973 total. Because his marriage was made public, many people blamed his slump on it. "Not true," Woodrow emphasized. "Some people were pointing their fingers at me saying that being married was the reason I was playing the way I was. But that wasn't it at all.

"The reason was because I had made All-American the year before, and there were certain players out there trying to get me. They were trying to show their coaches they could do a good job and make a name for themselves. The main problem was that I was trying too hard. I was trying to please a lot of people.

"Through all the turmoil and what was put in the newspapers about our marriage, my wife and I stuck it out. We had to. And if anybody helped me out during that time, it was Coach Crane. He told me to never quit no matter how hard it was 'raining.' I didn't quit, I didn't give up. We got through it all."

As a team in 1974 Alabama won 11 straight games and once again faced Notre Dame, this time in the Orange Bowl. In another classic the Irish downed the Tide, 13-11. Oklahoma, even though on probation, won the Associated Press national championship. Alabama finished fifth in the final poll.

Despite the slump Woodrow was highly decorated at the end of his junior season. He was named to the first team Associated Press All-SEC squad and was recognized as a first-teamer by two All-American teams—the Walter Camp Football Foundation and United Press International. Others making the UPI squad included future professional greats Randy White of Maryland, Archie Griffin of Ohio State, Steve Bartkowski of California, and Joe Washington of Oklahoma.

By the beginning of Woodrow's senior season (1975) the entire Tide defense was solid. Six linebackers—Gus White, Greg Montgomery, Colenzo Hubbard, Conley Duncan, Dewey Mitchell, and Woodrow—were all considered first-teamers by Bryant. Into the season White (5'10", 260 pounds) moved up to the middle guard spot and joined Leroy Cook, Bob Baumhower, Charley Hannah, Dick Turpin, and Paul Harris as the ingredients of the ever-continuing "Redwood Forest."

Add to those the Tide defensive backfield—Wayne Rhodes, Mark Prudhomme, Tyrone King, Alan Pizzitola, Andy Gothard, and Mike Tucker—and the result is the nation's top defense in 1975 (allowing only 6.0 points per game).

For the third consecutive year Alabama finished with an 11-1 mark. Take away a 20-7 national television loss to Missouri on opening night, and the Tide defense allowed less than five

*Woodrow Lowe (47) is joined by a host of Tide rein-
forcements—Ronny Robertson (55), Gus White (68), and Mike
Dubose (54)—to stop an Ole Miss ballcarrier.*

points per game. The offense, led by Richard Todd, Johnny
Davis, Willie Shelby, Mike Stock, and Ozzie Newsome, complemented the defense by scoring more than 30 points per game.

But perhaps the most important accomplishment of the
1975 team was that for the first time since the 1966 season,
Alabama won its bowl game. In the first Sugar Bowl played in
the New Orleans Superdome, the Crimsons edged Penn State,
13-6, sending a loud cheer through the French Quarter and all
the way back to Tuscaloosa. The bowl win streak would continue for six more seasons until the 1982 Cotton Bowl when the
Tide fell to Texas, 14-12.

Injuries slowed Woodrow for most of his senior season,
but he still managed to make 67 tackles, fourth best on the team
(behind Bob Baumhower, Leroy Cook, and Conley Duncan).
He had one interception, caused three fumbles, and recovered
one fumble.

Woodrow led the team with 13 tackles against Penn State

in the Sugar Bowl and was named the game's most valuable defensive player. Paul Crane, more than just a coach to Woodrow, fondly remembers Woodrow's performance against the Nittany Lions...and his performance the day before.

"Woodrow really played outstanding the latter part of his senior year and especially the bowl game," Crane said. "He played like his old self again.

"But he had quite an experience the day before the game," Crane chuckled. "We were going from the hotel to practice at the Superdome. Woodrow just missed the bus, and he started running to try to catch up. Every time he almost caught us the bus would pull off before he could get to it.

"He ran all the way from the hotel to the Superdome and got there in time for practice. The next day he played as fine a game as anybody could play."

Woodrow finished his Alabama career with a record of 43 wins and five losses, four Southeastern Conference championships and a UPI national championship. In his four years as a fierce competitor and feared hitter, the three-time All-American made 315 tackles, threw opposing runners for 47 yards in losses, had six interceptions, broke up seven passes, caused six fumbles, recovered six fumbles, and blocked one field goal attempt.

An intensive weight training program added about five pounds each year to Woodrow's stocky frame, and by his senior season he tipped the scales at 220 pounds. Somewhere down the line he grew an inch to an even six-feet. One inch is not much, but it goes a long way when every professional football team looks at the upcoming class each year. And the jump to the six-foot mark was ever so important for Woodrow and his professional fortunes.

Woodrow's official height and weight for the Senior Bowl was 6'0", 220 pounds. In the game, he played only two quarters but was "satisfied with the performance." Next up was the wait until April and the NFL draft.

Woodrow's abilities were proven. His height and weight were considered a bit small for professional standards, but he had a big plus going for him...the Alabama tradition. In Woodrow's four years at Alabama 25 teammates played or would eventually play at least one year of professional football.

Fourteen offensive players, ten defensive players, and one kicker (Greg Gantt, N.Y. Jets) rekindled an Alabama tradition that had slowed somewhat since the late sixties.

The 14 offensive Tiders in this group were Butch Norman (Winnipeg), Buddy Brown (Winnipeg), John Hannah (New England), Wilbur Jackson (San Francisco and Washington), Sylvester Croom (New Orleans), Willie Shelby (Cincinnati), Richard Todd (N.Y. Jets), Johnny Davis (Tampa Bay and San Francisco), Tony Nathan (Miami), Jeff Rutledge (Los Angeles), Ozzie Newsome (Cleveland), Bob Cryder (New England), Buddy Aydelette (Green Bay), and Steve Whitman (San Diego).

Ten defensive players were in this group of 25—Ricky Davis (Tampa Bay), Mike Washington (Tampa Bay), Mike Raines (Ottawa), Bob Baumhower (Miami), Charley Hannah (Tampa Bay), Paul Harris (Tampa Bay), Marty Lyons (N.Y. Jets), Terry Jones (Green Bay), Rich Wingo (Green Bay), and Barry Krauss (Baltimore).

Woodrow's name can be added to this impressive group. The San Diego Chargers, starved for their first winning season since 1969, picked Woodrow in the fifth round of the 1976 draft. The move prompted Alabama head coach Paul Bryant to comment, "San Diego's getting Woodrow Lowe in the fifth round is like getting a ten-dollar gold piece for ten cents."

Woodrow made an immediate contribution to the Chargers. Since 1969 they had won a total of 24 games, an average of only four wins per year. The hapless Chargers were 2-12 in 1975, and their defense gave up more than 24 points per game.

Hello Woodrow...and good-bye to the Chargers' lousy defense. Their 1976 record was up to 6-8 in Woodrow's rookie season, then steadily improved to 7-7 in 1977, 9-7 in 1978, 12-4 in 1979, 11-5 in 1980, and 10-6 in 1981. They won consecutive AFC West championships in 1979, 1980, and 1981 with what is known as "Air Coryell," an offensive strategy designed and installed by head coach Don Coryell. Using the talents of quarterback Dan Fouts and receivers Kellen Winslow, Charlie Joiner, Wes Chandler, and former Auburn star James Brooks, the Chargers set 10 NFL offensive records in 1981.

So where does Woodrow fit in the "Air Coryell" game plan? "Don is definitely an offensive-minded coach,"

Woodrow admitted, "but he's putting more emphasis on defense. The '81 season showed that he is (second in AFC in rushing defense and fifth in the NFL)."

Woodrow is today up to 227 pounds and is still considered "small" for a professional linebacker. But he doesn't necessarily agree with that assessment. "I can't understand why they have me as being small," he asked. "My first three years I thought I was small, but I played real well. Then I began to see other players coming up that weren't as big as me.

"I guess I'm not the ideal size for a linebacker, but I think with today's passing game in pro football there is a need for outside linebackers that can cover those backs coming out of the backfield. I've been playing six years (as of 1981), and I don't think my size has hurt me yet."

Woodrow's opponents on the field sure don't think he's small. He has earned his keep in the NFL and is becoming, according to Charger management, "one of the best outside linebackers in football." He was an AFC Pro Bowl alternate in 1980 and 1981 and was the Chargers' second-best tackler in 1981 with 133. At the conclusion of the 1981 season Woodrow had started in 90 of a possible 92 games (since coming into the league in 1976). The two games he missed were because of a sore hip.

Since "Charging" into the NFL in 1976, Woodrow has played against some great receivers and quarterbacks. He lists former Alabama and Auburn greats Tony Nathan (Miami) and Joe Cribbs (Buffalo) as the toughest receivers he's faced ("because of their speed coming out of the backfield") and former Alabama star Kenny Stabler (New Orleans) as the toughest quarterback to defense ("because he can really thread the ball").

The Chargers in 1982 are again aiming toward the Super Bowl, a game which eluded them in the 1981 season when they fell in the AFC finals to Cincinnati, 27-7. In the loss the Chargers had to travel to Riverfront Stadium in Cincinnati where the wind-chill factor was 59 degrees below zero. Cincinnati went on to the Super Bowl and bowed to San Francisco, 26-21.

Assuming he is injury free, Woodrow will have several more chances to win the coveted Super Bowl championship. But for younger brother Eddie, 1982 is his last chance to claim number one. The game Eddie plays—college football—may be a step behind the professional game, but the reward is equal, no matter what the level of competition.

And if there has ever been a kid who wanted to play his heart out for the University of Alabama, he is Eddie Lowe. "There's no way he's supposed to be out there playing major college football," said Jeff Rouzie, Eddie's linebacker coach from 1979 to 1981. "He's only 5'9" and 190 pounds, yet he's out there doing it—and doing it good. He's the kind of kid that takes what he's got and does more with it than he's supposed to do. Pound for pound Eddie gets more out of himself than anybody I've ever been around."

Rouzie's remarks become more meaningful once you consider that he *played* (1970, 1971, 1973) with linebackers such as Greg Montgomery, Chuck Strickland, Wayne Hall...and Woodrow. And from 1977 to 1981 he *coached,* among others, future professionals Rich Wingo (Green Bay), Barry Krauss (Baltimore), Randy Scott (Green Bay), and Thomas Boyd (Green Bay).

In other words, Rouzie puts Eddie right up there with the best in terms of attitude, desire, and dedication. Eddie is, as Paul Bryant puts it, "a real winner."

Eddie's sports career started similarly to Woodrow's. "I started playing football in the fifth grade, when Woodrow was a junior in high school," Eddie said. "We used to play all kinds of sports around the neighborhood. (Future Tide teammate) Billy Jackson grew up right across the street from us, and one year Woodrow coached a baseball team we had. I think we lost about three or four games in four years. He used to whip us good, and he ran us all the time.

Jackson, an All-SEC performer for the Tide in 1980, was one of Eddie's best friends while growing up in Phenix City. "When Woodrow was playing high school ball, he would bring all the plays home and we would get out in the field and run them," said Jackson, now a running back for the Kansas City Chiefs. "I guess that's where we got our start in football."

Eddie in 1978 graduated Central High after a three-year record of 17-10-1 under Coach Wayne Trawick. He was a 5'9", 175-pound linebacker and like Woodrow was not heavily recruited.

239

"The only school that was interested in me was Kansas," Eddie said. "Then a guy from Kentucky came down to Phenix City to meet me. I was in the weight room at the time, and he came up and asked me if I knew Eddie Lowe. I said, 'I'm Eddie Lowe.' He just looked at me and said, 'No way.' I didn't hear any more from him.

"I had always been an Alabama fan, even before Woodrow came here," Eddie continued. "When I found out Billy (Jackson) was going to play at Alabama, I wanted to come also. And Alabama had also been writing (close friend) Jeremiah (Castille), who was a junior at Central then. I kinda thought he'd be coming to Alabama too."

Whereas Pat Dye's assignment in 1971 was to sign Woodrow to a scholarship, Paul Crane's mission in the fall of 1977 was just the opposite. He had to turn down the same opportunity for Eddie.

"I had to tell Eddie we weren't going to offer him a scholarship," Crane said, "and he was really crushed about it. He was small but still a real fine high school player. He was a player that we just couldn't take a chance on that year.

"He desperately wanted to come to Alabama. We tried to get him to walk on, but he really couldn't afford it."

Eddie was naturally disappointed that Alabama didn't offer him a scholarship. "I knew I was small, but I still wanted to play for them," he said. "Billy (Jackson) kept telling me I could play here.

"After Alabama turned me down, I wanted to play anywhere in the SEC so I would get a chance to play *against* them. That's the way I felt. If Auburn had offered me a scholarship, I would have gone there."

The only school to offer Eddie a scholarship was the University of Tennessee at Chattanooga (UTC). "Alabama tried to get me to walk on, but at the time I didn't want to turn down my scholarship offer with Chattanooga," Eddie said. "They were the only big school that wanted me.

"I still think that the only reason I got a scholarship there was because of Frank Sadler, Woodrow's coach at Central. When I was in high school, Coach Sadler was at Kendrick High School in Columbus (Georgia) and we played against them every year. Then he became an assistant at Chattanooga. If he

240

had not known me, I don't think UTC would have wanted me."

Paul Crane left the Alabama staff in January of 1978 to coach at Ole Miss under former Alabama teammate and close friend Steve Sloan. Jeff Rouzie, who had been helping Crane with the linebackers in 1977, took Crane's spot as linebacker coach. When Rouzie saw Eddie perform in the 1978 high school All-Star game in Tuscaloosa, he began wondering if they hadn't made a mistake.

"Eddie just tore people up in the All-Star game," Rouzie recalled. "He was playing cornerback and had a great game.

"(Defensive secondary coach) Bill Oliver and I watched practice every day before the game. One day Bill looked over to me and said, 'I'm not so sure we didn't make a mistake. I'm not so sure if Eddie couldn't play strong safety for us.'

"But it was too late then. He had already signed with Chattanooga."

Eddie went on to Chattanooga and earned a starting spot at linebacker after only two games. The Moccasins rolled to a 6-0-1 record and had a 15-game unbeaten streak going.

"That's when the big controversy came up," Eddie said. "Some of the black players boycotted practice, and the coach suspended them from the team. There were only eight blacks (out of 33) that stayed on the team, and I was one of them."

The boycott resulted when head coach Joe Morrison suspended black defensive back Ken Mitchell from the squad for missing two practices. Mitchell claimed he had a sore neck, but he did not report the injury to the team's trainer as required. Twenty-five of the 33 blacks on the squad boycotted a practice in sympathy for Mitchell. Morrison said the 25 athletes would be reinstated if they made up the practice by running wind sprints the next morning. Only five accepted the offer, and the 20 no-shows were kicked off the team.

The Moccasins, minus most of their starters, had their 15-game unbeaten streak snapped the next Saturday when they fell to McNeese State, 28-24. They then lost three of the last four games to finish with a 7-3-1 record.

Eddie finished the season as the team's leading tackler, but he still wasn't happy. Dreams of playing football for the University of Alabama had never left his mind.

"Eddie just had it in his mind that he was going to come to

241

Alabama and play, no matter what it took," commented Jeff Rouzie. "During his freshman year at Chattanooga we couldn't talk to him (because of NCAA rules), but he had a friend at home that he talked to about coming to Alabama."

The "friend" Rouzie spoke of was Buddy Helton, a resident of Phenix City and Columbus, Georgia, businessman. Helton helped recruit Woodrow for Alabama in 1971 and did the same with Eddie in 1977.

"I thought Eddie could play at Alabama all the time," Helton said. "He was real downhearted when Paul (Crane) told him that Alabama couldn't give him a scholarship. He didn't act like he was upset, but he was really down in the dumps.

"When he was at Chattanooga, he would call me every weekend and tell us how he was doing, bless his heart. He wanted to come to Alabama awfully bad."

The boycott was just icing on the cake for Eddie to leave Chattanooga. "I had already made up my mind to walk on at Alabama," he said. "When the boycott came up, it made me want to leave just that much more."

Billy Jackson was delighted to see Eddie make the decision to walk on at Alabama. "I had told Eddie all along that I knew he could play at Alabama," Jackson said. "I had played against Eddie, and I knew the type person he was. I knew he had the willpower and the determination.

"He was small at the time, but we had played together before and I had been hit harder by him than by guys a lot bigger. I knew he could play."

After receiving permission from Chattanooga, Eddie transferred to Alabama in January of 1979. "I really didn't know what to expect when I got here," Eddie said.
"The way we practiced here was totally different (than at Chattanooga). I didn't know anything about a quickness drill, or the different colored jerseys and what they stood for. And it was two or three weeks before I knew what the list (depth chart) on the board meant.

"I didn't know anybody here except Billy (Jackson) and (basketball players from Phenix City) Ken Johnson and Eddie Adams. I had met some guys during the All-Star game, but I didn't get real close to them. I didn't know what everybody thought about me."

Eddie Lowe's dream was to follow older brother Woodrow's steps and play football for the University of Alabama.

Billy Jackson and Jeff Rouzie well remember what everybody thought of Eddie. "He came out there and earned everyone's respect within a couple of days," Jackson recalled. "He was quiet, but everyone knew he was there."

"Eddie impressed some people real quick," Rouzie added. "Even at that time we didn't really think he was big enough to play linebacker. We were going to try him at strong safety to see how well he caught on. He wasn't quite fast enough for that, but he sure had a knack for the ball—just like his brother Woodrow. He showed us excellent lateral movement and tremendous quickness. He always found a way to get the job done."

As a transfer Eddie was required by NCAA rules to sit out

the 1979 season. "That didn't bother me much," Eddie said. "Sure, I wish I could have been out there (in 1979), but I knew what I was going to have to go through. I liked football so much that I went out and practiced just like I wasn't redshirted."

Jeff Rouzie knew he had a winner in Eddie Lowe. "The offensive team hated to practice against Eddie during his redshirt season," Rouzie chuckled, "because they never could block him. He made every tackle on the field. They even got real upset with him. After the first week or so, Eddie knew all the plays and he would stop them every time."

Following a convincing 24-9 victory over Arkansas in the Sugar Bowl, the undefeated and untied 1979 Alabama squad was named national champion by both the AP and UPI polls. It was the first time since 1964 and only the third time (1961 was the first) since the polls began that both had agreed on a Tide team being named number one.

Because he was redshirted, Eddie didn't receive a national championship diamond ring ("but I sure want one in 1982"), but he used the 1979 season as a learning experience. "I learned a lot that year," Eddie said. "Every day I practiced against a real tough offense. Dwight Stephenson, Mike Brock, Buddy Aydelette, Jim Bunch, Vince Boothe, and Tim Travis were across the line. Steadman Shealy, Major Ogilvie, Steve Whitman, and Billy (Jackson) were in the backfield. Going against them every day really helped me."

Redshirted players don't receive much publicity, therefore Eddie was virtually unknown to Tide followers. His first official entrance to Alabama football (free from redshirt status) was the 1980 A-Day spring game when he led the White team with 10 tackles. From then on people wouldn't refer to him just as "Woodrow Lowe's little brother." He now had a name and identity of his own.

Thanks to rigorous weight training since finishing high school, Eddie was up to 190 pounds entering his 1980 sophomore season. He played second-team weakside linebacker (behind All-American Thomas Boyd) and finished the season with 46 tackles, including four for losses of 18 yards.

"Eddie didn't play a great deal (in 1980)," said Jeff Rouzie, "but when he played, he played very well. He did a great job on kickoff coverage and punts. And when he was in there at linebacker, he did a great job. Of course Thomas Boyd played ahead of him, and Randy Scott and Robbie Jones shared the other spot. Eddie worked himself right in there to play."

Most teams dream of a 10-2 season, but to Alabama in 1980 it was a big disappointment. After rolling to seven straight wins (continuing the nation's longest winning streak at 28 games), the Tide stumbled in Jackson against Mississippi State. The 6-3 setback was Alabama's first SEC loss since the Georgia game of 1976.

Notre Dame's domination over Alabama continued into 1980 when the Fighting Irish blanked the Tide, 7-0, in Birmingham. The Crimsons bounced back to defeat Auburn, 34-18, and Southwest Conference champions Baylor in the Cotton Bowl, 30-2. The Georgia Bulldogs represented the SEC in the Sugar Bowl and defeated Notre Dame to win the 1980 national championship.

Eddie continued his fine play into 1981 spring training. His outstanding performance in the A-Day game (15 tackles) and his stimulating efforts the entire spring earned him the coveted Lee Roy Jordan Headhunter award. He joined the names of Randy Scott (twice), Rich Wingo, and Chuck Strickland as the only linebacker recipients of the award since its inception in 1971.

Next up was the historic 1981 season. Never before in college football history was a season more written and talked about than in 1981. The main topic of conversation was naturally Coach Paul "Bear" Bryant's quest to become the winningest college coach of all time. Entering the 1981 season he needed nine victories to reach the magic 315 mark.

Talk of the record held by Amos Alonzo Stagg first surfaced in late 1977 when Bryant broke the news to a high school prospect on the telephone. "A prospect in South Florida asked me if I was going to be his coach for four years," Bryant said. "...I told him I would be. He's the first person I told.

"I certainly have no intentions of hanging it up, but it certainly isn't a 'me' thing with me, but it's turned out that way. I talked to the University president (Dr. David Mathews), my wife (Mary Harmon), and my staff. I feel better than I've felt in a long time. It was recruiting time and some schools were using that against us, so I thought I'd go ahead and clear the air. I really don't know what the record is right now, and it should be

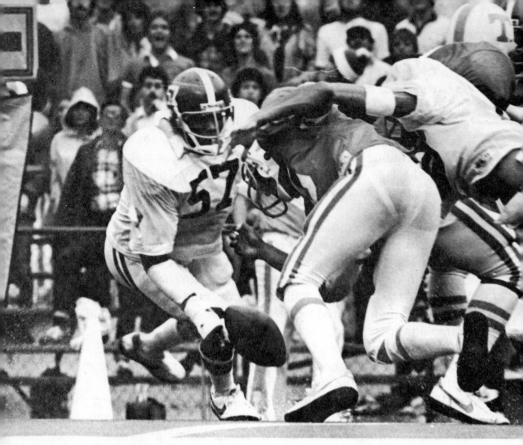

On a rain-soaked turf in Knoxville, Eddie Lowe (57) eyes a loose ball. Alabama blanked the Vols, 27-0, in the 1980 game.

obvious that I didn't have anything like that in mind when I made the schedule out for the next few years."

When Bryant made those comments in early 1978, he needed 42 victories to break the record. The countdown began...31 after the 1978 season, 19 after the 1979 season, 9 after the 1980 season...and finally the 1981 season was upon him.

"Everybody on the team wanted Coach Bryant to break the record," Eddie said, "because he deserved it. I really wanted to see him accomplish it.

"We didn't worry about it at the first of the year. We knew that if we won, the record would take care of itself."

Using that philosophy the Tide squad traveled to LSU for its season opener and smashed the Tigers on national television, 24-7. The third largest crowd (78,066) in Tiger Stadium history watched in disbelief as the Tide rolled to a 17-0 halftime lead, then coasted for the victory.

Eddie, Jeremiah Castille, Thomas Boyd, and Robbie Jones paced a tough Tide defense that shut LSU out until 13 seconds remaining in the game. Eddie made eight tackles in his junior season debut. "That game got us off to a good start," Eddie said. "We played pretty well and didn't think about the record."

Alabama rolled into Legion Field the next week as a 26-point favorite over Georgia Tech...and limped out as a three-point loser. The 24-21 upset of the Tide was considered by many to be college football's biggest upset of 1981 (Tech didn't win another game that year). Alabama outplayed the Yellow Jackets on paper, but a tragic fourth quarter (traditionally a Tide strength) spelled doom for the Crimsons. Penalties (84 yards worth), three lost fumbles, and erratic play all afternoon kept the Tide from putting the game away.

Eddie stopped Tech runners for eight tackles, but in the end it was the Tide that was stopped. "The Tech game really hurt," Eddie said. "I don't think we took them lightly. They just beat us.

"I think the game happened for the best. It did the team a lot of good. We realized we were going to have to get serious."

Eddie sure got serious the next week in Lexington against the Kentucky Wildcats. Starting in place of suspended All-American Thomas Boyd, Eddie made 15 tackles (10 unassisted) and was a thorn in Kentucky's side the whole afternoon. The Wildcats went ahead 10-9, early in the fourth quarter, only to fall behind on Peter Kim's fourth field goal of the game. A last-minute touchdown sealed a 19-10 victory for the Tide.

The defense scored 16 of Alabama's 28 points as the Vanderbilt Commodores fell in Nashville, 28-7. Eddie made three tackles in the game and intercepted a pass, setting up a five-play scoring drive. Jackie Cline, Russ Wood, and Benny Perrin all made big defensive plays as the Tide ran its record to 3-1 and left Bryant only six victories short of the magic 315.

On the Wednesday before the Ole Miss game the *Atlanta Constitution* printed a story alleging morale and racial problems on the Tide team. The allegations were forcefully put to rest the following Saturday when Alabama ripped Ole Miss, 38-7, prompting Rebel quarterback John Fourcade to com-

Eddie Lowe (57) stretches his 5'9" frame to tip a pass thrown by Georgia Tech quarterback Mike Kelley, who is pressured by the Tide's Randy Edwards (96).

ment, "The guy from Atlanta did a great job getting Alabama ready to play. They have no morale problems."

The journalistic cloud sent from Atlanta hung over Tuscaloosa for several days. "The story was blown way out of proportion," Eddie remarked. "There wasn't anything to it at all. I don't know how it came up. I know it shocked me and the rest of the team.

"The blacks and whites got together fine. Naturally there were fights and arguments on the football field, but they didn't have anything to do with color. There were blacks against blacks and whites against whites, but once they got in the locker room it was over. That's just a part of football. There was no racial tension whatsoever that I could see.

"The story," Eddie emphasized strongly, "gave us some incentive against Ole Miss."

Against the Rebels the Tide built a 17-0 lead at the half, 24-0 after three quarters, and led, 38-0, with under a minute to play. In the game Alabama had five different quarterbacks handing the ball off to 14 different runners and throwing to six different receivers. All in all it was just a fun day for the charged-up Alabama team.

Just as the Crimson Tide was looking like its old self again, another team came and spoiled all the fun. Southern Mississippi's Steve Clark calmly booted a 40-yard field goal with only eight seconds remaining to give the Golden Eagles a 13-13 "moral" victory over the Tide. It was the first time since the 1970 season that Alabama had failed to win back-to-back games at Legion Field.

Eddie played like a man possessed against Southern Miss and finished with 14 solo tackles and three assists.

The Tide was now 4-1-1 and in trouble. After the Southern Miss tie, the *soonest* Bryant could break the record was against archrival Auburn. One slip-up against Tennessee, Rutgers, Mississippi State, Penn State, or Auburn, and the chase would extend until bowl time. Two goofs and...wait 'till next year.

Relatively easy wins over Tennessee (38-19) and Rutgers (31-7) preceded the Southeastern Conference showdown against Mississippi State. The Bulldogs had clipped the Tide, 6-3, in 1980, and revenge was the talk of the day. In a jam-packed arena of tension and excitement, the Crimsons overcame 11 fumbles (losing seven) and edged the Bulldogs, 13-10.

The contest was never decided, however, until the closing seconds when Eddie and Tide All-American safety Tommy Wilcox combined for a heart-stopping play that left the Alabama fans—and players—totally exhausted.

Al Browning, sports editor of the *Tuscaloosa News,* summed up the entire game into just a few words. "With 19 seconds remaining in the game and Mississippi State at the Alabama nine-yard line," Browning wrote, "(State quarterback John) Bond attempted the eighth consecutive pass in a drive that had covered 70 yards. He threw the ball in the middle of the field, a tad left, and aimed at tight end Jerry Price. (Eddie) Lowe batted the ball with his right hand, and Wilcox intercepted it at the goal line."

Eddie finished with eight tackles and was in another world after the game. "I have no idea what happened," Eddie told Browning. "My memory is just a blur. I just remember throwing my right hand up. And I remember being scared they would score. I just thank God it happened like it did."

Eddie fondly recalls the moment after his 5'9" frame had reached the maximum and tipped the potential game-winning pass. "I remember the night before," Eddie chuckled, "Robbie Jones and I went to see the movie, *Halloween, Part Two*, and it was real scary.

"After the game I told Robbie, 'Man, my heart can't keep taking this.' He looked up and said, 'You ain't lying.' The movie and the game back-to-back was almost too much."

The Tide was idle the next Saturday, resting up for its national television showdown against Penn State. An Alabama victory would give Bryant win number 314 and tie him with Amos Alonzo Stagg on the all-time victory list.

In front of a record Beaver Stadium crowd of 85,133, the revived Tide shocked the fifth-ranked Nittany Lions, 31-16. Behind the pinpoint passing of quarterback Walter Lewis and the clutch receiving of Jesse Bendross and Joey Jones, Bama blitzed to a 24-3 halftime advantage and never looked back.

But it was a gallant defensive effort in the third quarter that brought back sweet memories for Tide fans...and bitter ones for Penn State followers. The Nittany Lions, trailing 24-3, took seven shots at the Alabama end zone from the four-yard line. The first three attempts netted three yards and a first down.

Three more cracks failed, and on fourth-and-inches Bama defensive end Mike Pitts hit Penn State halfback Curt Warner for a one-yard loss. Deja vu to the 1979 Sugar Bowl? Yes indeed.

Warren Lyles, the Tide noseguard, danced off the field, somersaulting his 260-pound body like that of an Olympic gymnast. Bryant, who later said, "I wanted to hug each of them," tipped his hat to the men dressed in White. "Efforts like that are what football is all about," he continued. "It meant a lot to me, and it should mean a lot to them."

It sure meant a lot to Eddie Lowe, who started with Boyd in place of an injured Robbie Jones. "All games are special," Eddie said, "but we especially wanted to beat Penn State. They were an Eastern team, and that's where all the sportswriters are. The goal-line stand really turned the game around.

"I didn't realize the game tied the record for Coach Bryant. A lot of the other players didn't realize it either."

They sure realized it the next week, though, as the pressure of "the" game was bearing down harder than ever. Hollywood couldn't have written a better script for the event. It was finally Bryant's long-awaited chance to surpass Amos Alonzo Stagg, a legend that earned his 314 wins at Springfield College, the University of Chicago, and College of the Pacific. Stagg, who in 1891 teamed with James A. Naismith to help invent the game of basketball, was 90 when he retired in 1952 and 103 when he died.

It was the 68-year-old Bryant against enemy Auburn and its new coach, Patrick Fain Dye, a former Bryant pupil for nine seasons (1965-1973). It was the finale of a season that had had its ups and downs, pressures, heartaches, and discipline problems, all of which prompted Bryant to say, "I'll be glad when it's over. This has been the most difficult season of my career."

And finally it was Alabama 28, Auburn 17. The mission, launched in 1945 when Bryant's Maryland squad defeated Guilford College, was accomplished. The *Birmingham News* headline on Sunday, November 29, 1981, said it best: "Auburn and Stagg second to Bear."

The Alabama win was not without its dramatics, however. Auburn went ahead, 17-14, early in the fourth quarter and an upset—postponing history for a while—loomed a possibility.

Never hurried, Bama quarterback Walter Lewis marched the Tide 75 yards in seven plays for the go-ahead and stay-ahead-forever touchdown. His 38-yard scoring toss to Jesse Bendross was Lewis' sixth (and most important) touchdown

Eddie Lowe (57) congratulates fellow linebacker Robbie Jones (97) after a sack in the historic 28-17 win over Auburn.

pass of the season.

Three minutes later the 21-17 advantage was extended to the final 28-17 when Tide sophomore running back Linnie Patrick gained 47 yards of a 49-yard drive, scoring the touchdown on a twisting, churning 15-yard run that was described by Jim Goostree, Tide trainer since 1957, as "one of the best I've seen."

The best he had ever witnessed, Goostree attested, occurred only a few seconds earlier when Patrick ran over, around, and through at least six Auburn defenders for 32 yards to the Auburn 15-yard line. "In all my years at Alabama," Goostree beamed, "that run for 32 yards by Patrick was the greatest I have seen."

Even though the Tide fell behind, Eddie wasn't worried. "We weren't worried about falling behind," he said. "Auburn always played us like that. The past three years (1978-1980) were the same way. We knew what we had to do, and we did it."

The post-game celebration was one which millions heard

or read about but only a handful actually saw. Eddie was one of the lucky ones. "It was wild in the locker room," he said. "The first thing we did, though, was kneel down and Coach Bryant led us in a prayer. Then the celebration started—people were screaming and yelling. President Reagan even called and congratulated Coach Bryant.

"It was one of the biggest thrills of my life because I knew that I was a part of it all."

While Eddie was whooping it up in the locker room beneath the massive Legion Field stands, Woodrow was whooping it up more than 2,000 miles away in San Diego. Even though he watched the historic occasion on television, Woodrow felt all along like he was there.

"I jumped up and down," Woodrow exclaimed. "I was so happy for everybody involved, and I was real proud for Eddie.

"Coach Bryant surely went down in the history books. I'm sure every player that Coach Bryant has ever coached was looking at the game that day. If I could have played, I would have.

"I consider it an honor to have been associated with Coach Bryant," Woodrow continued, "and I was glad I had the opportunity to contribute to some of those 315 victories.

"Coach Bryant is a man of principle and uses it to the fullest. He's a man I'll always admire. He gave me some aspects of life that I hope to pass on down to my children."

Woodrow, Linda, and children Woodrow, Jr. (11-11-75) and Briana (10-4-79) reside in San Diego. Until 1981 the Lowes came back to Alabama during the off-season to their home in Seale, a small community a few miles southwest of Phenix City. But Woodrow, Jr., born during his daddy's senior season at Alabama, started school in the fall of 1981, and that has kept Woodrow and Linda quite a busy couple.

Eddie, meanwhile, is expected to be a big factor in the 1982 Tide defense, assuming his ailing knee has improved. He finished the 1981 season as the team's third leading tackler with 85 stops, only one less than Thomas Boyd. A Christmas Eve-day knee injury in preparation for the Tide's Cotton Bowl clash with Texas not only kept Eddie out of the game (a 14-12 loss), but he missed the entire 1982 spring training as well.

Jeff Rouzie, who left the Bama staff after the 1981 season to enter the oil business in Texas, had nothing but praise for Ed-

Prior to another classic "teacher vs. pupil" match-up, Alabama head coach Paul "Bear" Bryant chats with Auburn head coach Pat Dye. The teacher came out on top, 28-17, and became the winningest coach in collegiate football history, with Alabama family members such as Eddie Lowe adding momentum to victory.

die's performance in 1981. "I really don't know what we would have done without Eddie last (1981) season," he said. "He was the mainstay in our defense. I can think of time after time where he came up with the big play.

"The reason Eddie gets more out of himself than anybody I've seen is because of his attitude. He's got a very positive attitude about everything he tries to do. He's deeply religious and has a tremendous amount of self-confidence. Whether it's his athletic ability, or just him as a person, I have the highest respect for Eddie. He does the little extra. He never gives up."

Sylvester Croom, in his seventh year as a Tide assistant coach, inherited Rouzie's linebacker responsibilities and is counting on Eddie to keep up his steady play in 1982. "Based on what he's done in the past," Croom said in early 1982, "we're really counting on Eddie to be a big factor in our defense and in our overall play as a team.

"We feel like when he's full-speed and healthy again (after his knee heals), he will be a winner. He's one of those kind of young men that never thinks he's too good to work. He's always worked hard and has given his best.

"Eddie has an intense desire to win and be the best at whatever he does. He won't take any shortcuts, and he won't settle for anything less than his best."

Eddie hopes his "best" will one day vault him into professional football. Billy Jackson was a big hit in 1981 as a rookie with Kansas City, and he thinks his good friend Eddie can play pro ball despite his small size. "I know Eddie can play," Jackson said. "All the way back to high school Eddie's been doing things people didn't think he could. He would always tell me that because of his size 'They can knock me down, but that's not enough. They've got to knock me out.' That's the attitude he takes. Yes, I know he can play pro ball."

Eddie doesn't expect to be drafted, but he hopes to walk on with some team and do his best. "I try to be dedicated in what I do," Eddie said. "Woodrow told me to keep the Lord in front of me and not worry about my size.

"I feel that if it's God's will, I'll play pro ball. The main thing I want to do is believe in His word, and I know everything will work out. Whether it's good or bad, I always thank Him. He's first in my life."

So far in life everything has "worked out" quite well for both Eddie and Woodrow. Woodrow's dream of playing professional football and Eddie's dream to play football at Alabama are being fulfilled.

And no matter how many times the date November 28, 1981, or the number "315" is mentioned, Woodrow and Eddie equally share a place in football history.

Epilog:
A Farewell To Bryant

The atmosphere on the campus of the University of Alabama was a bit uneasy on the morning of January 26, 1983. The night before, Alabamians had been startled by the news that University of Alabama athletic director and head football coach Paul "Bear" Bryant was admitted to Druid City Hospital complaining of chest pains. His condition on this cool Wednesday morning, however, had improved, and Bryant fans were resting easier. For years Bryant's trips to the hospital were highly publicized, most being routine checkups. No one thought this one to be any different, but as always there remained a bit of uneasiness.

After all, Bryant *was* University of Alabama football. Despite his crediting the players and assistant coaches as the reasons for Alabama's unparalleled success, everyone—including those players and assistants—would say that it was, without a doubt, Bryant's show.

His was a theatrical masterpiece in which he picked the characters, the costumes, and the stage. He directed the readings, practices, dress rehearsals, and, ultimately, the play itself. For 25 years he received rave reviews; so many, in fact, that his audiences didn't know how to react when one of his characters missed a line or stumbled over a stage prop. Bryant's plays were performed Off Broadway, On Broadway, and everywhere in between. People kept coming back for more; standing ovations were as much a part of Bryant football as for a Broadway smash hit.

Bryant often said that winning wasn't everything, but it sure beat anything that came in second. Alabama fans were accustomed to this philosophy, and any change from the norm, such as a Bryant visit to the hospital, was cause for concern. Bryant's presence, or the thought of his presence, always offered an extra sense of security to Alabamians over the years— like a warm quilt on a cold night.

Shortly after 2:00 p.m. on this Wednesday afternoon, a shocking bulletin came over the radio. Bert Bank, owner of WTBC radio station in Tuscaloosa, reported from Druid City Hospital that Coach Bryant had taken a turn for the worse at 12:24 p.m. and had suffered a massive heart attack. Efforts by a team of 10 doctors and nurses to revive the 69-year-old legend had failed. At 1:30 p.m. CST, the winningest coach in college football history was pronounced dead.

Only six weeks after announcing his retirement and only four weeks after winning his last game, Coach Paul "Bear" Bryant was dead. He died before he had the chance to do all those things Alabama football kept him from through the years. Bryant's death cast a shadow of gloom across the country that idolized him as college football's all-time winner.

Bryant's final season at Alabama, by his own standards, was disappointing. An 8-4 mark, a goal for many schools, was (and will always be) frowned upon at Alabama. And it was Bryant himself who led the frowners, all the way to hanging up his houndstooth hat following the December 29 Liberty Bowl.

After wins over Georgia Tech, Ole Miss, Vanderbilt, and Arkansas State, the Tide's first big test came on October 9 against Penn State at Birmingham's Legion Field. The Nittany Lions were looking for revenge from the 1981 Tide victory... and the 1979 Sugar Bowl...and the 1975 Sugar Bowl. The matchup was a battle of highly-ranked, unbeaten squads playing in front of a national television audience.

Following the game, Penn State was still searching for that revenge. The Tide broke open a close contest by scoring 18 points in the final quarter to bury the Lions, 42-21. People were calling this Tide squad possibly the best ever.

From that point on, the fortunes of Penn State and Alabama went in entirely opposite directions. The Nittany Lions, paced by the heroics of quarterback Todd Blackledge and running back Curt Warner, blitzed through the remainder of their schedule without a loss, then defeated the SEC champion

Georgia Bulldogs in the Sugar Bowl to win the 1982 national championship.

Alabama, on the other hand, fell flat on its face. The schedule did not end after the Penn State game, but many Tide fans wished it had; the "quit-while-you're-ahead" thought. In the next six games, the Crimsons defeated only Cincinnati and Mississippi State. Losses to SEC rivals Tennessee, LSU, and Auburn ended the Tide's decade-old dominance of those teams. Even the thought-to-be-unbreakable winning streak of 57 straight games at Bryant-Denny Stadium was snapped by the Southern Mississippi Golden Eagles. The sub-par season took its toll on Alabama fans, players, assistant coaches....and *the* coach, Paul "Bear" Bryant.

Following the 20-10 loss to LSU, Bryant shocked everyone by stating that "some changes ought to be made at the top (of the football program), and I'm at the top." He had said something very similar following the 1969 season, but this time he insisted he was serious. When asked if this meant he was considering retirement, Bryant replied, "I'll do anything it takes to get something done, to improve, to get better."

Very few people took Bryant seriously, but rumors of his retirement continued to fly throughout the remainder of the season. Almost everyone thought he would coach one more year and close out his career at the state-required retirement age of 70. No one actually expected what was to happen less than three weeks later.

What were to be the routine late-night television newscasts on Tuesday, December 14, 1982, suddenly changed when the Associated Press reported that the following morning Coach Bryant would announce his retirement and be succeeded by former Alabama All-American and current New York Giants head coach Ray Perkins. The report became the lead news story in Alabama and the lead sports story throughout the nation.

The following morning, December 15, 1982, the winningest coach in college football did, indeed, announce his retirement after 25 glorious years at the Tide helm. Dressed in a bright red sport coat and accompanied by University of Alabama president Joab Thomas, Bryant took the podium and stated his reasons for stepping down.

"There comes a time in every profession when you need to hang it up and that time has come for me as head football coach at the University of Alabama," Bryant stated. "My main purpose as Director of Athletics and Head Football Coach here at Alabama has been to field the best possible teams, to improve each player as a person and to produce citizens who will be a credit to our present day society.

"We have been successful in most of those areas, but now, I feel the time is right for a change in our football leadership...."

Bryant took all the blame for the four losses and said he had "done a poor job of coaching." He said the players "deserved better coaching than they've been getting," and that his stepping down was "an effort to see that they get better coaching from someone else."

The "someone else" Bryant referred to was none other than Walter Ray Perkins, who was simultaneously holding a press conference in New York announcing his resignation as head coach of the National Football League's New York Giants. "I'm following—I repeat—following the greatest coach in college football," Perkins stated. "I'm merely following the man. I'm just the next guy after him, that's all. I just hope I can come close to carrying on the tradition that he has established and maintained."

If anyone would have known about that Alabama tradition, it was Ray Perkins. Born in Mount Olive, Mississippi, and raised in Petal, Mississippi, Perkins came to the University of Alabama in the fall of 1962 as an All-American halfback from Petal High School. After a head injury forced him to redshirt in 1963, Perkins came back and made a big contribution as a wide receiver to Alabama's 1964 and 1965 national championship squads, and the undefeated, untied, and unrewarded 1966 team.

All-America and All-SEC honors came during his junior and senior seasons, and in 1967 Perkins was drafted in the seventh round by the NFL's Baltimore Colts. He spent five seasons with the Colts as a receiver for Johnny Unitas, playing in two NFL title games and Super Bowl appearances.

After a knee injury cut short his professional career, Perkins coached one year at Mississippi State, four years with the New England Patriots, and one year as offensive coor-

In a surprise move on Wednesday, December 15, 1982, University of Alabama President Joab Thomas (left) and Coach Paul "Bear" Bryant announced Bryant's retirement as head football coach. At the same time, Thomas announced that Bryant would be succeeded by former Tide All-American and current New York Giants head coach, Ray Perkins.

dinator of the San Diego Chargers.

Perkins' coaching talents were rapidly becoming noticed around the NFL, and in early 1979 the New York Giants gave him a call. He accepted what many call the most lucrative coaching job in America and in only three seasons accomplished what no other Giants coach had been able to do in the previous 18 years—lead the club to the NFL playoffs. Giants fans were amazed, and suddenly Perkins was the toast of New York.

From a 4-12 record in 1980 (after going 6-10 in his first season) he led the Giants to a 9-7 record and the playoffs in 1981, and a 4-5 record in the strike-shortened 1982 season. But before the 1982 season even ended, Perkins accepted the call from "momma," in a way similar to Coach Bryant's acceptance in late 1957.

And when "momma" called, Perkins was ready. The New York media, however, couldn't quite understand the change.

260

"When I took the job I guess they all thought I was crazy," Perkins said. "There I was taking this huge pay cut to go back and coach my alma mater.

"What they didn't seem to understand was that I was answering my heart. To me, being a success is doing what I want to do. It's not measured by how much money I make. And this is something I've wanted to do. It's been in the back of my mind for four or five years.

"I knew that it would somehow work out—I didn't know how—but I felt it would. Somewhere, a long time ago, I knew Carolyn [Perkins' wife] and I would work our way back there. I'm looking at it as a once-in-a-lifetime opportunity. I'm happy it worked out like it did. I'm more excited now than I've been in the 41 years of my life. I'm honored they selected me."

The new—and the old. Ray Perkins and Coach Paul "Bear" Bryant, together for their first press conference, answer questions from reporters. Only five days earlier Perkins had been hired to succeed Bryant as head football coach.

Ray Perkins (88) leaves behind a helpless Nebraska defender in the Tide's 34-7 victory in the 1967 Sugar Bowl. Sixteen years later Perkins was named to succeed Paul Bryant as University of Alabama head football coach.

"They" were a five-man search committee appointed by University President Joab Thomas to name a successor to the retiring Coach Bryant. Other members besides Dr. Thomas were University trustees Winton "Red" Blount of Montgomery and Ernest Williams of Tuscaloosa; Faculty Chairman of Athletics Dr. Charley Scott; and Dr. Gaylon McCollough of Birmingham, a former player under Bryant and teammate of Perkins. Seven men were interviewed for the job, four of those on the current Alabama staff.

On Thursday, December 9, 1982, Dr. Thomas called Perkins and asked him to fly down and speak with the committee. After receiving permission from Giants management, Perkins flew to Birmingham on Sunday, December 12, to talk with the search committee. The next day, after the committee's decision had been made, Dr. Thomas called Perkins and offered him the job. The following day, December 14, Perkins accepted the job and on Wednesday, December 15, the official announcement was made. Ray Perkins was Alabama's new head man.

The night before, many people had heard the news reports concerning Bryant's expected retirement, but no one, not even the Tide coaches and players, knew it for sure until early Wednesday morning. "I heard it on the late news Tuesday night and it shocked me," said linebacker Eddie Lowe, the Tide's leading tackler in 1982. "Still, I thought it was just a rumor because we had heard it so many times throughout the season.

"When I went downstairs for a snack I saw a notice posted on the bulletin board saying we had a meeting the next morning at 7:15 with Coach Bryant. When I saw that, I knew it must be true because we were in the middle of final exams and we wouldn't have otherwise been meeting at that time of the day.

"I felt like Coach Bryant thought it was best for the University for him to retire. And you sure couldn't hold that against him. I hated to see him do it, because I wanted him to win as many games as he could. His retiring really got us fired up for the Liberty Bowl. We wanted to win the last one for him."

"Win one for the Bear" became the theme of the 1982 Liberty Bowl against Illinois. Twenty-four years after beginning his bowl career at Philadelphia's Liberty Bowl, Bryant was coincidentally returning to the same bowl, since moved to Memphis, to end his celebrated career. What would have normally been a routine, but less than glamorous appearance by the Tide, turned into the most important sports event of the year. Many were calling it "the biggest story in Memphis since Elvis died."

Nearly 300 media requests for the game poured in from all over the nation, so many in fact that former Bryant aide Charley Thornton, since moved to Texas A&M as associate athletic director, was called in to help with the barrage. Bryant, naturally, was the center of attention.

Vowing to end the season on a positive note, make up for three straight losses, and of course "win one for the Bear," the Alabama Crimson Tide fought off several Fighting Illini charges in the game's waning moments to capture a thrilling 21-15 victory. The mission was accomplished—Coach Paul "Bear" Bryant bowed out in style by winning his final game, ending a career of 323 wins, 85 losses, and 17 ties. His 232-46-9 record at his alma mater translates into a remarkable 82.3 percent winning record.

A relieved Bryant met with hundreds of reporters after the game. "The players won in spite of me," he said, repeating the cliche probably for the 323rd time since he began his head coaching career in 1945. "Before the game I told the players that whether they liked it or not, people were always going to remember them for this game because of the circumstances. I was flattered they wanted to win one for me, but I told them I

The winningest coach in college football history, Paul "Bear" Bryant, is carried off the field after a 21-15 victory over Illinois in the 1982 Liberty Bowl. The win marked Bryant's 323rd win as a head coach, and his 232nd victory at his alma mater. Only four weeks later Bryant would die of a massive heart attack.

wanted them to win it for themselves, because they were the ones that were going to have to live with it.

"After the game I told them how proud I was for them. And I'm proud of them not just for tonight but for many other games through the years. Our players came back and played hard and showed some class."

Bryant's final game, attended by a bowl record 54,123 fans and seen by an estimated 50 million television viewers across the nation and around the world on the Armed Forces Network, was indeed a living tribute to the man who had devoted so many years of his life to football and the University of Alabama.

Even though Bryant had passed the Alabama football reins

over to Perkins, he announced his staying on as the school's athletic director. During Liberty Bowl week in Memphis Bryant hinted he would probably leave the position before the 1983 football season so he "wouldn't interfere." Perkins was very much looking forward to working with Coach Bryant and calling on him for advice. He never really got the chance.

Three weeks after Perkins went to work as the University's 20th football coach, Bryant passed away in Tuscaloosa's Druid City Hospital. The news came as such a shock to everyone because earlier in the morning Bryant was described by his cardiologist, Dr. William Hill, as "in good spirits, joking with the nurses, and free of pain."

According to Hill and to most everyone's surprise, Bryant had experienced "serious health problems" for the previous three years, including a stroke in 1980 which required frequent medication. "I think his accomplishments and the record he achieved the last few years—and personally knowing the difficulty he worked under—makes his achievement all the more remarkable," Hill said. "He was a very courageous man. I doubt there are many people who could have overcome what he did in the last three years to accomplish the feat Paul Bryant did."

Even though Bryant frequently said he would "croak in a week" if he ever quit coaching, Dr. Hill did not blame Bryant's death on his retirement. "I don't think the pressures of his retirement contributed to the heart attack," he said. "He had been free of pressures lately. He was looking forward to hunting trips, recreational trips. The coach was fully 69 years old—certainly not a young man."

Tributes for "The Coach" poured in from across the nation. President Ronald Reagan said Americans had "lost a hero who always seemed larger than life—a coach who made legends out of ordinary people." Former president Gerald Ford called Bryant a "superstar in the history of American football." Ford continued by saying "his achievements have been indelibly written in the history of American sports."

Dr. Tim Davis, Tide placekicker from 1961 to 1963 and now a Birmingham physician, spoke of Bryant's impact on people. "He was a man who meant so much to so many people," Davis said. "He gave us such an example to follow. The things he believed in and practiced were the things he taught to give us a good start in life. He epitomized everything success was. Even now, I feel he's looking over my shoulder. When you've done something good, and someone says, 'Coach Bryant would be proud of you,' I say, 'Coach Bryant would have expected it of me.' You never thought anything else."

Charley Thornton, longtime Bryant aide and now associate athletic director at Texas A&M, called Bryant "more than just a football coach; more than just a friend. I think the nation lost a legend in the same mold as John Wayne or George Patton. He taught living and how to handle moments like this (Bryant's death). Anybody can get by when things are going good but he taught you how to reach down and get that little something extra. He took a whole lot of us when we were still children and made men out of us."

Lee Roy Jordan and Paul Crane were two of Bryant's favorite players. Their love for the man is evident. "He was like a second father to me, to all of us," Jordan said. "Coach Bryant was far more than just a great football coach. He stressed character, honesty, and integrity, and he instilled in you the ability to fulfill your potential as a player and a person. This was the basis his program was built around. He had an unparalleled ability to get a group of people to make a commitment to working toward a goal and then unifying them for a 100 percent performance."

Crane philosophically assessed Bryant as "kind of like a big rock out there in the ocean of life. He could always be counted on. If you were hanging at the end of a rope over the edge of a cliff, he'd always be the one you'd call first. There was never a time when I'd call him and ask for assistance and not get it."

Many of Bryant's fiercest rivals—past and present— heaped praise on the man very few of them were ever able to defeat. "Wherever he coached," said former Georgia Tech head coach Bobby Dodd, "he elevated the standards of both his program and those who had to play against him. You had to get better to compete with his teams. The success the SEC has enjoyed for the past 20 years is a credit to Paul Bryant."

Auburn's Pat Dye, a Bryant assistant for nine years and the last coach to defeat Bryant, remarked "it is very evident what Coach Bryant meant to me, the game of football, and to the lives of so many people he has touched through the years. His presence made this world a better place to live. He was like all great people who have come through American history—though he may be gone, his teachings will last forever in the lives of those he touched. He received recognition for the games he won and the honors he received, but the greatest thing about him was the many things he did for people that no one knew about."

LSU head coach Jerry Stovall called Bryant's death "an irreparable loss to athletics and to America. Coach Bryant as a man influenced more young men as players and coaches than any man who ever touched the game. We all suffered a great loss in his death, but we were blessed for 69 years with his presence."

Alabama Governor George C. Wallace, saying Bryant "brought great fame and honor to Alabama," ordered all flags in the state to be flown at half mast. University President Joab Thomas was on a business trip in Australia and upon hearing the news of Bryant's death said, "The entire University community, the state of Alabama, and indeed, the country grieve at this shocking and terrible loss. It is impossible for me to fully convey what Paul Bryant meant to this institution and the innumerable contributions he made to the lives of everyone he encountered. He was more than the finest coach who ever lived. He was a great teacher, a great man and a dear personal friend. Our hearts go out in deepest sympathy to his family." Dr. Thomas added later that the news of Bryant's death was reported in Australia's major newspapers.

The day after the coach's death, more than 6,000 teary-eyed students, faculty, staff, and friends of the University attended a service in Memorial Coliseum to pay their tributes to the great legend. Thousands more passed through Hayes Funeral Home in Tuscaloosa to catch a glimpse of the carnation-covered casket. Members of the Bryant family, their friends, and former and present coaches graciously greeted the visitors. Many people, some having never met the man, filed in—and out—in total silence. Even the weather—dark and damp—matched the feelings of everyone.

The funeral, held on Friday morning, January 28, 1983,

Coach Paul "Bear" Bryant's funeral procession began in Tuscaloosa and ended at Birmingham's Elmwood Cemetery. An estimated 500,000 to 700,000 persons witnessed either the funeral, the three-mile-long procession, or the graveside services.

will be written and talked about for years to come. An estimated 500,000 to 700,000 people witnessed either the funeral, procession, or graveside services. Downtown Tuscaloosa's First United Methodist Church was the site for the funeral services with the overflow listening from within nearby First Baptist and First Presbyterian Churches.

Hundreds of former players and coaches—their names reading like a "Who's Who" in college football—attended. Among Bryant's former players were Lee Roy Jordan, John David Crow, Joe Namath, Barry Krauss, Richard Todd, Jackie Sherrill, Marty Lyons, Billy Neighbors, Bill Battle, and Gary Rutledge. All 10 Southeastern Conference head coaches— Emory Bellard, Billy Brewer, Jerry Claiborne, Pat Dye, Vince Dooley, George MacIntyre, Johnny Majors, Charley Pell, Ray Perkins, and Jerry Stovall—were in attendance, as well as many of their assistants.

George Allen, former Washington Redskins head coach, represented President Reagan. Retired coaches John Vaught, Woody Hayes, Bud Wilkinson, Darrell Royal, Frank Broyles, Bobby Dodd, Charlie McLendon, and Duffy Daugherty as well as current Bryant "pupil" coaches Danny Ford, Howard Schnellenberger, Steve Sloan, Jim Fuller, and Bill Oliver all paid their last tributes to the man who had taught them so much—not just about football, but about life.

The funeral service was short and simple with only one eulogy delivered by Reverend Joe Elmore, pastor of the First United Methodist Church. Eight Crimson Tide players— Tommy Wilcox, Paul Carruth, Walter Lewis, Jerrill Sprinkle, Mike McQueen, Paul Fields, Jeremiah Castille, and Darryl White—served as active pallbearers. News representatives from all over the nation including the *New York Times*, the *Chicago Tribune*, Cable News Network, ABC, CBS, and NBC watched as the services came to a close and the 300-car procession began.

Thousands of spectators lined Tenth Street, five and six deep, from downtown Tuscaloosa to McFarland Boulevard. Homemade signs and posters indicated the spectators' love and admiration for Bryant. A group of children had roped off some steps at Calvary Baptist Church. Their sign was simple and to the point—"Reserved for Little Friends." The University community, walking past buildings draped in black, turned out in

Active pallbearers for Coach Bryant's funeral were (clockwise from bottom): Mike McQueen, Paul Fields, Jeremiah Castille, Darryl White, Tommy Wilcox, Paul Carruth, Walter Lewis, and Jerrill Sprinkle. Honorary pallbearers were the remaining members of the 1982 Alabama team.

droves. As the procession passed two of the university's most popular landmarks—Bryant-Denny Stadium and Memorial Coliseum—tears fell from the eyes of onlookers. "Goodbye, Coach, we love you," the sign read as a man held his fist high in the air.

Six Greyhound buses of former and current players and coaches, visiting dignitaries, and friends of the Bryant family headed the procession onto McFarland Boulevard towards Interstate 59. Schoolchildren waved American flags. Traffic on both sides came to a complete standstill. One youngster held up a sign saying "God needed an offensive coordinator."

The entourage moved onto Interstate 59 towards Birmingham. Truckdrivers, normally on a tight schedule, parked their rigs on the side of the road and showed total respect for a man they probably knew very little about. Fans dressed in red and white and with index fingers pointing upwards held signs saying "You'll always be number one in our hearts." Every overpass along the 60-mile route was packed with people. Construction workers on an unfinished overpass near Birmingham held their hardhats to their hearts. A rough piece of plywood painted with green spraypaint said it all: "Bear, we love you and will miss you."

The crowds swelled as the three-mile-long procession moved closer to Elmwood Cemetery in Birmingham. Some 5,000 persons were already waiting at the cemetery, many since the early morning hours. The number zoomed to near 10,000 once the services began. Alabama State Troopers and City of Birmingham Police tried in vain to keep back the crowds. Helicopters hovered above the outskirts of the cemetery, heeding the Bryant family's request not to fly over the burial site during the services. A ban on cameras was also requested, but could not be enforced. It was just too big of an event.

The actual ceremony, conducted by Reverends Joe Elmore, Joe Raines, and Duncan Hunter, lasted only 10 minutes. After reading Psalms 100 and the eighth chapter of Romans, the thousands were led in recitals of the 23rd Psalm and the Lord's Prayer. Family members, including Coach Bryant's wife Mary Harmon and children Paul Bryant, Jr., and Mrs. Mae Martin Tyson, headed back to their automobiles while friends offered condolences.

Hundreds remained to watch the casket lowered, the grave filled, and the thousands of mostly red and white flowers arranged upon the gravesite. Giant floral wreaths in the shape of Bryant's famous houndstooth hat and the letter "A" were prominent along with those arrangements in the colors of several rival Southeastern Conference schools. Birmingham cemetery officials estimated that 100,000 persons throughout the weekend visited Elmwood Cemetery's Block 30, Lot 57-126, the final resting place for a man known as *Poppa* to his family, *Paul* to his closest friends, *Coach* to his players and associates, and *the Bear* to his millions of followers.

The Bryant family was so touched by all the visible support and affection that Paul Bryant, Jr. appeared on statewide television expressing his family's thanks. "The display of affection towards Poppa that we witnessed today was both touching and comforting and not one of us will forget it," he said. "We were particularly touched by the thousands of people along the motorcade route from First United Methodist Church in Tuscaloosa to the Elmwood Cemetery in Birmingham. All of those people, young and old, made us more aware of the love relationship Poppa had with Alabama."

Tributes and requests for moments of silence spread throughout the land. On the night after the funeral UCLA head football coach Terry Donahue asked the hometown Pauley Pavilion basketball crowd and a CBS national television audience for a moment of silence in memory of Coach Bryant. The Tide basketball team, wearing black shoulder patches, rose to the occasion and "won one for the Bear" by knocking off the top-ranked Bruins, 70-67. Two days later millions watched and listened as a tribute for the Coach was spoken at Super Bowl XVII in Pasadena. Five of Bryant's former players—Miami's Bob Baumhower, Don McNeal, Tony Nathan, and Dwight Stephenson; and Washington's Wilbur Jackson—were involved in the 27-17 Redskins victory. On Thursday, February 3, University President Joab Thomas announced plans for the university to build an $11 million facility in honor of Bryant, naming it the "Paul W. Bryant Center." Designed to house offices for continuing education and alumni activities, and the Paul W. Bryant Museum, the Center had Bryant's full approval before his death, according to

Dr. Thomas.

Coach Bryant was a big influence on many of the "family" members in *BAMA UNDER BEAR: Alabama's Family Tides*, none perhaps more than Billy Neighbors. "Coach Bryant's death was like my own father died," said Neighbors, a 1983 inductee into the Alabama Sports Hall of Fame. "I don't think I'll feel the shock for years to come. He played such a role in my life.

"I didn't have a father while I was at Alabama and Coach Bryant knew it. He knew where I came from and the difficulties my family had. Our upbringings were very similar and he knew... and understood. We became friends. I truly loved that man."

Billy's son Wes was one of 17 Alabama freshmen (out of a class of 21) redshirted in 1982. "Yes, of course I was disappointed I didn't get to play under Coach Bryant," Wes said. "For years he meant so much to our family. Growing up, that's all I heard my father talk about, and of course I wanted to play under Coach Bryant. I hope I was able to contribute to Coach Bryant's last team by being out there at practice every day. But I realize his decision to redshirt me was for the best. I'll have a better chance to play later because of it. I'm excited about Coach Perkins coming in and carrying on the Alabama tradition."

Wes Neighbors is not the only one excited about the University's future football fortunes. But one thing is for sure—Coach Paul "Bear" Bryant will surely be missed. His retiring as head coach was a tremendous display of unselfishness and loyalty to his university. He felt the program was on the downswing, and claimed it was his fault.

For years rival schools in their recruiting talks had used Bryant's eventual retirement as a knock against Alabama. Bryant did not want this to continue, so instead of "coaching forever" (as he said many times he would), he stepped down, laying the foundation for Ray Perkins to carry on the Alabama tradition.

If there was any consolation in Bryant's retirement, it was found when he announced he would be staying on as athletic director. But before he could even get his shotgun out of the closet, or crank up the boat for a much-loved fishing trip, the Coach passed away, leaving a void that will never fully be filled.

For years to come Bryant's standards will be the ones by which all others are measured and compared. First and foremost, his record of 323 wins is one of the most remarkable in football history, and may never be broken. His six national championships at Alabama, the numerous All-American and All-Conference players he produced, the list of some 45 of his pupils that went on to become head coaches...the string of accomplishments goes on and on.

Of course Bryant never took the credit for any of those 323 wins. The glory was always reserved for the players, and, as Bryant said many times, "their mommas and poppas, their girlfriends, their high school teachers, etc." Bryant stayed in touch with so many of those players, always available when they needed him. It was like one big happy "family," with Bryant playing the father role.

Two days after retiring, Bryant wrote a letter to several members of his "family." Dennis Homan, a teammate of Ray Perkins and All-SEC selection in 1965 and 1966, was one of the players who received the letter. Homan allowed the *Tuscaloosa News* to print the letter in its January 27, 1983, edition. The letter:

Dear Dennis,

As I contemplate my many years as a football coach during the post-retirement period, it is not surprising that my former players and my former associates are the first people that come to my mind. Since you are one of those people, I want to personally thank you for the contributions you have made to my happy, rewarding career.

Also, I want to tell you how proud I am of you and I want to challenge you to become an even bigger winner in life.

Frankly, I am sometimes embarrassed by the accolades that have been given to me, because never is enough said about the people who worked so hard for me, individuals like you.

I will always count you as a member of my football family, and I eagerly await the construction of a museum being constructed in your honor on the

274

campus of the University of Alabama.

Again, thanks and may all of your future days prove successful.

Sincerely,
Paul Bryant

P.S.
Mary Harmon sends her love to you both.

The contents of that letter is what Coach Bryant was all about. He was, in fact, the greatest coach in the history of college football. Americans of all ages, races, and classes looked up to him as one who molded boys into men; men into greater men. It has been said that Coach Bryant did not coach football— he coached people. Football was just the means by which he taught these people; a gift from God that no one else used as well as he did.

Many of Coach Bryant's contributions to football will not be noticed until 10, 15, or even 20 years down the road. Perhaps Grambling head football coach Eddie Robinson summed it up best: "As long as they kick the ball off," he said, "there will always be some of Coach Bryant's philosophy in the game."

And one of Coach Bryant's most famous contributions— Ray Perkins—has been given the challenging task of continuing the Alabama winning tradition. Bryant will forever be a big influence on Perkins—whether it be in his coaching style or lifestyle. "Coach Bryant, for those associated with him, was much more than just a genius with the Xs and Os," Perkins stated. "He was one of a kind.

"And when history looks back, I think what he's contributed to society will make it an even greater tribute to the man. Just how much he will be missed probably won't be felt for quite a while to come."

Appendix

UNIVERSITY OF ALABAMA FOOTBALL LETTERMEN
UNDER COACH PAUL "BEAR" BRYANT

Since the University of Alabama fielded its first football team in 1892, some 1,171 lettermen have earned their places in Crimson Tide football history. The late Coach Paul "Bear" Bryant was at the University for only 25 of those 88 years, yet nearly half (576) of all lettermen played under Coach Bryant. Below is a list of these 576 lettermen. The order of information is name, position, hometown (at that time), and years lettered. If a player earned first-team All-America status, it is indicated with an asterisk (*) before his name. If he was All-Southeastern Conference (All-SEC), it is listed after his name. The following information required many, many hours of research by the University of Alabama Sports Publicity Office, the Alumni Office, the Gorgas Library, Mr. Jeff Coleman, and many others.

A

ADCOCK, Mike (OT)
 Huntsville, Ala., 1981-82
ABBRUZZESE, Raymond (HB)
 Philadelphia, Pa., 1960-61
ADKINSON, Wayne (HB)
 Dothan, Ala., 1970-71-72
ALLEN, Charles G. (T)
 Athens, Ala., 1957-58-59
ALLEN, Steve (G)
 Athens, Ala., 1961-62-63
ALLISON, Scott (OT)
 Titusville, Fla., 1978-79-80
ALLMAN, Phil (DB)
 Birmingham, Ala., 1976-77-78
ANDREWS, Mickey (HB)
 Ozark, Ala., 1963-64
AYDELETTE, William Leslie
 "Buddy" (TE)
 Mobile, Ala., 1977-78-79

B

BAILEY, David (SE) All-SEC
 Bailey, Miss., 1969-70-71

BARNES, Ronnie Joe (DE)
 Abbeville, Ala. 1973-74
BARNES, WILEY (C)
 Marianna, Fla., 1978-79
BARRON, Marvin (G-T)
 Troy, Ala., 1970-71-73
BARRON, Randy (DT)
 Dadeville, Ala., 1966-67-68
BATES, TIM (LB)
 Tarrant, Ala., 1964-65
BATEY, Joseph Dwight "Bo"
 (OG)
 Jacksonville, Ala., 1976
BATTLE, Wm. "Bill" (E)
 Birmingham, Ala., 1960-61-62
BAUMHOWER, Robert Glenn
 (DT) All-SEC
 Tuscaloosa, Ala., 1974-75-76
BEAN, Dickie (HB)
 Childersburg, Ala., 1966
BEARD, Jeff (DT)
 Bessemer, Ala., 1969-70-71
BEARD, Ken (T)
 Bessemer, Ala., 1963
BEAZLEY, Joe (DT)
 Woodbridge, Va., 1979-80-81-82

BECK, Ellis (HB)
 Ozark, Ala., 1971-72-73
BEDDINGFIELD, David (QB)
 Gadsden, Ala., 1969
BEDWELL, David (DB)
 Cedar Bluff, Ala., 1965-66-67
BELL, Stanley (E)
 West Anniston, Ala., 1959
BENDROSS, Jesse (SE)
 Hollywood, Fla., 1980-81-82
BENTLEY, Edward K., Jr. (DB)
 Sylacauga, Ala., 1970
BERREY, Fred Benjamin
 "Bucky" (K)
 Montgomery, Ala., 1974-75-76
BILLINGSLEY, Randy (HB)
 Sylacauga, Ala., 1972-73-74
BIRD, Ron (T)
 Covington, Ky., 1963
BISCEGLIA, Steve (FB)
 Fresno, Calif., 1971-72
BLAIR, Bill (DB)
 Nashville, Tenn., 1968-69-70
BLEVINS, James Allen (T)
 Moulton, Ala., 1957-58-59
BLITZ, Jeff (DB)
 Montgomery, Ala., 1972

BLUE, Al (DB)
  Maitland, Fla., 1981-82
BOLDEN, Ray (DB)
  Tarrant, Ala., 1974-75
BOLER, Clark (T)
  Northport, Ala., 1962-63
BOLER, Thomas (OT)
  Northport, Ala., 1980
BOLES, John "Duffy" (HB)
  Huntsville, Ala., 1973-75
BOLTON, Bruce (SE)
  Memphis, Tenn., 1976-77-78
BOOKER, David (SE)
  Huntsville, Ala., 1979
BOOKER, Steve (LB)
  Huntsville, Ala., 1981-82
BOOTH, Baxter (E)
  Athens, Ala., 1956-57-58
BOOTHE, Vince (OG)
  Fairhope, Ala., 1977-78-79
BOSCHUNG, Paul (DT)
  Tuscaloosa, Ala., 1967-68-69
BOWMAN, Steve (FB) All-Sec
  Pascagoula, Miss., 1963-64-65
BOX, Jimmy (E)
  Sheffield, Ala., 1960
★ BOYD, Thomas (LB) All-SEC
  Huntsville, Ala., 1978-79-80-81
BOYLSTON, Robert W. "Bobby"
  (T)
  Atlanta, Ga., 1959-60
BRADFORD, James J. "Jim"
  (OG)
  Montgomery, Ala., 1977
BRAGAN, Dale (LB)
  Birmingham, Ala., 1976
BRAGGS, Bryon (DT) All-SEC
  Montgomery, Ala.,
  1977-78-79-80
BRAMBLETT, Gary (OG)
  Dalton, Ga., 1979-80-81-82
BRANNEN, Jere Lamar (E)
  Anniston, Ala., 1957-58
BREWER, Richard (SE)
  Sylacauga, Ala., 1965-66-67
BRITT, Gary (LB)
  Mobile, Ala., 1977
BROCK, Jim (OG)
  Montgomery, Ala., 1981
BROCK, Mike (OG) All-SEC
  Montgomery, Ala., 1977-78-79
BROOKER, Johnny (K)
  Demopolis, Ala., 1982
BROOKER, Wm. T. "Tommy" (E)
  Demopolis, Ala., 1959-60-61
BROWN, Bill (DB)
  Dekalb, Miss., 1982

★ BROWN, Halver "Buddy" (G)
  All-SEC
  Tallahassee, Fla., 1971-72-73
BROWN, Jerry (TE)
  Fairfax, Ala., 1974-75
BROWN, Larry (TE)
  Pembroke Pines, Fla.,
  1979-80-81-82
BROWN, Randy (T)
  Scottsville, N.Y., 1968
BRUNGARD, David A. (FB)
  Youngstown, Ohio 1970
BRYAN, Richard (DT)
  Verona, N.J., 1972-74
BUCHANAN, Richard Woodruff
  "Woody" (FB)
  Montgomery, Ala., 1976
BUCK, Oran (K)
  Oak Ridge, Tenn., 1969
★ BUNCH, Jim (OG) All-SEC
  Mechanicsville, Va.,
  1976-77-78-79
BUSBEE, Kent (DB)
  Meridian, Miss., 1967
BUSBY, Max (OG)
  Leeds, Ala., 1977
BUTLER, Clyde (OT)
  Scottsboro, Ala., 1970

C

CALLAWAY, Neil (LB-DE)
  Macon, Ga., 1975-77
CALLIES, Kelly (DT)
  Fairhope, Ala., 1977
CALVERT, John (G) All-SEC
  Cullman, Ala., 1965-66
CANTERBURY, Frank (HB)
  Birmingham, Ala., 1964-65-66
CARROLL, Jimmy (C)
  Enterprise, Ala., 1965-66
CARRUTH, Paul Ott (RB)
  Summit, Miss., 1981-82
CARTER, Joe (RB)
  Starkville, Miss., 1980-81-82
CARY, Robert H., Jr.
  "Robin" (DB)
  Greenwood, S.C. 1972-73
CASH, Jeraull Wayne "Jerry"
  (E)
  Bogart, Ga., 1970-71
CASH, Steve (LD)
  Huntsville, Ala., 1980
★ CASTILLE, Jeremiah (DB)
  All-SEC
  Phenix City, Ala., 1979-80-81-82
CAVAN, Peter Alexander (HB)
  Thomaston, Ga., 1975-76-77

CAYAVEC, Bob (OT)
  All-SEC
  Largo, Fla., 1980-81-82
CHAFFIN, Phil (FB)
  Huntsville, Ala., 1968-69-70
CHAMBERS, Jimmy (C)
  Fort Payne, Ala., 1967
CHAPMAN, Roger (K)
  Hartselle, Ala., 1977-78
CHATWOOD, David (FB)
  Fairhope, Ala., 1965-66-67
CHILDERS, Morris (B)
  Birmingham, Ala., 1960
CHILDS, Bob (LB)
  Montgomery, Ala., 1966-67-68
CIEMNY, Richard (K)
  Anthony, Kans., 1969-70
CLARK, Cotton (HB)
  Kansas, Ala., 1961-62
CLARK Tim (SE)
  Newnan, Ga., 1978-79-80-81
CLAY, Hugh Stephen (G)
  Gadsden, Ala., 1969
CLEMENTS, Mike (DB)
  Center Point, Ala., 1978-79-80
CLINE, Jackie (DT)
  McCalla, Ala., 1980-81-82
COCHRAN, Donald G. (G)
  Birmingham, Ala., 1957-58-59
COKELY, Donald (T)
  Chickasha, Okla., 1970-71
COLBURN, Rocky (DB)
  Cantonment, Fla., 1982
★ COLE, Richard (DT)
  Crossville, Ala., 1964-65
COLEMAN, Michael (SE)
  Anaheim, Ca., 1978
COLEY, Ken (DB)
  Birmingham, Ala., 1979-80-81-82
COLLINS, Danny (DE)
  Birmingham, Ala., 1976-77
COLLINS, Earl (FB)
  Mobile, Ala., 1980-81
COOK, Elbert (LB)
  Jacksonville, Fla., 1960-61-62
★ COOK, Leroy (DE) All-SEC
  Abbeville, Ala., 1972-73-74-75
COOK, Wayne (TE)
  Montgomery, Ala., 1964-65-66
COWELL, Vince (OG) All-SEC
  Snellville, Ga., 1978-79-80
COX, Allen (OT)
  Satsuma, Ala., 1972
CRANE, Paul (C-LB) All-SEC
  Prichard, Ala., 1963-64-65
CRENSHAW, Curtis (T)
  Mobile, Ala., 1961

★ CROOM, Sylvester (C) All-SEC
Tuscaloosa, Ala., 1972-73-74
CROW, John David, Jr. (HB)
El Cahon, Calif., 1975-76-77
CROWSON, Roger (FB)
Jackson, Miss., 1968
CROSS, Andy (LB)
Birmingham, Ala., 1972
CROYLE, John (DE)
Gadsden, Ala., 1971-72-73
CRUMBLEY, Allen (DB)
Birmingham, Ala., 1976-78
CRYDER, Robert J. (OG)
O'Fallon Township, Ill.,
1975-76-77
CULLIVER, Calvin (FB)
East Brewton, Ala.,
1973-74-75-76
CULWELL, Ingram (HB)
Tuscaloosa, Ala., 1961-62

D

DASHER, Bob (OG)
Plymouth, Miss., 1981
DAVIS, Bill (K)
Columbus, Ga., 1971-72-73
DAVIS, Fred, Jr. (T)
Louisville, Ky., 1964
DAVIS, Johnny Lee (FB)
Montgomery, Ala., 1975-76-77
DAVIS, Mike (K)
Columbus, Ga., 1975
DAVIS, Ricky (S) All-SEC
Bessemer, Ala., 1973-74
DAVIS, Steve (K)
Columbus, Ga., 1965-66-67
DAVIS, Terry Ashley (QB)
All-SEC
Bogalusa, La., 1970-71-72
DAVIS, Terry Lane (E)
Birmingham, Ala., 1970
DAVIS, Tim (K)
Columbus, Ga., 1961-62-63
DAVIS, William (DT)
Fort Deposit, Ala., 1978
DAVIS, William "Junior" (T)
Birmingham, Ala., 1967-68
DAWSON, Jimmy Dale (LB)
Excel, Ala., 1973
DEAN, Mike (DB)
Decatur, Ga., 1967-68-69
DEAN, Steve (HB)
Orlando. Fla., 1972-73
DeNIRO, Gary (DE)
Youngstown, Ohio,
1978-79-80
DICHIARA, Ron (K)
Bessemer, Ala., 1974

DILL, Jimmy (E)
Mobile, Ala., 1962-63
DISMUKE, Joe (OG)
Gadsden, Ala., 1982
DIXON, Dennis (TE)
Orange, Calif., 1967-68
DORAN, Stephen Curtis (TE)
Murray, Ky., 1969-70
★ DOWDY, Cecil (OT) All-SEC
Cherokee, Ala., 1964-65-66
DRINKARD, Reid (OG)
Linden, Ala., 1968-69-70
DUBOSE, Mike (DE)
Opp, Ala., 1972-73-74
DUNCAN, Conley (LB) All-SEC
Hartselle, Ala., 1973-74-75
DUNCAN, Jerry (OT)
Sparta, N.C., 1965-66
DUKE, Jim (DT)
Columbus, Ga., 1967-68-69
DURBY, Ron (T)
Memphis, Tenn., 1963-64
DYAR, Warren E. (TE)
Florence, Ala., 1972-73
DYESS, Johnny (RB)
Elba, Ala., 1981
DYESS, Marlin (HB)
Elba, Ala., 1957-58-59

E

ECKENROD, Michael Lee (C)
Chattanooga, Tenn., 1973
EDWARDS, Randy (DT)
Marietta, Ga., 1980-81-82
ELDER, Venson (FB)
Decatur, Ga., 1982
ELIAS, Johnny (MG)
Columbus, Ga., 1981-82
ELMORE, Grady (K-HB)
Ozark, Ala., 1962-63-64
EMERSON, Ken (DB)
Columbus, Ga., 1969-70

F

FAGAN, Jeff (RB)
Hollywood, Fla., 1979-80-81-82
FAUST, Donald W. (FB)
Fairhope, Ala., 1975-76-77
FAUST, Douglas, (DT)
Fairhope, Ala., 1972
FERGUSON, Charles M. (OG)
Cuthbert, Ga., 1968-69
FERGUSON, Mitch (RB)
Augusta, Ga., 1977-79-80
FERGUSON, Richard (OG)
Fort Payne, Ala., 1969
FIELDS, Paul (QB)
Gardendale, Ala., 1982

FLANAGAN, Thad (SE)
Leighton, Ala., 1974-75-76
FLORENCE, Craige (DB)
Enterprise, Ala., 1981-82
FORD, Danny (OT) All-SEC
Gadsden, Ala., 1967-68-69
FORD, Mike (DE) All-SEC
Tuscaloosa, Ala., 1966-67-68
FORD, Steven (DB)
Tuscaloosa, Ala., 1973-74
FOWLER, Conrad (SE)
Columbiana, Ala., 1966-67-68
FOWLER, Les (DB)
Hartselle, Ala., 1976
FRACCHIA, Mike (FB) All-SEC
Memphis, Tenn., 1960-61-63
FRALEY, Robert (QB)
Winchester, Tenn., 1974-75
FRANK, Milton (G)
Huntsville, Ala., 1958-59
FRANK, Morris
Huntsville, Ala., 1962
★ FREEMAN, Wayne (OG)
All-SEC
Fort Payne, Ala., 1962-63-64
FRENCH, Buddy (K)
Decatur, Ala., 1963-64
FULLER, Jimmy (T)
Fairfield, Ala., 1964-65-66
FULLER, Leon (HB)
Nederland, Texas, 1959-60

G

GANTT, Greg (K) All-SEC
Birmingham, Ala., 1971-72-73
GAY, Stan (DB)
Tuskegee, Ala., 1981-82
★ GELLERSTEDT, Sam (NG)
All-SEC
Montgomery, Ala., 1968
GERASIMCHUK, Davis (OG)
All-SEC
Lomita, Calif., 1975-76
GILBERT, Danny (DB)
Geraldine, Ala., 1968-69-70
GILLILAND, Rickey (LB)
Birmingham, Ala., 1976-77-78
GILMER, Creed (DE)
All-SEC
Birmingham, Ala., 1964-65
GOSSETT, Don Lee (MG)
Knoxville, Tenn., 1969
GOTHARD, Andrew "Andy" (DB)
Alexander City, Ala., 1975-76
GRAMMER, James W. (C)
All-SEC
Hartselle, Ala., 1969-71

GRAMMER, Richard (C)
Hartselle, Ala., 1967-68-69
GRAY, Alan (QB)
Tampa, Fla., 1979-80-81
GRAY, Charles (E)
Pell City, Ala., 1956-57-58
GREEN, Louis E. (OG)
Birmingham, Ala., 1975-76-77
GROGAN, Jay (TE)
Cropwell, Ala., 1981-82
GUINYARD, Mickey (RB)
Atlanta, Ga., 1981-82

H

★ HALL, Mike (LB)
All-SEC
Tarrant, Ala., 1966-67-68
HALL, Randy Lee (DT)
Huntsville, Ala., 1972-73-74
HALL, Wayne (LB)
Huntsville, Ala., 1971-72-73
HAMER, Norris (DE)
Tarrant, Ala., 1967-68
HAMILTON, Wayne (DE)
Okahumpka, Fla., 1977-78-79
HAND, Jon (DT)
Sylacauga, Ala., 1982
HAND, Mike (LB-OG)
Tuscumbia, Ala., 1968-69-70
HANEY, James (RB)
Rogersville, Ala., 1979
HANNAH, Charles (DT)
All-SEC
Albertville, Ala., 1974-75-76
HANNAH, David (OT)
All-SEC
Albertville, Ala., 1975-77-78-79
★ HANNAH, John (OG)
All-SEC
Albertville, Ala., 1970-71-72
HANNAH, William C. (T)
Indianapolis, Ind., 1957-58-59
HANRAHAN, Gary (OG)
Pompano Beach, Fla., 1973
HARKNESS, Fred (MG)
Winfield, Ala., 1980
HARPOLE, Allen "Bunk" (DG)
Columbus, Miss., 1965-66-67
HARRISON, Bill (DT)
Ft. Walton Bch., Fla., 1976
HARRIS, Charles (DE)
Mobile, Ala., 1965-66-67
HARRIS, Don (DT)
Vincent, Ala., 1968-69-70
HARRIS, Hudson (HB)
Tarrant, Ala., 1962-63-64

HARRIS, Jim Bob (DB)
All-SEC
Athens, Ga., 1978-79-80-81
HARRIS, Joe Dale (SE)
Uriah, Ala., 1975
HARRIS, Paul (DE)
Mobile, Ala., 1974-75-76
HAYDEN, Neb (QB)
Charlotte, N. C., 1969-70
HEATH, Donnie (C)
Anniston, Ala., 1960
HENDERSON, Josh (DB)
Panama City, Fla., 1982
HENDERSON, Wm. T., "Bill" (TE)
Tuscaloosa, Ala., 1975-77
HENRY, Butch (E)
Selma, Ala., 1961-62-63
HIGGINBOTHAM, Steve (DB)
All-SEC
Hueytown, Ala., 1969-70-71
HIGGINBOTHAM, Robert (DB)
Hueytown, Ala., 1967-68
HILL, John (RB)
Centre, Ala., 1979-80
HILL, Roosevelt (LB)
Newnan, Ga., 1982
HINES, Edward T. (DE)
LaFayette, Ala., 1970-72
HODGES, Bruce (DE-T)
Sarasota, Fla., 1977
HOLCOMBE, Danny (OG)
Marietta, Ga., 1980-81-82
HOLSOMBACK, Roy (G)
West Blocton, Ala., 1959-60
HOLT, Darwin (LB)
Gainesville, Tx., 1960-61
HOLT, James Jay "Buddy" (P)
Demopolis, Ala., 1977-79
★ HOMAN, Dennis (SE)
All-SEC
Muscle Shoals, Ala., 1965-66-67
HOMAN, Scott (DT)
Elkhart, Ind., 1979-80-81-82
HOOD, Sammy (DB)
Ider, Ala., 1982
HOPPER, Mike (E)
Huntsville, Ala., 1961-62-64
HORSTEAD, Don (RB)
Elba, Ala., 1982
HORTON, Jimmy (DE)
Tarrant, Ala., 1971
HUBBARD, Colenzo (LB)
Mulga, Ala., 1974-75-76
HUFSTETLER, Thomas R., Jr. (C)
Rossville, Ga., 1977-78
HUNT, Morris Parker (OT)
Orlando, Fla., 1972-73

HUNTER, Scott (QB)
Prichard, Ala., 1968-69-70
HURLBUT, Jack (QB)
Houston, Texas, 1962-63
HURST, Tim (OT)
DeArmandville, Ala, 1975-76-77
HUSBAND, Hunter (TE)
Nashville, Tenn., 1967-68-69
HUSBAND, Woodward A.
"Woodie" (LB)
Nashville, Tenn., 1969-70

I

IKNER, Lou (RB)
Atmore, Ala., 1977-78
ISRAEL, Jimmy Kent (QB)
Haleyville, Ala., 1966
ISRAEL, Thomas Murray (G)
Haleyville, Ala., 1969

J

JACKSON, Billy (RB)
All-SEC
Phenix City, Ala., 1978-79-80
JACKSON, Bobby (QB)
Mobile, Ala., 1957-58
JACKSON, Mark (C)
Houston, Tex., 1981-82
JACKSON, Wilbur (HB)
All-SEC
Ozark, Ala., 1971-72-73
JACOBS, Donald (QB)
Scottsboro, Ala., 1979-80
JAMES, Kenneth Morris (T)
Columbus, Ga., 1969-70
JILLEBA, Pete (FB)
Madison, N. J., 1967-68-69
★ JOHNS, Bobby (DB)
All-SEC
Birmingham, Ala., 1965-66-67
JOHNSON, Billy (C)
Selma, Ala., 1965-66-67
JOHNSON, Cornell (HB)
High Point, N. C., 1959-60
JOHNSTON, Donny (HB)
Birmingham, Ala., 1966-69
JONES, Amos (RB)
Aliceville, Ala., 1980
JONES, Joe (RB)
Thomaston, Ga., 1978-79-80
JONES, Joey (SE)
Mobile, Ala., 1980-81-82
JONES, Kevin (QB)
Louisville, Ky., 1977-78
JONES, Robbie (LB)
Demopolis, Ala., 1979-80-81-82
JONES, Terry Wayne (C)
Sandersville, Ga., 1975-76-77

★ JORDAN, Lee Roy (LB)
All-SEC
Excel, Ala., 1960-61-62
★ JUNIOR, E. J. III (DE)
All-SEC
Nashville, Tenn., 1977-78-79-80

K

KEARLEY, Dan (DT)
All-SEC
Talladega, Ala., 1962-63-64
KELLEY, Joe (QB)
Ozark, Ala., 1966-67-68
KELLEY, Leslie (FB)
Cullman, Ala., 1964-65-66
KENNEDY, President John F.
(Honorary)
Washington, D. C., 1961
KERR, Dudley (K)
Reform, Ala., 1966-67
KILLGORE, Terry (C)
Annandale, Va., 1965-66-67
KIM, Peter (KS)
Honolulu, HI., 1980-81-82
KING, Emmanuel (DE)
Leroy, Ala., 1982
KING, Tyrone (DB)
All-SEC
Docena, Ala., 1972-73-74-75
KNAPP, David (HB)
Birmingham, Ala., 1970-71-72
KRAMER, Michael T. (DB)
Mobile, Ala., 1975-76-77
★ KRAPF, James Paul (C)
All-SEC
Newark, Del., 1970-71-72
KRAUSS, Barry (LB)
Pompano Beach, Fla., 1976-77-78
KROUT, Bart (TE)
All-SEC
Birmingham, Ala., 1978-79-80-8
KUBELIUS, Skip (DT)
Morrow, Ga., 1972-73
KULBACK, Steve Joseph (DT)
Clarksville, Tenn., 1973-74

L

LaBUE, John (RB)
Memphis, Tenn., 1976
LaBUE, Joseph II (HB)
Memphis, Tenn., 1970-71-72
LAMBERT, Buford (OT)
Warner Robins, Ga., 1976
LAMBERT, Randolph (C)
Athens, Ga., 1973-74
LANCASTER, John (DE)
Tuscaloosa, Ala., 1979

LANGSTON, Griff (SE)
Birmingham, Ala., 1968-69-70
LAW, Phil (OT)
Montgomery, Ala., 1971
LAWLEY, Lane (SE)
Citronelle, Ala., 1970
LAYTON, Dale (E)
Sylacauga, Ala., 1962
LAZENBY, K. J. (OT)
Monroeville, Ala., 1974-75-76
LEE, Mickey (FB)
Enterprise, Ala., 1968-69
LEGG, Murray (DB)
Homewood, Ala., 1976-77-78
LEWIS, Al (G)
Covington, Ky., 1961-62-63
LEWIS, Walter (QB)
Brewton, Ala., 1980-81-82
LOWE, Eddie (LB)
Phenix City, Ala., 1980-81-82
★ LOWE, Woodrow (LB)
All-SEC
Phenix City, Ala., 1972-73-74-75
LUSK, Thomas Joseph II (DE)
Clarksville, Tenn., 1970-72
LYLES, Warren (NG)
All-SEC
Birmingham, Ala., 1978-79-80-81
LYONS, Martin A. "Marty" (DT)
St. Petersburg, Fla., 1977-78

M

MADDOX, Sam H. (TE)
Orlando, Fla., 1976-77
MALLARD, James (SE)
Tampa, Fla., 1980
MANN, Frank (K)
Birmingham, Ala., 1968-69-70
MARCELLO, Jerry (DB)
McKeesport, Pa., 1973
MARDINI, Georges (PK)
Damascus, Syria, 1980
MARKS, Keith (SE)
Tuscaloosa, Ala., 1979-82
MARSHALL, Fred H. (C)
Montgomery, Ala., 1970-71
MARTIN, Gary (HB)
Dothan, Ala., 1961-62-63
MARTIN, Kenny (FB)
Hemet, Calif., 1966-67
MAURO, John (DE)
South Bend, Ind., 1978-79-80
MAXWELL, Raymond Edward (OT)
Flat Rock, Ala., 1973-74-75
MIKEL, Bobby (DE)
Ft. Walton Beach, Fla., 1976
MILLER, Noah Dean (LB)
Oneonta, Ala., 1973

MITCHELL, David Dewey (LB)
Tampa, Fla., 1975-76-77
★ MITCHELL, John (DE)
All-SEC
Mobile, Ala., 1971-72
MITCHELL, Ken "Tank" (G)
Florence, Ala., 1964
MONTGOMERY, Greg (LB)
Macon, Ga., 1972-73-74-75
MONTGOMERY, Robert M. (DE)
Shelbyville, Ky., 1970
MOONEYHAM, Marlin (FB)
Montgomery, Ala., 1962
MOORE, Harold (FB)
Chattanooga, Tenn., 1965-66
MOORE, John (HB)
Montgomery, Ala., 1962
MOORE, Mal (QB)
Dozier, Ala., 1962
MOORE, Pete (FB)
Hopkinsville, Ky., 1968-69
MOORE, Randy (TE)
Montgomery, Ala., 1970-73
MOORE, Ricky (FB)
Huntsville, Ala., 1981-82
MOORE, Robert "Bud" (E)
Birmingham, Ala., 1958-59-60
MORGAN, Ed (FB)
Hattiesburg, Miss., 1966-67-68
MORRISON, Duff (HB)
Memphis, Tenn., 1958-59-61
MORTON, Farris (E)
Sardis, Ala., 1962
MOSELEY, Elliott (C)
Selma, Ala., 1960
MOSLEY, John (HB)
Thomaston, Ala., 1964-65-66
MOSS, Stan (LB)
Birmingham, Ala., 1965-66-67
MOTT, Steve (C)
New Orleans, La., 1980-81-82
MURPHY, Philip (HB)
Anniston, Ala., 1973
★ MUSSO, Johnny (HB)
All-SEC
Birmingham, Ala., 1969-70-71

Mc

McCLENDON, Frankie (T)
Guntersville, Ala., 1962-63-64
McCOLLOUGH, Gaylon (C)
Enterprise, Ala., 1962-63-64
McCOMBS, Eddie (OT)
Birmingham, Ala., 1978-79-80
McCRARY, Tom (DT)
Scottsboro, Ala., 1982

McELROY, Alan (PK)
Tuscaloosa, Ala., 1978-79
McGEE, Barry (OG)
Birmingham, Ala., 1975
McGILL, Larry (HB)
Panama City, Fla., 1962-63
McGRIFF, Curtis (MG)
Cottonwood, Ala., 1977-78-79
McINTYRE, David (OT)
Columbus, Miss., 1975-76
McKEWEN, Jack II (T)
Birmingham, Ala., 1968
McKINNEY, Robert B., Jr. (DB)
All-SEC
Mobile, Ala., 1970-71-72
McLAIN, Rick (TE)
Walnut Hill, Fla., 1974-75
McLEOD, Ben (DE)
Pensacola, Fla., 1965
McMAKIN, David (DB)
All-SEC
Tucker, Ga., 1971-72-73
★ McNEAL, Don (DB)
All-SEC
McCullough, Ala., 1977-78-79
McQUEEN, Mike (OT)
Enterprise, Ala., 1981-82
McRAE, Scott (LB)
Huntsville, Ala., 1982

N

★ NAMATH, Joe Willie (QB)
All-SEC
Beaver Falls, Pa., 1962-63-64
NATHAN, Tony (HB)
Birmingham, Ala., 1975-76-77-78
NEAL, Rick (TE)
Birmingham, Ala., 1976-77-78
★ NEIGHBORS, Billy (T)
All-SEC
Northport, Ala., 1959-60-61
NELSON, Benny (HB)
All-SEC
Huntsville, Ala., 1961-62-63
NELSON, Rod (K)
Birmingham, Ala., 1974-75-76
★ NEWSOME, Ozzie (SE)
All-SEC
Leighton, Ala., 1974-75-76-77
NIX, Mark (RB)
Altoona, Ala., 1979-80-81
NORMAN, Haywood Eugene
"Butch" (DE)
Luverne, Ala., 1973
NORRIS, Lanny S., (DB)
Russellville, Ala., 1970-71-72

O

O'DELL, Richard (E)

Lincoln, Ala., 1959-60-62
ODOM, Ernest Lavont (E)
Birmingham, Ala., 1973
OGDEN, Ray (HB)
Jesup, Ga., 1962-63-64
OGILVIE, Morgan Oslin "Major"
(RB), All-SEC
Birmingham, Ala., 1977-78-79-80
O'LINGER, John (C)
Scottsboro, Ala., 1959-60-61
OLIVER, William "Brother" (DB)
Livingston, Ala., 1960-61
ORCUTT, Ben (RB)
Arlington Heights, Ill., 1981
O'REAR, Jack (QB)
Tarrant, Ala., 1974-76-77
OSER, Gary (C)
New Orleans, La., 1976
O'STEEN, Robert "Gary" (FB)
Anniston, Ala., 1957-58-59
O'TOOLE, Mike (DB)
Palmerdale, Ala.. 1982
OWEN, Wayne (LB)
Gadsden, Ala., 1966-67-68

P

PALMER, Dale (LB)
Calera, Ala., 1978
PAPPAS, Peter George (SE)
Birmingham, Ala., 1973
PARKER, Calvin (DE)
Eastoboga, Ala., 1976-78
★ PARKHOUSE, Robin (DE)
All-SEC
Orlando, Fla., 1969-70-71
PARSONS, Don (G)
Houston, Texas, 1958
PATRICK, Linnie (RB)
Jasper, Ala., 1980-81-82
PATTERSON, Jim (OG)
Annandale, Cal., 1971
PATTERSON, Steve (OG)
Omaha, Neb., 1972-73-74
PATTON, James "Jap" (E)
Tuscumbia, Ala., 1959-61
PELL, Charles B. (T)
Albertville, Ala., 1960-61-62
★ PERKINS, Ray (E)
All-SEC
Petal, Miss., 1964-65-66
PERRIN, Benny (DB)
Decatur, Ala., 1980-81
PERRY, Anthony "Lefty" (DB)
Hazel Green, Ala., 1973
PETTEE, Robert A. "Bob" (G)
Bradenton, Fla., 1960-61-62
PHILLIPS, Gary (G)
Dothan, Ala., 1958-59-60

PIPER, Billy (HB)
Poplar Bluff, Mo., 1960-62-63
★ PITTS, Mike (DE)
All-SEC
Baltimore, Md., 1979-80-81-82
PITTMAN, Alec Noel (LB)
New Orleans, La., 1970
PIZZITOLA, Alan (DB)
All-SEC
Birmingham, Ala., 1973-74-75
POOLE, John Paul (E)
Florence, Ala., 1955-58
POPE, Herman "Buddy" (OT)
Bradenton, Fla., 1973-74-75
PRESTWOOD, Thomas A. (DE)
Chattanooga, Tenn., 1975
PROPST, Eddie (DB)
Birmingham, Ala., 1966-67
PRUDHOMME, John Mark (DB)
Memphis, Tenn., 1973-74-75
PUGH, George (TE)
Montgomery, Ala., 1972-73-74-75
PUGH, Keith Harrison (SE)
Evergreen, Ala., 1977-78-79

Q

QUICK, Cecil Van (DE)
Collins, Miss., 1970

R

RABURN, Gene (FB)
Jasper, Ala., 1965-66
RAINES, James Patrick (C)
Montgomery, Ala., 1970-71-72
RAINES, Vaughn Michael (DT)
All-SEC
Montgomery, Ala., 1972-73
RANAGER, George (SE)
Meridian, Miss., 1968-69-70
RANKIN, Carlton (QB)
Piedmont, Ala., 1962
★ RAY, David (SE-K)
All-SEC
Phenix City, Ala., 1964-65
REAVES, Pete (G)
Bessemer, Ala., 1958
REED, Wayne (Mgr.) 1981
REILLY, Mike (DG)
Mobile, Ala., 1966-67-68
REITZ, John David (DE-OT)
Morristown, Tenn., 1965-66-67
RHOADS, Wayne R. (DE)
Jackson, Miss., 1969-70
RHODEN, Steve (K)
Red Bay, Ala., 1981
RHODES, D. Wayne, Jr. (DB)
All-SEC
Decatur, Ga., 1973-74-75
RICE, William Jr., "Bill" (E)

Troy, Ala., 1959-60-61
RICH, Jerry (HB)
Atalla, Ala., 1959
RICHARDSON, Ron (DB)
Columbus, Ga., 1971
RICHARDSON, W.E. (HB)
Jasper, Ala., 1959-60-61
RIDGEWAY, Danny Howard (K)
Fyffe, Ala., 1973-74-75
RILEY, Mike (DB)
Corvallis, Ore., 1974
RIPPETOE, Benny (QB)
Greenville, Tenn., 1971
ROBBINS, Joe (C)
Opp, Ala., 1978-79-80
ROBERTS, Kenneth (C)
Anniston, Ala., 1956-57-58
ROBERTS, Larry (TE)
Dothan, Ala., 1982
ROBERTSON, Ronald Dale (LB)
Signal Mtn., Tenn., 1973-74
RODDAM, Ronnie (C)
Birmingham, Ala., 1968-69
RODRIGUEZ, Mike (MG)
Melbourne, Fla., 1981-82
ROGERS, Eddie Bo (LB)
Bessemer, Ala., 1966-67
ROGERS, John David (OG)
All-SEC
Montgomery, Ala., 1972-73-74
ROGERS, Richard (OG)
Boise, Idaho, 1973
RONSONET, Norbie (E)
Biloxi, Miss., 1958-59-60
ROOT, Steve (LB)
Indio, Calif., 1971
ROSSER, Jimmy Lynn (OT)
Birmingham, Ala., 1969-70-71
ROUZIE, Jefferson Carr (LB)
Jacksonville, Fla., 1970-71-73
ROWAN, Robert "Robby" (DB)
Huntsville, Ala., 1972
ROWELL, Terry (DT)
Heidelberg, Miss., 1969-70-71
RUFFIN, Larry Joe (OG)
Fayette, Ala., 1973-74-75
RUMBLEY, Roy (OG)
Moss Point, Miss., 1981-82
RUSTIN, Nathan (DT)'
Phenix City, Ala., 1966-67
RUTLEDGE, Gary (QB)
Birmingham, Ala., 1972-73-74
RUTLEDGE, Jack (G)
Birmingham, Ala., 1959-60-61
RUTLEDGE, Jeffery R. (QB)
Birmingham, Ala.,
1975-76-77-78

S
SADLER, David A. (OG)
Cadiz, Ky., 1975-76-77
★ SAMPLES, Alvin (OG) All-SEC
Tarrant, Ala., 1967-68-69
SANDERS, Terry (K)
Birmingham, Ala., 1981-82
SANSING, Walter (FB)
West Blocton, Ala., 1958
SASSER, Mike (DB)
Brewton, Ala., 1966-69
SAWYER, Bubba (SE)
Fairhope, Ala., 1969-71
SCHAMUN, Eric (DB)
Blue Island, Ill., 1977
SCHAMUN, Russ (SE)
Napa, Calif., 1974-76
SCHMISSRAUTER, Kurt (OT)
Chattanooga, Tenn., 1981-82
SCISSUM, Willard (OG)
Huntsville, Ala., 1981-82
SCOTT, Randy (LB) All-SEC
Decatur, Ga., 1978-79-80
SCROGGINS, Billy (SE)
Jacksonville, Fla., 1967-68
SEARCEY, Bill (OG)
Savannah, Ga., 1978-80
SEAY, Buddy (HB)
Dadeville, Ala., 1969-70
SEBASTIAN, Mike (DT)
Columbus, Ga., 1978
SEWELL, Ray (QB)
Breman, Ga., 1976
SHANKLES, Don (E)
Fort Payne, Ala., 1967
SHARPE, Jimmy (OG)
Montgomery, Ala., 1960-61-62
SHARPLESS, John Waylon, Jr. (SE)
Elba, Ala., 1972-73
SHEALY, Steadman (QB)
All-SEC
Dothan, Ala., 1977-78-79
SHELBY, Willie (HB) All-SEC
Purvis, Miss., 1973-74-75
SHERRILL, Jackie (FB-LB)
Biloxi, Miss., 1963-64-65
SHINN, Richard (DT)
Columbiana, Ala., 1980-82
SIDES, John "Brownie" (DT)
Tuskegee, Ala., 1966-67
SIMON, Kenny (RB)
Montgomery, Ala., 1979-81
SIMMONS, Jim (T)
Piedmont, Ala., 1962-63-64
SIMMONS, Jim (TE)

Yazoo City, Miss., 1969-70-71
SIMMONS, Malcolm (P)
Montgomery, Ala., 1981-82
SIMS, Wayne (G)
Columbiana, Ala., 1958-59
SINGTON, Dave (T)
Birmingham, Ala., 1956-57-58
SINGTON, Fred Jr. (T)
Birmingham, Ala., 1958-59
SISIA, Joseph (T)
Clark, N.J., 1960
SKELTON, Robert "Bobby" (QB)
Pell City, Ala., 1957-59-60
★ SLOAN, Steve (QB) All-SEC
Cleveland, Tenn., 1963-64-65
SMALLEY, Jack, Jr. (LB)
Douglasville, Ga., 1976-77
SMILEY, Anthony (DE)
Birmingham, Ala., 1981-82
SMITH, Barry S. (C)
Anniston, Ala., 1977-78-79
SMITH, Bobby (DB)
Fairhope, Ala., 1978-79
SMITH, Bobby (QB)
Brewton, Ala., 1956-57-58
SMITH, James Sidney (C)
Warner Robins, Ga.,
1974-75-76
SOMERVILLE, Tom (OG)
White Station, Tenn.,
1965-66-67
SPENCER, Tom (DB)
Fairfax, Va., 1979
SPIVEY, Paul Randall (FB)
Montgomery, Ala., 1972-73
SPRAYBERRY, Steve (OT)
All-SEC
Sylacauga, Ala., 1972-73
SPRINKLE, Jerrill (DB)
Chamblee, Ga., 1980-81-82
SPRUIELL, Jerry (E)
Pell City, Ala., 1960
STABLER, Ken "Snake" (QB)
All-SEC
Foley, Ala., 1965-66-67
STANFORD, Robert "Bobby" (OT)
Albany, Ga., 1969-72
STAPP, Laurien "Goodie" (QB-K)
Birmingham, Ala., 1958-59-60
STEAKLEY, Rod (SE)
Huntsville, Ala., 1971
STEPHENS, Bruce (G) All-SEC
Thomasville, Ala., 1965-66-67
STEPHENS, Charles (E)
Thomasville, Ala., 1962-63-64

282

STEPHENS, Gerald (C)
Thomasville, Ala., 1962
★ STEPHENSON, Dwight (C)
All-SEC
Hampton, Va., 1977-78-79
STEVENS, Wayne (E)
Gadsden, Ala., 1966
STICKNEY, Ravis "Red" (FB)
Key West, Fla., 1957-59
STOCK, Mike (HB)
Elkhart, Ind., 1973-74-75
STOKES, Ralph Anthony (HB)
Montgomery, Ala., 1972-74
STONE, Rocky (G)
Birmingham, Ala., 1969
STRICKLAND, Charles
"Chuck"
(LB) All-SEC
East Ridge, Tenn., 1971-72-73
STRICKLAND, Lynwood (DE)
Alexander City, Ala., 1965
STRICKLAND, William Ross (T)
Birmingham, Ala., 1970
SULLIVAN, Johnny (DT)
Nashville, Tenn., 1964-65-66
★ SURLAS, Tom (LB) All-SEC
Mt. Pleasant, Pa., 1970-71
SUTTON, Donnie (SE)
Blountsville, Ala., 1966-67-68
SUTTON, Mike (DB)
Brewton, Ala., 1978
SWAFFORD, Bobby "Hawk"
(SE)
Heflin, Ala., 1967-68
SWANN, Gerald (DB)
Ashville, Ala., 1982

T

TAYLOR, James E. (HB)
Citronelle, Ala., 1973-74-75
THOMAS, Daniel Martin (C)
Clinton, Tenn., 1970
THOMPSON, Louis (DT)
Lebanon, Tenn., 1965-66
THOMPSON, Richard "Dickey"
All-SEC
Thomasville, Ga., 1965-66-67
TILLMANN, Homer Newton
"Chip" (OT)
Panama City, Fla., 1976-77
TODD, Richard (QB) All-SEC
Mobile, Ala., 1973-74-75
TOLLESON, Tommy (SE) All-SEC
Talladega, Ala., 1963-64-65
★ TRAMMELL, Pat (QB) All-SEC
Scottsboro, Ala., 1959-60-61
TRAVIS, Timothy Lee "Tim" (TE)
Bessemer, Ala., 1976-77-78-79

TRIMBLE, Wayne (QB)
Cullman, Ala., 1964-65-66
TRODD, Paul (PK)
Eufaula, Ala., 1981
TUCKER, Michael V. (DB)
Alexandria, Ala., 1975-76-77
TUCKER, Richard Glenn "Ricky'
(DB) All-SEC
Florence, Ala., 1977-78-79-80
TURNER, Craig (RB)
Gaithersburg, Md., 1982
TURPIN, John R. (FB)
Birmingham, Ala., 1977-78
TURPIN, Richard "Dick" (DE)
Birmingham, Ala., 1973-74-75

U

UMPHREY, Woody (P)
Boubonnais, Ill., 1978-79-80

V

VAGOTIS, Chris (OG)
Canton, Ohio, 1966
VALLETTO, Carl (E)
Oakmont, Pa., 1957-58
VARNADO, Carey Reid (C)
Hattiesburg, Miss., 1970
VERSPRILLE, Eddie (FB)
Norfolk, Va., 1961-62-63
VICKERS, Doug (OG)
Enterprise, Ala., 1981-82
VINES, Jay (OG)
Birmingham, Ala., 1978

W

WADE, Steve (DB)
Dothan, Ala., 1971-72
WADE, Tommy (DB)
Dothan, Ala., 1967-68-70
WALKER, Hardy (OT)
Huntsville, Ala., 1981
WALL, Larry "Dink" (FB)
Fairfax, Ala., 1961-62-64
WASHCO, Gerard George (DT)
West Orange, N.J., 1973-74-75
★ WASHINGTON, Mike (DB)
All-SEC
Montgomery, Ala., 1972-73-74
WATKINS, David (DE)
Rome, Ga., 1971-72-73
WATTS, Jimmy (DE)
Gulf Breeze, Fla., 1981-82
WATSON, Rick (FB)
Birmingham, Ala., 1974-75-76
WEIGAND, Tommy (HB)
Enterprise, Ala., 1968
WESLEY, Wm. Earl "Buddy"
(FB)
Talladega, Ala., 1958-59-60

WHALEY, Frank (DE)
Lineville, Ala., 1965-66
★ WHEELER, Wayne (SE)
All-SEC
Orlando, Fla., 1971-72-73
WHITE, Darryl (SE)
Tuscaloosa, Ala., 1981-82
WHITE, Gus (MG)
Dothan, Ala., 1974-75-76
WHITE, Jack (OG)
Louisville, Miss., 1971
WHITE, Tommy (FB)
West Blocton, Ala.,
1958-59-60
WHITMAN, Steven K. (FB)
Huffman, Ala.,, 1977-78-79
WIESEMAN, Bill (G)
Louisville, Ky., 1962-63
★ WILCOX, Tommy (DB)
All-SEC
Harahan, La., 1979-80-81-82
WILDER, Ken (OT)
Columbiana, Ala., 1968-69
WILDER, Roosevelt (FB)
Macon, Ga., 1982
WILKINS, Red (E)
Bay Minette, Ala., 1961
WILLIAMS, Charlie (FB)
Bessemer, Ala., 1980
WILLIAMS, John Byrd (G)
Decatur, Ala., 1965-66
WILLIAMS, Steven Edward (DB)
Moline, Ill., 1969-70-71
WILLIAMSON, Richard (SE)
Fort Deposit, Ala., 1961-62
WILLIS, Perry (SE)
Dadeville, Ala., 1967
WILSON, George "Butch" (HB)
Hueytown, Ala., 1960-61-62
WILSON, Jimmy (OG)
Haleyville, Ala., 1961-62
WINGO, Richard Allen "Rich"
(LB)
Elkhart, Ind., 1976-77-78
WISE, Mack (HB)
Elba, Ala., 1958
WOOD, Russ (DE)
Elba, Ala., 1980-81-82
WOOD, William Dexter (SE)
Ozark, Ala., 1970-72
WOODRUFF, Glen (TE)
Aliceville, Ala., 1971
WRIGHT, Steve (T)
Louisville, Ky., 1962-63

Y

YELVINGTON, Gary (DB)
Daytona Beach, Fla., 1973-74

283

Year By Year Under Bryant

1958—WON 5, LOST 4, TIED 1

3	L. S. U.	13	Mobile (N) Sept. 27
0	Vanderbilt	0	Birmingham (N) Oct. 4
29	Furman	6	Tuscaloosa (N) Oct. 11
7	Tennessee	14	Knoxville Oct. 18
9	Miss. State	7	Starkville Oct. 25
12	Georgia	0	Tuscaloosa Nov. 1
7	Tulane	13	New Orleans (N) Nov. 8
17	Georgia Tech	8	Atlanta Nov. 15
14	Memphis State	0	Tuscaloosa Nov. 22
8	Auburn	14	Birmingham Nov. 29
106		75	

1959—WON 7, LOST 2, TIED 2

3	Georgia	17	Athens Sept. 19
3	Houston	0	Houston (N) Sept. 26
7	Vanderbilt	7	Nashville (N) Oct. 3
13	Chattanooga	0	Tuscaloosa Oct. 10
7	Tennessee	7	Birmingham Oct. 17
10	Miss. State	0	Tuscaloosa Oct. 24
19	Tulane	7	Mobile (N) Nov. 7
9	Ga. Tech	7	Birmingham Nov. 14
14	Memphis State	7	Tuscaloosa Nov. 21
10	Auburn	0	Birmingham Nov. 28
* 0	Penn State	7	Liberty Bowl Dec. 19
95		59	

1960—WON 8, LOST 1, TIED 2

21	Georgia	6	Birmingham Sept. 17
6	Tulane	6	New Orleans (N) Sept. 24
21	Vanderbilt	0	Birmingham (N) Oct. 1
7	Tennessee	20	Knoxville Oct. 15
14	Houston	0	Tuscaloosa Oct. 22
7	Miss. State	0	Starkville Oct. 29
51	Furman	0	Tuscaloosa Nov. 5
16	Ga. Tech	15	Atlanta Nov. 12
34	Tampa	6	Tuscaloosa Nov. 19
3	Auburn	0	Birmingham Nov. 26
* 3	Texas	3	Bluebonnet Bowl Dec. 17
183		56	

1961—WON 11, LOST 0

NATIONAL CHAMPIONS
SEC CHAMPIONS

32	Georgia	6	Athens Sept. 23
9	Tulane	0	Mobile (N) Sept. 30
35	Vanderbilt	6	Nashville (N) Oct. 7
26	N. C. State	7	Tuscaloosa Oct. 14
34	Tennessee	3	Birmingham Oct. 21
17	Houston	0	Houston (N) Oct. 28
24	Miss. State	0	Tuscaloosa Nov. 4
66	Richmond	0	Tuscaloosa Nov. 11
10	Ga. Tech	0	Birmingham Nov. 18
34	Auburn	0	Birmingham Dec. 2
*10	Arkansas	3	Sugar Bowl, Jan. 1, '62
297		25	

1962—WON 10, LOST 1

35	Georgia	0	Birmingham (N) Sept. 22
44	Tulane	6	New Orleans (N) Sept. 28
17	Vanderbilt	7	Birmingham (N) Oct. 6
14	Houston	3	Tuscaloosa Oct. 13
27	Tennessee	7	Knoxville Oct. 20
35	Tulsa	6	Tuscaloosa Oct. 27
20	Miss. State	0	Starkville Nov. 3
36	Miami	3	Tuscaloosa Nov. 10
6	Georgia Tech	7	Atlanta Nov. 17
38	Auburn	0	Birmingham Dec. 1
*17	Oklahoma	0	Orange Bowl, Jan. 1, '63
289		39	

1963—WON 9, LOST 2

32	Georgia	7	Athens Sept. 21
28	Tulane	0	Mobile (N) Sept. 28
21	Vanderbilt	6	Nashville (N) Oct. 5
6	Florida	10	Tuscaloosa Oct. 12
35	Tennessee	0	Birmingham Oct. 19
21	Houston	13	Tuscaloosa Oct. 26
20	Miss. State	19	Tuscaloosa Nov. 2
27	Georgia Tech	11	Birmingham Nov. 16
8	Auburn	10	Birmingham Nov. 30
17	Miami	12	Miami Dec. 14
*12	Mississippi	7	Sugar Bowl, Jan. 1, '64
227		95	

1964—WON 10, LOST 1

NATIONAL CHAMPIONS
SEC CHAMPIONS

31	Georgia	3	Tuscaloosa (N) Sept. 19
36	Tulane	6	Mobile (N) Sept. 26
24	Vanderbilt	0	Birmingham (N) Oct. 3
21	N. C. State	0	Tuscaloosa Oct. 10
19	Tennessee	8	Knoxville Oct. 17
17	Florida	14	Tuscaloosa Oct. 24
23	Miss. State	6	Jackson (N) Oct. 31
17	L. S. U.	9	Birmingham Nov. 7
24	Georgia Tech	7	Atlanta Nov. 14
21	Auburn	14	Birmingham Nov. 26
*17	Texas	21	Orange Bowl (N), Jan. 1, '65
250		88	

1965—WON 9, LOST 1, TIED 1

AP NATIONAL CHAMPIONS
SEC CHAMPIONS

17	Georgia	18	Athens Sept. 18
27	Tulane	0	Mobile (N) Sept. 25
17	Mississippi	16	Birmingham (N) Oct. 2
22	Vanderbilt	7	Nashville (N) Oct. 9
7	Tennessee	7	Birmingham Oct. 16
21	Florida State	0	Tuscaloosa Oct. 23
10	Miss. State	7	Jackson (N) Oct. 30
31	L. S. U.	7	Baton Rouge Nov. 6
35	So. Carolina	14	Tuscaloosa Nov. 13
30	Auburn	3	Birmingham Nov. 27
*39	Nebraska	28	Orange Bowl (N), Jan. 1, '66
256		107	

1966—WON 11, LOST 0, TIED 0

SEC CHAMPIONS

34	La. Tech	0	Birmingham (N) Sept. 24
17	Mississippi	7	Jackson (N) Oct. 1
26	Clemson	0	Tuscaloosa Oct. 8
11	Tennessee	10	Knoxville Oct. 15
42	Vanderbilt	6	Birmingham Oct. 22
27	Miss. State	14	Tuscaloosa Oct. 29
21	L. S. U.	0	Birmingham Nov. 5
24	South Carolina	0	Tuscaloosa Nov. 12
34	Sou. Miss.	0	Mobile Nov. 26
31	Auburn	0	Birmingham Dec. 3
*34	Nebraska	7	Sugar Bowl, Jan. 2, '67
301		44	

*Indicates Bowl game   (N) Night game

1967—WON 8, LOST 2, TIED 1

37	Florida State	37	Birmingham (N) Sept. 23
25	Sou. Miss.	3	Mobile (N) Sept. 30
21	Mississippi	7	Birmingham Oct. 7
35	Vanderbilt	21	Nashville (N) Oct. 14
13	Tennessee	24	Birmingham Oct. 21
13	Clemson	10	Clemson Oct. 28
13	Miss. State	0	Tuscaloosa Nov. 4
7	L. S. U.	6	Baton Rouge (N) Nov. 11
17	So. Carolina	0	Tuscaloosa Nov. 18
7	Auburn	3	Birmingham Dec. 2
*16	Texas A&M	20	Cotton Bowl, Jan. 1, '68
204		131	

1968—WON 8, LOST 3

14	Va. Tech	7	Birmingham (N) Sept. 21
17	Sou. Miss.	14	Mobile Sept. 28
8	Mississippi	10	Jackson Oct. 5
31	Vanderbilt	7	Tuscaloosa Oct. 12
9	Tennessee	10	Knoxville Oct. 19
21	Clemson	14	Tuscaloosa Oct. 26
20	Miss. State	13	Tuscaloosa Nov. 2
16	L. S. U.	7	Birmingham Nov. 9
14	Miami	6	Miami (N) Nov. 16
24	Auburn	16	Birmingham Nov. 30
*10	Missouri	35	Gator Bowl Dec. 28
184		139	

1969—WON 6, LOST 5

17	Va. Tech	13	Blacksburg Sept. 20
63	So. Miss.	14	Tuscaloosa (N) Sept. 27
33	Mississippi	32	Birmingham (N) Oct. 4
10	Vanderbilt	14	Nashville (N) Oct. 11
14	Tennessee	41	Birmingham Oct. 18
38	Clemson	13	Clemson Oct. 25
23	Miss. State	19	Jackson (N) Nov. 1
15	L. S. U.	20	Baton Rouge (N) Nov. 6
42	Miami	6	Tuscaloosa Nov. 15
26	Auburn	49	Birmingham Nov. 29
*33	Colorado	47	Liberty Bowl Dec. 13
314		268	

1970—WON 6, LOST 5, TIED 1

21	Southern Cal.	42	Birmingham (N) Sept. 12
51	Virginia Tech	18	Birmingham (N) Sept. 19
46	Florida	15	Tuscaloosa (N) Sept. 26
23	Mississippi	48	Jackson (N) Oct. 3
35	Vanderbilt	11	Tuscaloosa Oct. 10
0	Tennessee	24	Knoxville Oct. 17
30	Houston	21	Houston Oct. 24
35	Miss. State	6	Tuscaloosa Oct. 31
9	L. S. U.	14	Birmingham Nov. 7
32	Miami	8	Miami (N) Nov. 14
28	Auburn	33	Birmingham Nov. 28
*24	Oklahoma	24	Astro-Bluebonnet Bowl (N) Dec. 31
334		264	

1971—WON 11, LOST 1
SEC CHAMPIONS

17	Southern Cal	10	Los Angeles (N) Sept. 10
42	Southern Miss.	6	Tuscaloosa Sept. 18
38	Florida	0	Gainesville Sept. 25
40	Mississippi	6	Birmingham Oct. 2
42	Vanderbilt	0	Nashville (N) Oct. 9
32	Tennessee	15	Birmingham Oct. 16
34	Houston	20	Tuscaloosa Oct. 23
41	Miss. State	10	Jackson (N) Oct. 30
14	L. S. U.	7	Baton Rouge (N) Nov. 6
31	Miami	3	Tuscaloosa Nov. 13
31	Auburn	7	Birmingham Nov. 27
* 6	Nebraska	38	Orange Bowl (N), Jan. 1, '72
368		122	

1972—WON 10, LOST 2
SEC CHAMPIONS

35	Duke	12	Birmingham (N) Sept. 9
35	Kentucky	0	Birmingham (N) Sept. 23
48	Vanderbilt	21	Tuscaloosa (N) Sept. 30
25	Georgia	7	Athens Oct. 7
24	Florida	7	Tuscaloosa Oct. 14
17	Tennessee	10	Knoxville Oct. 21
48	Southern Miss.	11	Birmingham (N) Oct. 28
58	Miss. State	14	Tuscaloosa Nov. 4
35	L. S. U.	21	Birmingham Nov. 11
52	Virginia Tech	13	Tuscaloosa Nov. 18
16	Auburn	17	Birmingham Dec. 2
*13	Texas	17	Cotton Bowl Jan. 1, '73
406		150	

1973—WON 11, LOST 1
UPI NATIONAL CHAMPIONS
SEC CHAMPIONS

66	California	0	Birmingham (N) Sept. 15
28	Kentucky	14	Lexington Sept. 22
44	Vanderbilt	0	Nashville (N) Sept. 29
28	Georgia	14	Tuscaloosa Oct. 6
35	Florida	14	Gainesville Oct. 13
42	Tennessee	21	Birmingham Oct. 20
77	Virginia Tech	6	Tuscaloosa (N) Oct. 27
35	Miss. State	0	Jackson (N) Nov. 3
43	Miami	13	Tuscaloosa Nov. 17
21	L. S. U.	7	Baton Rouge (N) Nov. 22
35	Auburn	0	Birmingfham (N) Dec. 1
*23	Notre Dame	24	Sugar Bowl (N) Dec. 31
477		113	

1974—WON 11, LOST 1
SEC CHAMPIONS

21	Maryland	16	College Park Sept. 14
52	Southern Miss.	0	Birmingham (N) Sept. 21
23	Vanderbilt	10	Tuscaloosa Sept. 28
35	Ole Miss	21	Jackson Oct. 5
8	Florida State	7	Tuscaloosa Oct. 12
28	Tennessee	6	Knoxville Oct. 19
41	T. C. U.	3	Birmingham Oct. 26
35	Miss. State	0	Tuscaloosa Nov. 2
30	L. S. U.	0	Birmingham Nov. 9
28	Miami	7	Miami (N) Nov. 16
17	Auburn	13	Birmingham Nov. 29
*11	Notre Dame	13	Miami (N) Jan. 1, '75
329		96	

1975—WON 11, LOST 1
SEC CHAMPIONS

7	Missouri	20	Birmingham (N) Sept. 8
56	Clemson	0	Tuscaloosa (N) Sept. 20
40	Vanderbilt	7	Nashville Sept. 27
32	Ole Miss	6	Birmingham Oct. 4
52	Washington	0	Tuscaloosa Oct. 11
30	Tennessee	7	Birmingham Oct. 18
45	T. C. U.	0	Birmingham Oct. 25
21	Miss. State	10	Jackson (N) Nov. 1
23	L. S. U.	10	Baton Rouge (N) Nov. 8
27	Southern Miss.	6	Tuscaloosa Nov. 15
28	Auburn	0	Birmingham Nov. 29
*13	Penn State	6	Sugar Bowl (N) Dec. 31
374		72	

1976—WON 9, LOST 3

7	Ole Miss	10	Jackson (N) Sept. 11
56	SMU	3	Birmingham Sept. 18
42	Vanderbilt	14	Tuscaloosa Sept. 25
0	Georgia	21	Athens Oct. 2
24	Southern Miss.	8	Birmingham Oct. 9
20	Tennessee	13	Knoxville Oct. 16
24	Louisville	3	Tuscaloosa Oct. 23
34	Miss. State	17	Tuscaloosa Oct. 30
28	LSU	17	Birmingham Nov. 6
18	Notre Dame	21	South Bend Nov. 13
38	Auburn	7	Birmingham Nov. 27
*36	UCLA	6	Liberty Bowl (N) Dec. 20
327		140	

285

1977—WON 11, LOST 1
SEC CHAMPIONS

34	Ole Miss	13	Birmingham (N)	Sept. 10
24	Nebraska	31	Lincoln	Sept. 17
24	Vanderbilt	12	Nashville	Sept. 24
18	Georgia	10	Tuscaloosa	Oct. 1
21	Southern Cal	20	Los Angeles	Oct. 8
24	Tennessee	10	Birmingham	Oct. 15
55	Louisville	6	Tuscaloosa	Oct. 22
37	Miss. State	7	Jackson (N)	Oct. 29
24	LSU	3	Baton Rouge	Nov. 5
36	Miami	0	Tuscaloosa	Nov. 12
48	Auburn	21	Birmingham	Nov. 26
*35	Ohio State	6	Sugar Bowl	Jan. 2, '78
380		139		

1978—WON 11, LOST 1
AP NATIONAL CHAMPIONS
SEC CHAMPIONS

20	Nebraska	3	Birmingham (N)	Sept. 2
38	Missouri	20	Columbia	Sept. 16
14	Southern Cal	24	Birmingham	Sept. 23
51	Vanderbilt	28	Tuscaloosa	Sept. 30
20	Washington	17	Seattle	Oct. 7
23	Florida	12	Tuscaloosa	Oct. 14
30	Tennessee	17	Knoxville	Oct. 21
35	Virginia Tech	0	Tuscaloosa	Oct. 28
35	Miss. State	14	Birmingham	Nov. 4
31	L. S. U.	10	Birmingham	Nov. 11
34	Auburn	16	Birmingham	Dec. 2
*14	Penn State	7	Sugar Bowl	Jan. 1, '79
345		168		

1979—WON 12, LOST 0
AP & UPI NATIONAL CHAMPIONS
SEC CHAMPIONS

30	Georgia Tech	6	Atlanta (TV)	Sept. 8
45	Baylor	0	Birmingham (N)	Sept. 22
66	Vanderbilt	3	Nashville	Sept. 29
38	Wichita State	0	Tuscaloosa	Oct. 6
40	Florida	0	Gainesville	Oct. 13
27	Tennessee	17	Birmingham	Oct. 20
31	Virginia Tech	7	Tuscaloosa	Oct. 27
24	Miss. State	7	Tuscaloosa	Nov. 3
3	LSU	0	Baton Rouge	Nov. 10
30	Miami (Fla.)	0	Tuscaloosa (TV)	Nov. 17
25	Auburn	18	Birmingham	Dec. 1
*24	Arkansas	9	Sugar Bowl, Jan. 1, 1980	
383		67		

1980—WON 10, LOST 2

26	Georgia Tech	3	Birmingham	Sept. 6
59	Ole Miss	35	Jackson	Sept. 20
41	Vanderbilt	0	Tuscaloosa	Sept. 27
45	Kentucky	0	Birmingham	Oct. 4
17	Rutgers	13	Meadowlands	Oct. 11
27	Tennessee	0	Knoxville (TV)	Oct. 18
42	Southern Miss.	7	Tuscaloosa	Oct. 25
3	Miss. State	6	Jackson	Nov. 1
28	LSU	7	Tuscaloosa	Nov. 8
0	Notre Dame	7	B'ham (TV)	Nov. 15
34	Auburn	18	Birmingham	Nov. 29
*30	Baylor	2	Cotton Bowl, Jan. 1, 1981	
352		98		

1981—WON 9, LOST 2, TIED 1
SEC CHAMPIONS

24	LSU	7	B. Rouge (TV)	Sept.5
21	Georgia Tech	24	Birmingham	Sept. 12
19	Kentucky	10	Lexington	Sept. 19
28	Vanderbilt	7	Nashville	Sept. 26
38	Mississippi	7	Tuscaloosa	Oct. 3
13	S. Mississippi	13	Birmingham	Oct. 10
38	Tennessee	19	Birmingham	Oct. 17
31	Rutgers	7	Tuscaloosa	Oct. 24
13	Miss. State	10	Tuscaloosa	Oct. 31
31	Penn State	16	University Pk.	Nov. 14
28	Auburn	17	Birmingham	Nov. 28
*12	Texas	14	Cotton Bowl, Jan. 1, 1982	
296		151		

1982—WON 8, LOST 4

45	Georgia Tech	7	Atlanta	Sept. 11
42	Mississippi	14	Jackson	Sept. 18
24	Vanderbilt	21	Tuscaloosa	Sept. 25
34	Arkansas State	7	Birmingham	Oct. 2
42	Penn State	21	Birmingham (TV)	Oct. 9
28	Tennessee	35	Knoxville	Oct. 16
21	Cincinnati	3	Tuscaloosa	Oct. 23
20	Mississippi State	12	Jackson	Oct. 30
10	LSU	20	Birmingham	Nov. 6
29	Southern Miss	38	Tuscaloosa	Nov. 13
22	Auburn	23	Birmingham (TV)	Nov. 27
*21	Illinois	15	Liberty Bowl, Dec. 29, 1982	
338		216		

CAREERS OF ALABAMA COACHES

Coach	Coaching Years	Total Years	Games	Won	Lost	Tied	Percent
E.B. Beaumont	1892	1	4	2	2	0	.500
Eli Abbot	1893-1895,1902	4	19	7	12	0	.368
Otto Wagonhurst	1896	1	3	2	1	0	.667
Allen McCants	1897	1	1	1	0	0	1.000
W.A. Martin	1899	1	4	3	1	0	.750
M. Griffin	1900	1	5	2	3	0	.400
H.M. Harvey	1901	1	5	2	1	2	.600
W.B. Blount	1903-1904	2	17	10	7	0	.588
Jack Leavenworth	1905	1	10	6	4	0	.600
J.W.H. Pollard	1906-1909	4	29	20	4	5	.776
Guy Lowman	1910	1	8	4	4	0	.500
D.G. Graves	1911-1914	4	36	21	12	3	.625
Thomas Kelly	1915-1917	3	25	17	7	1	.700
Xen C. Scott	1919-1922	4	41	29	9	3	.744
Wallace Wade	1923-1930	8	77	61	13	3	.812
Frank Thomas	1931-1946	15	146	115	24	7	.812
H.D. Drew	1947-1954	8	91	55	29	7	.643
J.B. Whitworth	1955-1957	3	30	4	24	2	.167
Paul W. Bryant	1958-1982	25	287	232	46	9	.824
TOTALS		88	838	593	203	42	.733

No team 1898,1918,1944

ALABAMA'S FOOTBALL RECORDS YEAR-BY-YEAR

Year	Coach	Captain	Record	Pts.	Opp.
1892	E. N. Beaumont (Penn)	W. G. Little	2-2-0	96	37
1893	Eli Abbott (Penn)	G. H. Kyzer	0-4-0	24	74
1894	Eli Abbott	S. B. Slone	3-1-0	60	16
1895	Eli Abbott	H. M. Bankhead	0-4-0	12	112
1896	Otto Wagonhurst (Penn)	S. B. Slone	2-1-0	56	10
1897	Allen McCants (Alabama)	Frank S. White, Jr.	1-0-0	6	0
1898	No Team	T. G. Burk—Elected	No Team		
1899	W. A. Hartin (Virginia)	T. W. Wert	3-1-0	39	31
1900	M. Griffin	W. E. Drennen	2-3-0	52	99
1901	M. H. Harvey (Auburn)	W. E. Drennen	2-1-2	92	23
1902	Eli Abbott, J. O. Heyworth	J. R. Forman	4-4-0	191	49
1903	W. B. Blount (Yale)	W. S. Wyatt	3-4-0	60	114
1904	W. B. Blount	W. S. Wyatt	7-3-0	100	62
1905	Jack Leavenworth (Yale)	B. A. Burks	6-4-0	178	113
1906	J. W. H. Pollard (Dartmouth)	Washington Moody	5-1-0	97	82
1907	J. W. H. Pollard	Emile Hannon	5-1-2	70	64
1908	J. W. H. Pollard	Henry Burks	6-1-1	108	31
1909	J. W. H. Pollard	Derrill Pratt	5-1-2	68	17
1910	Guy S. Lowman (Springfield)	O. G. Gresham	4-4-0	65	107
1911	D. V. Graves (Missouri)	R. H. Bumgardner	5-2-2	153	31
1912	D. V. Graves	Farley W. Moody	5-3-1	156	55
1913	D. V. Graves	C. H. Van de Graaff	6-3-0	188	40
1914	D. V. Graves	C. A. "Tubby" Long	5-4-0	211	64
1915	Thomas Kelly (Chicago)	William L. Harsh	6-2-0	250	51
1916	Thomas Kelly	Lowndes Morton	6-3-0	156	62
1917	Thomas Kelly	Jack Hovater	5-2-1	168	29
1918	No Team	Dan Boone—Elected	No Team		
1919	Xen C. Scott (Western Reserve)	Isaac J. Rogers	8-1-0	280	22
1920	Xen C. Scott	Sid Johnston	10-1-0	377	35
1921	Xen C. Scott	Al Clemens	5-4-2	241	104
1922	Xen C. Scott	Ernest E. Cooper	6-3-1	300	81
1923	Wallace Wade (Brown)	Al Clemens	7-2-1	222	50
1924	Wallace Wade	A. T. S. Hubert	8-1-0	290	24
1925	Wallace Wade	Bruce Jones	10-0-0	297	26
1926	Wallace Wade	Emile "Red" Barnes	9-0-1	249	27
1927	Wallace Wade	Freddie Pickhard	5-4-1	154	73
1928	Wallace Wade	Earle Smith	6-3-0	187	75
1929	Wallace Wade	Billy Hicks	6-3-0	196	58
1930	Wallace Wade	Charles B. Clement	10-0-0	271	13
1931	Frank W. Thomas (Notre Dame)	Joe Sharpe	9-1-0	370	57
1932	Frank W. Thomas	John Cain	8-2-0	200	51
1933	Frank W. Thomas	Foy Leach	7-1-1	130	17
1934	Frank W. Thomas	Bill Lee	10-0-0	316	45
1935	Frank W. Thomas	James Walker	6-2-1	185	55
1936	Frank W. Thomas	Jas. "Bubber" Nisbet	8-0-1	168	35
1937	Frank W. Thomas	Leroy Monsky	9-1-0	225	33
1938	Frank W. Thomas	Lew Bostick	7-1-1	149	40
1939	Frank W. Thomas	Carey Cox	5-3-1	101	53
1940	Frank W. Thomas	Harold Newman	7-2-0	166	80
1941	Frank W. Thomas	John Wyhonic	9-2-0	263	85
1942	Frank W. Thomas	Joe Domnanovich	8-3-0	246	97
1943	No Team	No Team	No Team		
1944	Frank W. Thomas	Game Captains	5-2-2	272	83
1945	Frank W. Thomas	Game Captains	10-0-0	430	80
1946	Frank W. Thomas	Game Captains	7-4-0	186	110
1947	H. D. Drew (Bates)	John Wozniak	8-3-0	210	101
1948	H. D. Drew	Ray Richeson	6-4-1	228	170
1949	H. D. Drew	Doug Lockridge	6-3-1	227	130
1950	H. D. Drew	Mike Mizerany	9-2-0	328	107

1951	H. D. Drew	Jack Brown	5-6-0	263	188
1952	H. D. Drew	Bobby Wilson	10-2-0	325	139
1953	H. D. Drew	Bud Willis	6-3-3	178	152
1954	H. D. Drew	Sid Youngleman	4-5-2	123	104
1955	J. B. Whitworth (Alabama)	Nick Germanos	0-10-0	48	256
1956	J. B. Whitworth	Jim Cunningham Wes Thompson	2-7-1	85	208
1957	J. B. Whitworth	Jim Loftis-Clay Walls	2-7-1	69	173
1958	Paul W. Bryant (Alabama)	Dave Sington-Bobby Smith	5-4-1	106	75
1959	Paul W. Bryant	Marlin Dyess-Jim Blevins	7-2-2	95	59
1960	Paul W. Bryant	Leon Fuller-Bobby Boylston	8-1-2	183	56
1961	Paul W. Bryant	Pat Trammell-Billy Neighbors	11-0-0	297	25
1962	Paul W. Bryant	Lee Roy Jordan-Jimmy Sharpe	10-1-0	289	39
1963	Paul W. Bryant	Benny Nelson-Steve Allen	9-2-0	227	95
1964	Paul W. Bryant	Joe Namath-Ray Ogden	10-1-0	250	88
1965	Paul W. Bryant	Steven Sloan-Paul Crane	9-1-1	256	107
1966	Paul W. Bryant	Ray Perkins-Richard Cole	11-0-0	301	44
1967	Paul W. Bryant	Ken Stabler-Bobby Johns	8-2-1	204	131
1968	Paul W. Bryant	Mike Hall-Donnie Sutton	8-3-0	184	139
1969	Paul W. Bryant	Danny Ford-Alvin Samples	6-5-0	314	268
1970	Paul W. Bryant	Danny Gilbert-Dave Brungard	6-5-1	334	264
1971	Paul W. Bryant	Johnny Musso-Robin Parkhouse	11-1-0	368	122
1972	Paul W. Bryant	Terry Davis-John Mitchell	10-2-0	406	150
1973	Paul W. Bryant	Wilbur Jackson-Chuck Strickland	11-1-0	477	113
1974	Paul W. Bryant	Sylvester Croom-Ricky Davis	11-1-0	329	96
1975	Paul W. Bryant	Richard Todd-Leroy Cook	11-1-0	374	72
1976	Paul W. Bryant	Thad Flanagan-Charles Hannah	9-3-0	327	140
1977	Paul W. Bryant	Mike Tucker-Ozzie Newsome	11-1-0	380	139
1978	Paul W. Bryant	Marty Lyons-Jeff Rutledge-Tony Nathan	11-1-0	345	168
1979	Paul W. Bryant	Don McNeal-Steve Whitman	12-0-0	383	67
1980	Paul W. Bryant	Major Ogilvie	10-2-0	352	98
1981	Paul W. Bryant	Randy Scott-Warren Lyles	9-2-1	296	151
1982	Paul W. Bryant	Alan Gray Eddie Lowe	8-4-0	338	216
		Steve Mott			